Damien Lewis is a number one bestselling author whose books have been translated into over forty languages worldwide. For decades he worked as a war and conflict reporter for the world's major broadcasters, reporting from across Africa, South America, the Middle and Far East and winning numerous awards. His books include the World War Two classics *Churchill's Secret Warriors*, *SAS Nazi Hunters* and *Hunting the Nazi Bomb*. A dozen of his books have been made, or are being made, into movies or TV drama series and several have been adapted as plays for the stage. He has raised tens of thousands of pounds for charitable concerns connected with his writings.

ALSO BY DAMIEN LEWIS

SMOKY
THE
BRAVE

The World's Smallest Dog
The World's Biggest Heart

DAMIEN LEWIS

Quercus

First published in Great Britain in 2018 by Quercus.
This paperback edition published in 2019 by

Quercus Editions Ltd
Carmelite House
50 Victoria Embankment
London EC4Y oDZ

An Hachette UK company

PB ISBN 978 1 78648 310 2
Ebook ISBN 978 1 78648 309 6

11

Text designed and typeset by CC Book Production
Printed and bound in Great Britain by Clays Ltd, Elcograf S.p.A.

For the fallen of the 26th

Captain Sheldon P. Hallett
1st Lt. Donald W. Christians
1st Lt. William McDaniels
T/Sgt. Harry R. Rogers
1st Lt. Clair J. Bardsley
1st Lt. Lee G. Smith
2nd Lt. James H. Morrison
1st Lt. Karl M. Booth Jr
1st Lt. Madison E. Gillespey
2nd Lt. Clarence E. Cook
F/O James L. Wilson
F/O Henry R. Willis
1st Lt. Samuel Dunaway

They shall grow not old, as we who are left grow old:
Age shall not weary them, nor the years condemn.
At the going down of the sun and in the morning,
We will remember them.

Laurence Binyon

Photo Joe

Now, Photo Joe is an altitude fiend.
He flies way up high where he can't be seen.
He flies at thirty thousand in his P-three-eight,
Getting drunk on oxygen at a rapid rate.

He tells all the bombers of every hot spot.
He flies over places where the fighters will not.
The bombers have top-cover and the fighters have a gun,
But all Photo Joe can ever do is run.

There's a little more to this sad, sad story:
The bombers do the work and the fighters get the glory.
And here's another thing that you ought to know –
There aren't any medals for a Photo Joe!

Anon

AUTHOR'S NOTE & SOURCES

The time served by Allied servicemen and women during the Second World War was often traumatic. Memories tend to differ and apparently none more so than those concerning operations flown deep behind enemy lines. The written accounts that do exist of such missions tend to vary in their detail and timing, and locations and chronologies can prove contradictory. That being said, I have done my best to provide a proper sense of place, timescale and narrative to the story as depicted in these pages.

Where various accounts of a mission appear to be somewhat confused, the methodology I have used to determine when and how events took place is the 'most likely' scenario. If two or more testimonies or sources point to a particular time or place or sequence of events, I have opted to use that version as most likely. Where necessary I have very occasionally re-created small sections of dialogue to aid the story's flow.

The above notwithstanding, any mistakes herein are entirely of my own making, and I would be happy to correct them in future editions. Likewise, while I have endeavoured to locate the copyright holders of the photos, sketches and other images and material used in this book, this has not always been straightforward or easy. Again, I would be happy to correct any errors in future editions.

Of particular use during the writing of this book were the 5th Air Force, 26th Photo Reconnaissance Squadron's own accounts of the war years. These include the Flight Reports, Intelligence Reports and other official squadron records held at Maxwell Air Force Base, in Alabama, USA. The 26th being a photo reconnaissance squadron, the photo archive held at Maxwell AFB also proved particularly useful. So too did the 26th Photo Reconnaissance Squadron's own war diary, entitled simply 'Squadron History – Twenty-Sixth Photographic Squadron (L)'. Likewise, the squadron's more informal photographic and written legend of the war years, entitled '26th Photo', and published by 26th Photo Reconnaissance Squadron, proved hugely insightful.

ACKNOWLEDGEMENTS

In researching this book I was able to speak to and receive assistance from a number of individuals, who were especially generous with their time. My special thanks and gratitude are extended to all, and my apologies to those that I have inadvertently forgotten to mention.

This book could not have been written without William A. Wynne, who recounted his and Smoky's wartime story in his own book entitled *Yorkie Doodle Dandy; A Memoir*, which served as a reference for and is quoted in this book. William A. Wynne sadly passed away in 2021, but he is survived by his loved ones, who are determined to keep the memory of his and Smoky's wartime story alive and to cherish its legacy.

In no particular order I wish to thank the following, who assisted in many ways: research, proofreading, recollections and subject matter expertise. Author Taylor Dowling was kind enough to alert me to the existence of his superlative account of the British reconnaissance pilots of the Second World War, when we shared a platform at an Imperial War Museum Duxford event, and to discuss same.

Sim Smiley, for your expertise and inspiration, gleaned from the various archives in the USA. Simon Fowler, for your expertise and inspiration, gleaned from the various archives in the UK. Paul and Anne Sherratt, for your perceptive comments and guidance.

The staff at several archives and museums also deserve special mention, including those at the British National Archives, in Kew, London; and those at the Maxwell Air Force Base archives, Alabama, USA. I would like to make particular mention of Tammy Horton, archivist at Maxwell AFB, for your diligent help and assistance.

I'd like to thank in particular nonagenarian Rouse Voisey, a survivor of the the Second World War years in the southwest Pacific theatre, who was captured by the Japanese and survived many months of hellish forced labour, not to mention journeys on the so-called 'hell ships', shipwrecks and the Sumatra 'hell railway'. Thank you, again, Rouse, for sharing with me your extraordinary memories and recollections of your time serving in this theatre of war, over seventy years ago.

My gratitude also to my literary agent, Gordon Wise, and film and TV agent, Luke Speed, both of Curtis Brown, for helping bring this project to fruition, and to all at my publishers Quercus, including, but not limited to, Jon Butler, Charlotte Fry, Ben Brock and Hannah Robinson. My editor, Richard Milner, deserves very special mention, as does Josh Ireland: your unstinting enthusiasm for this story is, I hope, rewarded in these pages.

I am also indebted to those authors who have previously written about some of the topics dealt with in this book and whose work has helped inform my writing. These include, in alphabetical order of author: *Smoky the War Dog*, Nigel Allsopp

(New Holland Publishers, 2013); *Dogs of Courage*, Clare Campbell (Little, Brown, 2015); *Spies in the Sky*, Taylor Downing (Little, Brown, 2011); *Beyond the Call of Duty*, Isabel George (HarperCollins, 2010); *The Eight Ballers: Eyes of the Fifth Air Force*, John Stanaway and Bob Rocker (Schiffer Military History, 1999).

Enormous gratitude is also due to Fiona MacDonald and all at the charity Glenart and their Bravehound initiative, which helps match service dogs to deserving ex-servicemen, those who have either been wounded in combat or suffered from the modern-day trauma-related disabilities (akin to those I have described in this book as assailing some of the Second World War veterans). Thank you for those events that you organized to support the publication of this book: I'm honoured to be able to raise the profile of the fantastic and hugely valuable work that you do.

And thanks are due as always to the ever-patient Eva and to the wonderful David, Damien Jr and Sianna, for not resenting Dad spending too much of his time locked away . . . again . . . writing . . . again.

CHAPTER ONE

The image painted on the side of the aircraft's fuselage was eye-catching. It showed Donald Duck riding on a speeding cloud, one eye squinting down a camera lens as he snapped off a photo of the earth far below, his webbed feet thrust before him, dashing pilot's scarf and leather flight helmet flapping in the slipstream.

It was the patch of the 26th Photo Reconnaissance Squadron, part of the aptly named Hawkeye Group: their task was to dash across hostile territory at altitude, grabbing daring images of enemy positions – images that would prove key to winning the war.

The pilot flying the powerful but graceful P-38 Lightning – nicknamed the fork-tailed devil, *der Gabelschwanz-Teufel*, by the enemy, due to its distinctive twin tail planes – was one of the best. First Lieutenant Lee G. Smith, a hugely popular figure in the squadron, was blessed with dark good looks, his square-jawed features set below a steady, self-possessed gaze, offset by a thin, somewhat wry and lopsided smile.

Right now, Smith's jaw was locked tight as he wrestled with the Lightning's controls and the demands of flying such a mission.

It wasn't his aircraft's capabilities which worried First

Lieutenant Smith. Known as a hugely robust and forgiving airframe – the 'sweetest-flying plane in the sky' to many – the twin-engine Lightning could take any amount of mistreatment and abuse. It was the photo recce pilot's age-old adversaries – the weather, plus any marauding enemy aircraft that might be menacing the skies.

Smith banked tightly, turning his head as he did so, scanning the cloud-enshrouded earth as he tried to identify the distant target that he intended to capture on celluloid. At the same time he kept flicking his eyes to either side and behind, as he checked anxiously for hostile warplanes.

The standard combat model of the P-38 Lightning (the 'P' stood for pursuit) packed a devastating punch: one 20mm cannon and four Browning machine guns were positioned in the aircraft's bulbous nosecone, primed to unleash a torrent of heavy-calibre bullets at any adversaries. No wonder it had produced so many combat aces.

But Smith's aircraft – the F4 reconnaissance version – was a very different kind of machine. A bulky K 22 camera – as large as any man's torso and operated by a clunky lever bolted to the pilot's control column – was positioned where the weapons normally sat. In place of the gun button Smith had only a hot switch to enable him to fire off nothing more deadly than . . . photographs. And whereas normally the pilot was ensconced within a sarcophagus of protective armour, on the photo recce version of the Lightning that was all stripped away to save weight.

Less weight meant more speed, which was the key to surviving such solo dashes through enemy airspace, or so the photo recce fliers reasoned.

The eerie, alien suck and blow of the oxygen mask echoed in Smith's ears, accentuating the loneliness and isolation of flying such a mission. He was alone on the roof of the world up here – tearing along at pushing 435 miles per hour and 20,000 feet of altitude. Without the oxygen, he'd last barely minutes before losing consciousness.

At such height, the air outside the Lightning was at minus 12 degrees; far colder with the wind-chill factor. So frigid was it that the K22 camera crammed into the nosecone had its own bespoke heating system, to prevent the lenses from fogging up or the mechanism from freezing solid.

Smith was blessed with few such comforts. He was hunched in the unheated cockpit, his clawed hands aching from the glacial conditions and the hours spent gripping the flight controls, his thick sheepskin flying jacket buttoned tight.

The heavens stretched above him, a deep, icy blue. Towards the eastern horizon, the sun peeped a fiery eye above thick clouds, gilding their billowing tops a fierce orange. Smith had taken off early in an effort to catch his target in the fine morning light – the best time to secure the kind of images he was after.

But the cumulus stretched from 3,000 to 14,000 feet, where towering updrafts of moist tropical air punched high into the atmosphere, and Smith found himself having to steer a path around heavy rainstorms. Above the cloud cover the visibility was pretty good at around ten miles, but within the dark and torrential cloudbursts it was close to zero.

It was 12 March 1944, and all that month the squadron had been dogged by bad weather here in the southwest Pacific theatre. Repeatedly, pilots' Final Mission Reports had concluded with the dreaded words: 'Unsuccessful due to weather'. It was a phrase that did little to reflect the drama and heartache of being dogged by such treacherous conditions. Even worse was being forced to file the report: 'Did not take off due to weather'.

At least Smith had got airborne. But in spite of his best efforts, he feared today's flight was destined to earn that hateful epitaph: *Unsuccessful due to weather.*

He pressed on, eyes searching for a break in the cloud and determined to bring back something – anything – that might be of use to the Allied commanders presently plotting death and destruction to the enemy. At the same time he tried to ensure that his hunger to bring back some positive results didn't blind him to the dangers inherent in his task.

He had to avoid creating a 'contrail' – a double line of cloud formed when the water vapour from the Lightning's twin-engine exhausts condensed in the freezing blue and froze. Such a trail thrown across the heavens would appear like a giant arrow, leading the eyes of any watchers to the tiny, isolated speck of an aircraft.

Repeatedly, Smith scanned cloud cover, temperature and altitude, running a series of complex computations through his head. At the same time he kept his eyes peeled, checking if the enemy might have left any telltale signs of their own. Spotting their contrails would give him a few precious seconds warning, allowing him to push to full throttle and dive to shake off any pursuers.

The cockpit was freezing cold. Agonisingly so. Smith ran his aching eyes across the controls, checking for any that might have frozen solid, so giving him a potentially catastrophic mis-reading. Crystals of frozen moisture could even form around the Lightning's sharply raked canopy, frosting up the windows and obscuring his vision.

Momentarily, his gaze flicked downwards, to the map folded into the knee pouch of his flight suit. He'd been airborne for two hours, and it required pinpoint navigation to bring his Lightning directly over today's target – the Cape Gloucester headland, set to the far west of New Britain Island, one of the key enemy positions hereabouts.

Menaced by the 6,000-foot volcano of Mount Talawe, and clad in thick jungle and treacherous swamps, any pilot forced to eject over such terrain stood little chance of survival. Below lay a clutch of enemy airbases and ports, ones that Allied commanders hoped to secure as part of Operation Cartwheel, a series of island-hopping missions designed to isolate and neutralize Japanese strongpoints across the Pacific.

But planning such a complex series of amphibious and airborne assaults called for the kind of detailed intelligence that air recce photos supplied, which is why Smith had been sent out to brave the weather this morning.

Smith's camera pointed vertically downwards and was set to fire off a series of photographs at regular intervals, which would allow him to cover a continuous strip of terrain. Each shot would overlap with its predecessor, forming one uninterrupted image. Each large, 7 x 8.5-inch strip of celluloid would capture a patch of ground roughly one square mile. Such was the quality of the camera equipment that it could capture enough detail to identify individual vehicles moving across the terrain. But only if a weather window opened, and there was little sign of that happening right now.

Eventually, Smith was forced to turn for home – which presently consisted of the airbase at Nadzab, situated on the coast of New Guinea, which lay off the northern coast of Australia. Nadzab Airbase was never the easiest place to land: it had been hacked out of the deep jungle flanking the Markham River valley and was menaced by rugged mountains on either side.

Seven months earlier Allied forces had seized the area in a series of airborne assaults. In response, the Japanese – hungering for revenge following one of their first setbacks in the war – had launched a series of ferocious counter-attacks. Waves of Japanese warplanes flew repeated bombing missions, forcing the men of the 26th Photo Recce Squadron to pitch their tents directly beneath the jungle canopy, in an effort to hide from hostile eyes. Still they'd taken casualties, both men and machines getting blasted on the ground.

Yet there was little that the Photo Reconnaissance pilots could do to retaliate or to fight back. Their planes had been stripped of the guns that would have allowed them to do so – it was up to their comrades in the fighter squadrons. In the meantime, men like Smith had to carry on with the task at hand: speeding through enemy airspace to locate their target, capture it on film, and return as quickly as possible, so that their precious photos could be rushed into Allied commanders' hands.

As he set a course for home Smith checked his fuel gauges. After being airborne for several hours, dodging the weather and enemy aircraft alike, he might return only to find the airstrip cloaked in cloud. By then his aircraft might be sipping on fumes, and just at the moment when he was forced to delay landing. The Lightning used more than a gallon of fuel every minute, and

Smith needed to keep a constant watch on speed and bearing. There would be little scope for loitering above Nadzab, waiting for the cloud to clear.

It took a certain type of temperament to volunteer for such work. A certain kind of courage. Bomber and fighter pilots were accustomed to flying in formation, enjoying the company of fellow aircrew and a shield of friendly aircraft to ward off the enemy. By contrast, the recce pilot flew alone, unarmed and unescorted.

Serving in a photo recce squadron called for a rare combination of common sense, daring, self-reliance and initiative. Such pilots had to make a virtue out of the fact that their aircraft flew unarmed. If his P-38 carried guns, Smith would be tempted to turn and fight at the approach of an enemy warplane. As it was he had no option but to concentrate on avoiding combat, securing his photographs and speeding them back intact.

All too frequently recce pilots failed to return to base. They were flying solo missions across airspace where 'enemy fire and interception were probable and expected', as the mission briefings expressed it. More often than not those who failed to return were simply listed as Missing in Action (MIA). The chances were that no one would ever know what calamity had befallen them on their long and lonely flight.

If a pilot went down in the sea there was little likelihood of his body or any wreckage ever being found. If a plane came down on land, a report might filter in from local resistance fighters or villagers, and the wreckage might be identified from its tail number, but it was often difficult to determine whether the pilot had lost his life due to enemy action, mechanical failure or adverse weather.

Such dangers were all too real. A month earlier this had been brought home most powerfully, when the squadron's Commanding Officer (CO) had been lost in action. The 26th had been founded a year earlier, at Colorado Airbase, Colorado Springs, in western USA. First Lieutenant Sheldon P. Hallett had been appointed its founding officer, and he had been in command ever since.

Fresh-faced and youthful, yet with a direct intensity to his eyes, Hallett had nurtured a fierce pride in the 26th, one defined by rigour. His was the only photo recce squadron to have passed out of training in that autumn of 1943 with an 'Excellent' rating. On Sunday 31 October they had deployed from the US, sailing for a 'secret destination' on a luxury liner hastily converted into a troopship.

En route Hallett had spoken to his men of the eternal quest for excellence that he wanted the squadron to embody. From the moment they had arrived in theatre Hallett had led from the front, earning enormous respect from all who flew alongside him. But then, on 29 February 1944 had come shocking news: Hallett had been listed Missing in Action. In the blink of an eye the squadron had lost its Commanding Officer, and it would be some time before anything was learned of his fate.

Such unexpected losses could be shattering – especially within such a tight knit unit – but it was offset by the knowledge of the crucial role they were performing here. The squadron's war diary made proud mention of the 'highly important pictures of the enemy's activities and dispositions' that their pilots were bringing home. It was not an idle boast. The US Army Air Force's Official Service Journal concluded that photo reconnaissance furnished 'ninety percent of modern military intelligence. Armies do not move without it.'

So important was their work that President Roosevelt's son, Colonel Elliott Roosevelt, had been placed in charge of developing the craft of the photo recce squadrons, continuously pushing at the boundaries of what was known and possible. Such knowledge of the war-winning scope of their missions helped put steel in the pilots' souls.

As he set a course for home, Smith likewise had to draw on his own reserves of steel. He had to remain razor sharp and one hundred per cent focused. A moment's distraction could prove fatal. He was looking forward to landing back at base, in spite of the failure of his mission. After hours of intense concentration he was dogged by exhaustion, and he longed for the relief that came from simply making it back again in one piece.

He was just off Karkar Island, on the western fringes of the Bismarck Sea, when he spotted something. Far below the thick cumulus swirled for a moment and then cleared. In the break in the clouds a stretch of glistening ocean opened before him. Right in the midst of the water were the familiar forms of two ships, steaming resolutely onwards.

Smith studied the vessels. They were positioned five miles off the coast of Karkar Island and heading southeast – most likely making for Rabaul, on the eastern shores of New Britain, a base that the Japanese had captured from its Australian defenders in February 1942. Under Operation Cartwheel, Rabaul – one of the enemy's most significant strongholds – was to be isolated by air and by sea, its garrisons rendered impotent.

From such altitude the two ships appeared as little more

than pin pricks, but Smith doubted they were friendly. A year earlier a major sea battle had raged here, becoming known as the Battle of the Bismarck Sea. A fleet of Japanese warships and troop carriers had been steaming for Nadzab, to intercept Allied landings. The troopships and their destroyer escorts were caught by Allied warplanes. All eight transports were sunk and 3,664 Japanese soldiers and seamen had lost their lives.

But despite the losses they'd suffered, the armed forces of Imperial Japan remained resolutely committed to holding this region, and supply ships regularly braved the Bismarck Sea. To be certain of the two vessels' identities Smith needed to take a closer look. He put his Lightning into a shallow dive, dropping to 12,000 feet.

From that height he was almost certain of the identity of the ships below him. During training he'd memorized the photos and diagrams depicted in the Department of Naval Intelligence's 'Standard Classes of Japanese Merchant Ships'. The two vessels had all the appearance of the Type D freighter – a 2,300-tonne merchant ship codenamed *Sugar Charlie Love* in the manuals.

The freighters looked laden with war materiel, but you could never be too careful with such vessels, for the Japanese were in the habit of packing them with unexpected cargo, including Allied prisoners of war. Those fighting in the Pacific had heard of these 'hell ships': they transported British, American, Australian and other Allied POWs across the ocean, thousands crammed into bamboo cages stacked into hot and airless holds.

In the months following Pearl Harbor a vast swathe of terrain – from Burma in the north to New Guinea in the south – had been overrun by the Japanese. It seemed as if nothing could stop the Emperor Hirohito's forces: in spring 1942 the Japanese had launched a raid on Sydney harbour, using a fleet of *Ko-hyoteki* class mini-submarines. One Australian ship, HMAS *Kuttabul*, was sunk and the mini-subs had shelled shore positions.

The damage done wasn't great, but the message sent was heard loud and clear by the Australian people: their nation was under threat of invasion. As Japanese forces scored one triumph after another, hundreds of thousands of Allied troops had been taken prisoner. Those Allied POWs were used as slave labour. Working in nightmarish conditions, they were forced to clear the jungle and build airstrips and railways across territory seized by the Japanese.

The two vessels that Smith had discovered might be packed with such long-suffering Allied POWs. He dropped lower, setting his cameras running. Most such Japanese freighters boasted gun emplacements set in the stern and prow, but at his current altitude he was well out of range. As the camera whirred, he felt a kick of adrenalin. In spite of the terrible weather, he'd found something of possible interest and captured it on film.

Just as soon as he touched down at Nadzab, the ground crew would rush into action. They'd slip the precious roll of film out of the camera, jump into a jeep and dash across to the photolab that lay beneath the dark fringe of jungle. Within an hour at most the negatives would have been developed and dried, and the specialist photo-interpreters would be poring over whatever Smith had found here.

Painstaking research had enabled a calculation to be made of a ship's speed, based upon specific measurements of the wake revealed in such photographs. That combined with the vessels' bearing would give a good indication as to both where the ships were heading and their present position. It was then just a matter of whether attack aircraft could be scrambled in time to reach the two vessels while they were still within range.

But first, Smith had to fly like the wind to get his precious images home.

As his Lightning approached the hills that lay to the east of Nadzab Airbase, little did Smith suspect what lay far beneath him, secreted in the jungle shadows. Likewise, the warplane would be invisible to the stray soul hiding under the thick forest canopy. But her ears would be drawn to the distant roar of the twin engines, even as she crouched, fearfully, in the deserted foxhole in which she'd taken refuge.

Abandoned long ago, she appeared like a shapeless mass of tangled, dirty hair. After days lost in the jungle this starving, emaciated animal was barely recognizable. But she was still breathing and still fighting for her survival, and even in such a state a dog's hearing remains many times more powerful than that of any human.

Perhaps she raised her head a little further and pricked up her ears. If she did, she would doubtless have associated the roar of the P-38's twin aero-engines with what she longed for most in the world right then – human company, for she was accustomed to the sights, smells and sounds of an airbase such as this. Wonderful companions because they are so affectionate, she was of a kind of dog that hungers for human companionship, and hates being cut off from its two-legged companions.

Left alone for even a short while, she was of a breed that suffers from separation anxiety. After days marooned in the hot and airless jungle, and with little conception of how she had come to be there, the dog's disquiet and distress was acute. She longed for a human voice; a human touch; someone to scoop her up in friendly arms and to cherish her once more.

As the P-38 thundered onwards one thing was for certain: this tiny ball of matted, dirt-encrusted hair could have little inkling how her fate, and that of the reconnaissance squadron with whom Smith flew were inextricably linked, for all of that lay sometime in the future.

Abandoned in the jungle and lost to her erstwhile human protectors, the future was one of fearful uncertainties.

CHAPTER TWO

The angular form of a Willys jeep pulled out from the motor pool at Nadzab Airbase and took to a dirt track that threaded through the jungle. At the wheel sat Edward 'Ed' Downey, one of the airbase's ground crew. With a rugged boxer's features and a shock of unruly red hair, Downey was forever to be found with a Lucky Strike cigarette glued to his bottom lip.

Where they'd felled and burned the jungle to expand the airstrip, thick kunai grass crowded in on the track, its spear-like heads rising as high as ten feet and blinding Downey to his surroundings. He was more accustomed to the rolling hills of his native Pennsylvania and its heavy winter snows, than to the thick and stifling jungle and the claustrophobic fields of kunai grass. It made for hellish terrain in which to fight.

The track snaked this way and that as Downey gunned the jeep through the toughest sections, which had worsened with the rains. There seemed to be no happy medium to the weather here. When the sun was out it was as hot as an oven. When the clouds built it was oppressively humid, like being trapped in a giant sauna. And when the rains came it was as if God Himself had turned on a giant tap over the airbase.

In places the track was completely flooded and Downey had

to slow to a crawl to ease the jeep through chocolate-coloured water as thick as custard. It sloshed about up to the level of his axles. In places it was deep enough to reach to his mudguards, the jeep's powerful 'Go Devil' engine straining to keep the vehicle in motion.

Such terrain took a heavy toll on the unit's vehicles, and Downey wasn't entirely surprised when the one that he was driving coughed and spluttered and came to a sloughing halt. Not for the first time since he had been deployed here, he clambered out of the driver's seat and went to open the vehicle's hood, trying to avoid the worst of the mud as he did so.

He lifted it, latched it, and leaned over the engine, feeling the heat rise from the straight-four. He reached for and jiggled a couple of wires, checking if those serving the vehicle's battery were still making good contact. Such damp and humid conditions weren't great for keeping any kind of machinery serviceable, or weapons for that matter.

As he fiddled with the engine, a P-38 roared across the sky and touched down on the airstrip. One of the squadron's recce flights, no doubt. Maybe First Lieutenant Smith, making it early back to base. Surrounded by the tall kunai grass, Downey couldn't see the runway, and his concentration was focused on the engine compartment of the jeep.

He was just about to give the engine a try when he heard a sound from over his shoulder. It was so utterly unexpected, but he could have sworn that he'd heard a dog whining. The sound transported him back to his native Pennsylvania and his childhood years. To Downey, it was a far from welcome noise and one that sparked distinctly unpleasant memories.

He didn't mind admitting that he was a die-hard dog-hater. He couldn't fathom his fellow soldiers' affection for the four-legged curs, nor how they were always going on about how they missed the pets they'd left back home. It didn't make the slightest bit of sense to him. He was about to ignore the sound – surely he'd imagined it? – when he heard it again: a plaintive whimper coming from just behind where he stood.

Later, when asked, Downey was never able to explain why he went to investigate. But for whatever reason – curiosity, perhaps – he turned and sloshed his way through the mud to the side of the track. He peered, cautiously, into the shadows that seemed to be the source of the noise. There was an abandoned foxhole by the roadside, and Downey had learned to love and loathe those shell-scrapes in equal measure.

During the rains they were invariably thick with clinging, stinking mud. During the drier periods, they became home to a variety of crawling, stinging, slithering life, much of which was lethal. At the very least vicious red fire ants were bound to have set up camp, and he'd learned to his cost what sharing a foxhole with those critters entailed.

But the foxholes could also be real lifesavers. When the enemy warplanes attacked, you had two basic choices: remain where you were and dice with death, or dive into a foxhole and take your chances with whatever jungle life had made a home there.

As he peered into the gloom Downey spied movement. A pair of dark eyes, glinting in the dull light, gazed up at him, imploringly. They seemed disproportionately large for the sodden floor-mop of hair they seemed to inhabit. He heard the noise again – a dog's pitiful whine. If it hadn't been for that, Downey would have doubted whether this sad, benighted creature really was a dog at all.

Even as he stared at the animal, trying to fathom what in God's name the breed might be, Downey saw it try to clamber out of the pit, its tiny paws scrabbling desperately at the earth. It jumped at him, tiny head bobbing upwards once, twice, three times. Downey couldn't help but admire the creature's sheer tenacity and will to survive. Perhaps it was that which spoke to him and prompted him to act as he did.

Almost against his will he reached out a hand, scooped up the tiny dog, turned back to the jeep and tossed it unceremoniously onto the passenger's seat. That done, he went back to fiddling with the wires. It was most likely a dodgy connection, maybe to the spark plugs. He tinkered for a while longer, eventually persuading the engine to cough back into life, and with barely a glance at the dog he continued on his way.

One of the greatest ironies of Downey's discovery was that he shared a tent with a man who was arguably Nadzab's greatest dog-lover: Bill Wynne. Wynne and Downey had trained as aerial photographers back in the US, before deploying to theatre together. Downey fancied himself as something of an athlete and a swashbuckling adventurer. He had a wicked sense of humour and was cocky and sharp-tongued. He and the dashingly handsome Wynne were the best of friends.

Their only differences seemed to be over the hotly disputed topic of dogs. And knowing of Wynne's all-consuming passion for man's four-legged friend, Downey was loath to let his buddy set eyes on his newfound discovery. If he did, Downey felt sure that this irritating mop of a hairball would end up moving into the tent that he shared with Wynne.

He wasn't about to let that happen.

Upon returning to camp Downey parked up at the motor pool and yelled across to his friend who worked there, Sergeant Dare. 'Hey, Dare, I found this in a foxhole.' He thrust the diminutive animal into the sergeant's hands, then banged a fist onto the bonnet of his jeep. 'And this damn thing broke down.' Another vehicle for Dare to fix. Downey spent a few more minutes explaining how he'd found the animal, before concluding by saying: 'I don't know what it is, but I know I don't want it.'

With very little ceremony – he was glad to be shot of the shaggy canine enigma – Downey left the animal in Sergeant Dare's care. He headed for the tent he shared with his friend and dog-lover, Bill Wynne, determined not to breathe a word of his discovery.

It was a little over two years since the 7 December 1941 surprise Japanese attack on Pearl Harbor had catapulted America into the war. Ever since deploying to this far-flung corner of the globe – to avenge Japanese aggression, and in defence of Australia – those based at Nadzab had grown accustomed to the nightly air raids. Powerful blasts shook the very foundations of the camp. The 26th's end of the airbase was stocked with any amount of highly combustible and explosive materials – gasoline for the trucks and jeeps, aviation fuel for the P-38 Lightnings, plus photographic film, paper and chemicals. A lucky hit would result in a cataclysmic explosion.

Their accommodation tents had been given suitably ironic names: 'GI Manor' or 'Target For Tonight'. If any soldier managed to sleep through the nightly air-raid sirens and remain in his cot, he'd certainly be wrenched awake by the time the first bombs had fallen. He'd make a mad dash for the comparative safety of the coconut log and earthen-roofed air-raid shelters, as the flash of detonating munitions tore the dark night apart.

Daylight raids were rarer. Generally, the only aircraft to menace the skies during daytime were the enemy's 'Washing Machine Charlies' – most often a lone Mitsubishi G4M twin-engine bomber, the nearest Japanese equivalent to the P-38 photo recce aircraft (although slower and more vulnerable). Those flights were the enemy's attempts to do exactly what the 26th were charged to do here – to spy on their adversaries.

Among the war debris scattered around the airbase, the men had retrieved some prized souvenirs. Foremost were the white cotton flags emblazoned with the symbol of Imperial Japan – a blood-red rising sun. Then there were the aircraft recognition manuals that had been issued to the Japanese troops, illegible with their vertical columns of spidery writing. But the accompanying diagrams of Allied warplanes dropping sticks of bombs over Japanese positions left little to the imagination.

You never knew what you might find here, abandoned in a Japanese foxhole. But neither Ed Downey nor Sergeant Dare had ever expected this – a mysterious and diminutive dog, with what must once have been a long and luxurious coat of hair that fell to her ankles, but which now was a mass of dirt-encrusted knots and tangles.

Left with his new charge, Sergeant Dare wondered what on earth he was to do with such a dog in a place like this. He had his hands full with his duties at the motor pool, and the harsh rigours of jungle warfare hardly made this a fit place for pets. There was a saying popular among Allied troops then serving in the region: 'Heaven is Java; hell is Burma; but no one returns alive from New Guinea.' It sure wasn't an ideal location to try to nurse some life back into a sickly little dog.

Of course, there was a very real chance that the mystery dog shared its origin with the Rising Sun flags and aircraft recognition manuals the men had found around the base. After all, the Japanese were known to afford dogs similar veneration as Western cultures tend to.

In Japanese tradition a number of animals were renowned as lucky charms. The *Maneki-neko* – the beckoning cat – was a symbol of success, prosperity and happiness. The *Komainu*, known as Foo Dogs in English, were the ubiquitous lion-like statues that flanked the doors of Japanese Shinto and Buddhist shrines. Foo Dogs – as with their living brethren – guarded such places against those who would do them harm, even when their human occupants were absent.

Traditionally, the size of the Foo Dog was irrelevant: even a miniature one could do the job well. Maybe this tiny bundle of canine mystery had served a similar purpose for the Japanese forces garrisoned at Nadzab? Maybe the good luck that she supposedly brought had finally run out the day the fearsome armada of USAAF C47 Skytrains had released their paratroopers over this jungle-clad valley?

On the morning of 5 September 1943 a fearsome aerial barrage had saturated the Nadzab area with bombs. Immediately after, US warplanes had strung a thick smokescreen across the valley, into which the C47s had dropped their paratroopers in human waves. The US and Australian airborne troops had routed the Japanese defenders, even as General Douglas MacArthur, supreme Allied commander in the region, had circled overhead in a B-17 Flying Fortress, keeping watch as 'his kids' went into action.

The assault had been declared a 'signal step on the road to Victory' by the Allies. Once captured, Nadzab Airbase, which lies on the northeastern coast of what was then called New Guinea – today's Papua New Guinea – was rapidly expanded, until eventually four all-weather airstrips were in use, making it the most important Allied airbase in the region.

The loss of Nadzab Airbase, and the neighbouring port of Lae, had constituted a game-changer. No longer would Japanese commanders concentrate on new offensives aimed at overrunning nearby Australia and cutting it off from America – something which they had come so very close to achieving. Instead, they would focus their efforts on holding their positions, and preventing the Allies from approaching any closer to the Japanese homeland. That was to be prevented at all costs.

The battle for Nadzab was a good seven months old by now, and if the mystery dog retrieved from the foxhole was some kind of Japanese lucky charm, how on earth had she stayed alive in the interim? Any way Sergeant Dare looked at it, the dog's very existence here just didn't seem to add up. Regardless, she had been handed into his care and for now at least the Nadzab motor pool would be the diminutive mutt's home.

Japanese Foo Dog or not, the immediate priority was ensuring her survival. Though seemingly overjoyed to be back among human companions, the tiny little dog was emaciated and terribly weakened. Dare fetched some water and leftover rations. The food at Nadzab was atrocious – real potatoes were an unheard-of treat in the mess, fresh meat a thing of their dreams – and some US Army rations were the best that he could manage.

Once the dog seemed passably fed and watered Dare figured the tiny animal needed a shave. She looked horribly hot, and her long coat seemed beyond saving. Holding her down, he proceeded to slice off the worst of the matted clumps, until all that remained were short tufts sticking out at odd angles. That done, he fashioned her a collar and lead of sorts, a section of old belt forming the former, and a strip of cord cut from a parachute's shroud-lines making the latter.

With the dog shaved, 'dressed', and secured to a nearby tyre, Dare settled back to his duties. His newfound canine companion looked somewhat alarmed by the turn of events, and especially at her unceremonious scalping, but at least she seemed visibly less distraught than when Downey had first dumped her in the motor pool. No doubt the mystery surrounding her surprise discovery would be answered in time.

Dare had his work cut out right now with tending to the 26th's vehicles. The entire squadron was slated to move north to Hollandia – present day Jayapura – the capital city of the northern half of New Guinea Island and the next objective of Operation Cartwheel. No one was kidding themselves that wresting Hollandia from Japanese hands was going to be easy, especially with the calibre of enemy forces that were based there.

Just months earlier Roosevelt, Churchill and China's leader, Generalissimo Chiang Kai Shek, had met to determine the aims and future conduct of the war in the Far East. The resulting

Cairo Declaration had pulled no punches. The Allied leaders had pledged to continue military operations until Japan's unconditional surrender was secured. Japan would 'be stripped of all the islands in the Pacific . . . all territories Japan has stolen from the Chinese,' and any other gains it had made.

The priority for the Allies was to cut off Japan from its chief source of oil supplies, which entailed driving ever northwards to take the Philippines. The archipelago of islands making up the Philippines lay between Imperial Japan and the oil fields to the east. If MacArthur could seize back that territory, he could block all oil supplies from reaching Japan. Deprived of fuel, the nation's warships, tanks and warplanes would grind to a halt, and the Allies would be free to march upon Tokyo.

Of course, Japanese commanders had realized the threat this posed, especially after an airborne attack of breathtaking audacity had demonstrated Japan's vulnerability. In what had become known as the Doolittle Raid, in April 1942 Lieutenant-Colonel James Doolittle had led a flight of sixteen B-25B Mitchell bombers, which had taken off from the carrier USS *Hornet*, deep in the western Pacific Ocean.

They'd reached Japan largely undetected and released their payloads over a selection of military targets spread across six major cities, including Tokyo itself. Intended as retaliation for Pearl Harbor, and as a dramatic stunt for the Allies to boost spirits at home, the raids proved wildly successful. Fifteen of the bombers flew on to China, where they were scheduled to land, and most of the aircrew returned to the USA in triumph.

While doing little lasting damage, the raid convinced the Japanese that their homeland was threatened and vulnerable. Land, naval and aerial reinforcements were rushed to the southwest Pacific region. Provoked into action, Admiral Isoroku Yamamoto had steamed with a powerful armada to attack the US-held airbase on Midway Island, in the Central Pacific. Yamamoto planned to seize Midway and extend the reach of Japanese air power into US territory. Instead, his forces had suffered a major defeat, losing four aircraft carriers – *Akagi*, *Kaga*, *Soryu* and *Hiryu*.

The Battle of Midway represented a serious blow to the Japanese, but the losses were covered up and the Japanese high command announced Midway as a stunning victory. Yet Yamamoto knew as well as anyone the import of such a major setback, and especially in light of the subsequent airborne and amphibious assaults typified by Operation Cartwheel. The Allied advances would have to be halted on the island of New Guinea, which meant that the stakes could not have been higher.

The man charged by Imperial Japan to hold the line among the rugged jungles of New Guinea was General Hatazo Adachi, a figure whose reputation went before him. Adachi came from humble roots. Born to an impoverished Samurai family, he'd worked his way into the ranks of the Japanese military the hard way. When Japan had invaded China, in July 1937, Adachi – then a colonel – had led from the front, spearheading the fierce and brutal fighting around the Chinese port city of Shanghai.

Injured in a mortar barrage, he became known as a soldier's soldier, sharing front-line combat and the miserable conditions suffered by his troops. After being promoted to major general he played a leading role in the hellish policies pursued by the Japanese Army in northern China – the 'Three Alls': 'kill all, burn all, loot all'. Adachi oversaw a scorched-earth policy known as the *Sanko Sakusen* – the annihilation campaign – which had been signed off by Japanese Emperor Hirohito himself.

The *Sanko Sakusen* had involved the razing of Chinese villages, the targeting of 'enemies pretending to be local people', and of 'all males between the ages of fifteen and sixty'. Infused with the same sense of racial and military superiority that enabled Japanese soldiers to treat Allied POWs so mercilessly, the *Sanko Sakusen* policy had claimed more than 2.7 million Chinese lives.

More recently Adachi had cause to taste the Allies' mettle. Upon deploying from China to New Guinea, he'd been caught by US warplanes in the Battle of the Bismarck Sea. He'd seen Japanese ships sunk by Allied aircraft and witnessed thousands of Japanese servicemen losing their lives. Adachi knew what he was up against in New Guinea: he was determined to give no quarter and to fight to the last man.

Despite the savagery that he had orchestrated in China, there was another, more measured, cultured side to Adachi. He was a skilful composer of poetry, excelling at Japanese traditional short verse – *tanka*. Unusually for a Japanese officer of the day, he was exceptionally close to his men. He was accustomed to drinking quantities of sake – rice wine – with the rank and file, and encouraging them to speak freely about their concerns.

In short, Adachi was a formidable adversary. He considered it an enormous honour to have been given command over New Guinea, especially 'at a time when the issue of the day was to be settled'. He relished the challenge of being posted to the 'point of strategic importance in order to ensure that the tide of the war moved in our [Japan's] favour'.

Hollandia – the next clutch of Japanese positions on General MacArthur's shopping list – was to be the acid test. There, General Adachi was determined to make the Allied saying 'Heaven is Java; hell is Burma; but no one returns alive from New Guinea' into a grim and bloody reality.

If the mystery hound now tethered at the Nadzab motor pool was indeed a Foo Dog, the men of the 26th would need all the good luck and protection that she might bring.

Shortly, they would be sailing for Hollandia and whatever hell awaited there.

CHAPTER THREE

Before the squadron could move anywhere, Bill Wynne came to investigate sketchy reports of a dog residing at the motor pool. Wynne's tentmate, Ed Downey, hadn't breathed a word about her presence, but news had a way of getting out. Wynne had heard rumours about a four-legged fugitive that had arrived from out of the blue – a mystery dog that Sergeant Dare had apparently christened 'Smokums', after her smoky grey-blue colouring.

Wynne's first reaction on meeting 'Smokums' was surprise. The tall, dark-haired GI had never laid eyes on an animal as odd-looking as the one presently tied to the motor pool tyre. As her tiny tongue lolled out, panting in the heat, Smokums repeatedly tried to jump up at her newest visitor, desperate to demonstrate how happy she was that someone, anyone, was paying her a little attention.

She was so small it was almost unreal. When standing, she came to no higher than Wynne's boot tops. He squatted down for a better look, getting face-to-face with the dog. This close up her eyes were half-obscured by the shock of shorn hair: he could make out a set of fuzzy, grinning features, in a face exuding an impish sense of curiosity and canine mischief. Wynne's close scrutiny was rewarded with a generous lick from her tiny pink tongue. He was more than a little intrigued.

'Well, what kind of beast is this?' he announced, speaking more to himself than to Sergeant Dare.

All he could see of the motor pool sergeant was a pair of booted feet sticking out from beneath a nearby jeep. He repeated the question, Dare responding by extricating himself from the dark and oily engine compartment, his eyes blinking in the fierce sunlight.

The motor pool sergeant proceeded to relate the tale of how the dog had been found in the jungle, but that no one seemed to have a clue as to how she had got there, let alone what breed she might be. As Dare spoke, Wynne studied the dog some more. She was a compact little animal, that was for sure. Too compact: she was clearly half-starved. But regardless, she carried herself well, conveying an air almost of self-importance, with her head held high.

That head was petite, the nose short and finely-boned, the tip a glistening black button. The V-shaped ears were a rich tan colour and covered in short hair, as were her legs. But it was the eyes that struck him most powerfully. A deep amber-brown, they had a fierce sparkle in them that spoke of an innate loyalty and a quick-witted intelligence.

'So, what d'you think she is?' Sergeant Dare asked, once he'd finished relating his tale.

Wynne shrugged. 'Well, it's a dog . . . But it looks kind of weird thanks to the haircut. Some kind of dizzy little poodle,' he ventured.

He caressed her for a moment. Word was that Dare wanted rid

of the animal and was seeking a buyer. Her stubby tail wagged furiously, but still he could tell that the tiny dog was sickly. She weighed almost nothing, and the impression of scrawniness was hardly helped by the appalling haircut. Plus she seemed racked with anxiety, weaving this way and that and spinning incessantly on her tired legs.

A hopeless lover of dogs, Wynne did his best to comfort and calm her. Despite her tiny stature, the animal's big personality seemed to shine through. She had to be one feisty and courageous animal, to have survived all alone in the jungle for however long she had. Beneath the ragged shorn coat and sickly pallor, he could sense the dog's true nature – one replete with charm and a real love of fun.

'I'm not sure she's very healthy,' he remarked, as he fingered her uneven tufts of hair. 'Where exactly did you say you found her again?'

Dare repeated the story of her discovery, as told him by Downey.

'I'm not sure she'll live,' Wynne ventured. 'She seems so weak. But hey, I'll give you two pounds Australian for her.'

'Make it three and she's yours,' Dare countered.

Wynne considered this for a second. The price wasn't the issue. In American money it amounted to less than ten dollars. He was more worried about the risks involved in taking the dog. He sensed that they would bond incredibly quickly, but he was worried that she might die on him, and he would be bereft. It wouldn't be the first time that he'd lost a beloved canine companion, and the trauma had left him wary: once bitten, twice shy.

On the other hand she was a fellow creature caught up in the horrors of war, and that tugged at his heartstrings. Wynne marvelled at the series of events that had led to Downey's jeep breaking down at the exact spot where he could hear the dog's whining, not to mention a dog-hater such as him deciding to rescue her. He didn't doubt that Downey had saved her life, for she wouldn't have lasted many more days in the heat of the jungle with no water to hand.

A part of him felt that fate somehow had brought him together with this dog. Yet at the same time he had an instinctive feeling that nature might take its course with this tiny little life. He couldn't face carrying Smokums back to his tent, only to have to bury her in the jungle in a day or two's time.

Hailing from Cleveland, Ohio – a city on the shores of Lake Erie, which sits astride the US-Canadian border – Bill Wynne had known few moments when dogs hadn't graced the family home. Indeed, he'd come to view the families in the neighbourhood by the type of dog they kept. A quiet, happy dog signified a quiet, happy home, and vice versa.

His parents were of Irish and Welsh ancestry, but his father, Martin Wynne, had left before Bill had had the chance to get to know him at all. He hadn't seen or heard from him since. By the time he was six, Wynne's mother, Beatrice, was supervising a large staff at a factory making chicken incubators. She struggled to manage work and to find childcare for Bill and his younger brother, Jim, while striving to give them the care and attention they deserved.

Finally, she'd made the tough decision to send the boys to the Parmadale Children's Village of St Vincent de Paul, a Catholic orphanage, in Parma, a suburb of Cleveland. The orphanage was run by an overworked but immensely patient staff of Catholic nuns and it was an all-boys affair. That being the case, Bill's sister, Mary, was sent to live with a grandparent. Caring for boys aged six to sixteen, Parmadale boasted its own school, gymnasium, swimming pool, accommodation blocks and a convent. The boys rarely had cause to leave the grounds.

At first Wynne was horribly lonely, and it was fortunate that the orphanage came complete with a veritable menagerie of animals. To the consternation of Sisters Lucy and Hubert the boys kept bringing all sorts of creatures into their dorm, including snakes, turtles and raccoons. One day some of the older lads had returned from a nightly forage with a pair of owls carefully wrapped in their jumpers. The birds proceeded to hoot all night long, until Sister Hubert insisted an owl-release expedition was in order.

Bill Wynne had grown closest to Parmadale's dog, Rags, a big, shaggy-haired Airedale, which, with his fluffy face and kindly eyes resembled a giant teddy bear. Rags loved kids and he and Wynne ran wild through the grounds. But one day a big, sullen fourteen-year-old had decided to take out his anger and frustration on the defenceless dog. He threw acid at Rags, and the memory of the poor animal running in panic and agony was seared forever in Wynne's mind.

Playing in the orphanage baseball team had taught Wynne that apparent losers could become winners, if blessed with the right frame of mind. With spirit and hope and guts they'd won the local championship, even without any parents on the sidelines to cheer them on. But the discipline at Parmadale had been harsh and that, combined with the loneliness that plagued him over the two years he spent there, meant that Wynne returned home somewhat introverted and withdrawn. Again, it was dogs that brought him out of himself.

Queenie was a stray who followed him home one day. His mother decided to let her young son keep the dog. In time Queenie had six pups, which looked like a crazed Chow-Brindle Bullmastiff-Stafford Terrier-Bulldog cross. Unsurprisingly, they grew up to be bundles of pure grit and muscle. Wynne named his favourite Pal. Pal nurtured a love all of things human, but he turned out to be a true hellhound with any male dogs that crossed his path. Fed mostly on table scraps, his teeth got into poor condition, which at least meant that he didn't do too much damage when fighting his rivals.

Cleveland was a sprawling expanse of a city, with lots of wide-open spaces. It was a paradise for groups of energetic young boys. Wynne and his friends would take Pal to the sand field, a large area of derelict ground several blocks square, and pocked with 'Indian mounds' – low, angular hillocks which made for adventurous bike rides. Nearby was a patch of scrubby woodland thick with songbirds, and an adjacent swamp, thronging with water fowl. They were great places for Pal, Wynne and their gang to explore.

Pal was a fast learner and an eager pupil. Wynne taught the dog to jump up and snatch his woollen hat, without harming a hair of his head, and then to drop it the moment he cried out 'Stop!' During the heavy snows that often hit Ohio in winter, Pal learned to ride a sled downhill and then drag it back up again crammed full of eager boys.

Smart and fiercely loyal, Pal even managed to discover where Wynne attended school. Everyday he'd be there at 3.30, waiting to escort his young master the mile walk home. But one day Pal wasn't waiting in his usual spot any more. Wynne hurried back to the house, only to find that Pal wasn't there either. For months he waited for Pal to return, but the dog had simply disappeared.

Losing Pal broke the young Wynne's heart. He was sickened by the loss, which he never forgot. And now, as he crouched in the motor pool tent at Nadzab contemplating Smokums, he was assailed by similar worries; similar fears. Could he really take the risk of being hurt like that again? Could he really risk getting another dog, especially in a place such as the war-torn New Guinea jungle?

In war, everything seemed heightened: fear, adrenalin, brotherly love, sadness, hunger, thirst, loss, trauma, boredom and excitement. Wynne wasn't exactly eager to go through everything that he had suffered with Pal all over again.

Bidding farewell to Smokums, he wandered back to his tent lost in thought. He felt torn. He vowed to give it twenty-four hours. He'd go and visit the motor pool tent the following day, to see how the little dog was faring. Yet even if she had survived, he wondered how a unit like the 26th – one that thirsted for excellence – would take to one of their own adopting a mystery hound.

Ever since its formation a year earlier, the 26th had been pinned as a 'hot' squadron, one earmarked for overseas deployment and a leading front-line role. The men had prepared themselves by undergoing weeks of exercises under canvas,

complete with daily hikes laden with weapons and rucksacks –
all designed to simulate the kind of conditions they might
encounter in the Pacific.

Wynne had trained as an airborne photography specialist, but
the single-seater P-38 Lightnings had no call for such a role. At
first, no one had been sure where best to utilize his skills: was
he going to be most use in the camera repair workshops or the
photo laboratory? As the lab was short of manpower he'd ended
up there, processing the reams of precious images that the pilots
brought back from their daring airborne sorties.

By its very nature photo recce work was top secret. Nothing – from the destinations of recce flights, to the images the
pilots secured, to the intelligence the photos revealed – could
be allowed to leak to the enemy. As a result, the squadron
had to observe exacting standards of security. Just about every
document emanating from the 26th – from Final Flight Reports
to the monthly intelligence briefings – was stamped 'CONFI-
DENTIAL', 'CLASSIFIED' or 'OPS SECRET'.

Only the highest calibre officers could be entrusted with
overseeing such levels of security. After First Lieutenant Hallett –
recently listed as missing in action (MIA) – First Lieutenant
Hartwell C. McCullough was one of the 26th's most senior
officers. McCullough was a former photo reconnaissance instructor at Peterson Field, Colorado, then the centre of US photo recce
excellence. Along with First Sergeant Joyce B. Howell, a squat,
forty-something dark-haired Texan, McCullough constituted
the heart and soul of this elite unit.

McCullough, who hailed from Louisiana in the American
Deep South, was an absolute stickler for discipline. Among his

many duties, McCullough was 'Custodian of Squadron Classified Documents' – the man charged with ensuring nothing of any import found its way into the enemy's hands.

McCullough ensured that rules and regulations, especially concerning security, were rigidly adhered to. Just that month he'd had to read the men the riot act, after wild rumours had swept through the ranks about the squadron's forthcoming move. Careless talk costs lives. It could also seriously dent morale.

Yet inevitably, there was also a real maverick streak to a unit like the 26th. The solitary seat-of-the-pants flying tended to attract single-minded, one-of-a-kind individuals, and the culture of daily risk-taking rubbed off on everyone, ground crew included.

Here at Nadzab, the men expressed their individualism in various idiosyncratic ways. Over the camp flew the iconic Texas colours – the Lone Star Flag – as opposed to the regular Stars and Stripes, reflecting the fact that sixteen of the squadron's two-hundred-plus personnel originated from Texas. In rare moments of downtime the Texans liked to gather beneath the flag to play poker and shoot the breeze. Hidden away in the jungle there was a still, for distilling moonshine – a fierce liquor the Texans like to quaff beneath their Lone Star Flag. Most prominent among the Texans was First Sergeant Joyce Howell, a self-confessed country-boy and a renowned practical joker who was in the habit of wandering about Nadzab wearing a pair of leather cowboy boots, as opposed to regulation army footwear.

But despite the squadron's decidedly maverick bent, Wynne could expect few special favours here at Nadzab, and who knew whether adopting a dog would pass muster? He ducked inside his tent – an inverted V of khaki green, sheltered beneath a forest giant laced with thick vines – and eyed Ed Downey, his so-called buddy and tentmate, accusingly.

'How come you didn't offer me the dog?' he demanded.

Downey turned an expressionless face on Wynne. 'I don't want a mutt in my tent,' he replied, flatly.

The whole thing was made even worse by the fact that Downey was well aware that Wynne hankered after a canine companion, for he was forever going on about it. Not only would Wynne have to risk the censure of the 26th's senior officers if he adopted the dog, he'd have to tackle his tent buddy, who clearly wasn't going to welcome a few pounds of cute and cuddly hairball into their communal living quarters.

First the dog had been abandoned in the jungle by persons unknown. Then she'd been discovered by a self-confessed dog-hater, and she hadn't exactly been welcomed with open arms in the motor pool, either. Right now she was for sale, but there weren't any buyers. Right now, it seemed as if Smokums wasn't particularly welcome anywhere. It struck Wynne that she was an orphan – and orphan from a foxhole – rather like he had once been, at least for a while.

Surely he was duty-bound to ride to her rescue?

CHAPTER 4

Before joining the military and training as an aerial photographer, Bill Wynne had done his utmost to use his canine experiences to help the US war effort. On his twentieth birthday he'd been given a dog by his sweetheart, Margie Roberts, who lived just ten doors down from his house on the same Cleveland street. It was 1942 and Wynne had answered the call to train the puppy, a Doberman-German Shepherd cross named Toby, as a war dog.

Bill and Toby signed up to the Cleveland All Breed Training School, part of a nationwide initiative established by the US military to boost the number of potential war dogs in circulation. The need was acute. At the time of Pearl Harbor the US had fewer than a hundred dogs serving in the Army, mostly sled dogs serving at snow-bound military bases in Alaska.

To begin with the US military had no plans for training any kind of expanded canine corps. Senior commanders had simply assumed that in the new high-tech form of warfare in this global conflict there would be little call for animals to serve. That thinking quickly changed. Dogs were wanted for wire-laying, message-carrying, mine-detection, sentry, first aid, scout, attack and trail duties, and demand for trained dogs far outstripped supply. Hence the War Dog Program was launched, informally known as the 'K9 Corps'.

A national publicity campaign solicited donations of semi-trained animals to join the Dogs for Defense initiative, run in conjunction with the American Kennel Club. Experience showed that German Shepherds, Dobermans, farm collies, Siberian Huskies, Malamutes and Eskimo dogs were the breeds most suited to such work.

Crosses of those breeds were equally acceptable, making Toby an ideal recruit. Wynne and his dog had started attending the Dogs for Defense obedience classes, which were held in a downtown Cleveland public square. Those open-air training sessions drew crowds of onlookers, attracting yet more owners and their dogs to volunteer for the War Dog Program.

Dogs for Defense received 18,000 donations, of which around half completed formal training with the military. Those disqualified were generally ruled out due to their small size, temperament, health, extreme excitability or for having a weak sense of smell. Wynne and Toby were halfway through the ten-week obedience classes when he had received his draft orders. Before Toby was able to graduate, his master had left to train for war.

In the spring of 1943 the US War Department decided that K9 units were needed for front-line duties, especially in the southwest Pacific theatre. Dogs could make a real difference in the close confines of the jungle, where visibility was often limited, but where scent and sound could still be detected over great distances.

Committing dogs to the jungle war presented a serious challenge. The K9 Corps didn't possess trainers with experience of such a tough and unforgiving environment, but they knew of those who did. At the British War Dog Training School they had been doing this far longer than anyone. Time was short and there seemed little point in trying to reinvent the wheel, so the US K9 Corps asked for help from Captain John B. Garle, one of the most experienced of the British trainers.

In February 1943 Captain Garle travelled to the US along with two fellow handlers and four veteran dogs, on what the American K9 Corps jokingly referred to as a 'lend-leash' basis. (Lend-lease was the system in which the US provided her allies with warships, warplanes, fuel and other vital war materiel, in return for leases granted on overseas bases owned by those Allied nations.)

Garle and his lend-leash team set to work at the War Dog Reception and Training Center, in Maryland, on the eastern coast of the USA. There they demonstrated how messenger dogs could be trained to carry urgent communiqués across the field of battle. Each dog had two handlers, to both of whom he or she demonstrated a fierce loyalty: one would give the dog a message to be carried, while the other would await its delivery. Such messenger dogs could cover great distances at high speed, presenting an elusive target to enemy snipers.

Garle and his team demonstrated how scout dogs could use their incredibly powerful senses of hearing and smell to identify hostile patrols at up to 1,000 yards away. Depending on the conditions – wind direction, vegetation cover, dampness of the ground – they could be used in amphibious landings to detect enemy positions on the shoreline, or on reconnaissance and combat patrols. But in all cases the dogs' effectiveness would depend upon how accustomed they were to gunfire and explosions.

Following the lend-leash training programme, the first American war dogs units had been dispatched to the Pacific, K9 teams going into action in New Guinea. Reports that filtered back from those units were highly positive. Both messenger and scout units gave 'consistently excellent performances'. Inevitably, such successes had made the dogs a target. A Marine Corps German Shepherd was shot by a Japanese sniper on Bougainville, an island off the east coast of New Guinea, and later would die of his wounds. There were dozens more such canine casualties.

In contrast to the US military, in the run-up to the war the Japanese had had a highly active K9 programme. The Japanese military had urged the public to donate their domestic pets, German Shepherds being the most sought after. As early as their 1937 invasion of China, some 10,000 highly trained dogs – mostly German Shepherds – served with the Imperial Japanese Army, as messengers, sentries, trackers and sled teams. The breed was praised as embodying the 'dauntless courage whose loyalty and bravery rank with the Imperial Soldier, and which would even make a fierce god weep'.

But that was the mighty German Shepherd; the diminutive dog tethered to a tyre at the Nadzab motor pool was an entirely different kind of beast. If Smokums had been a Japanese war dog, it stood to reason that a creature of her size could only have served as some kind of a mascot. As Bill Wynne wandered through Nadzab camp the morning after her surprise arrival, he didn't doubt that she was ready to serve a new master – that's if she'd survived the night just gone.

She had. Not only that, Sergeant Dare had decided that his need to be rid of the dog was ever more pressing. Indeed, he came seeking Wynne with a new proposition. There was a knock at the door of the photo trailer, Wynne's main place of work in the camp.

'Hey, Wynne, d'you want to buy the dog for two pounds?' Dare declared. He laughed, a little self-consciously. 'I need to get back in a poker game.' Dare had been losing and he wanted the money to help him reverse his recent ill-fortune.

Wynne eyed him, suspiciously. 'How is she looking today?'

Dare assured him that with a little half-decent food Smokums was making a remarkable recovery. Wynne was on duty, so he could hardly go and see for himself. He was a Private First Class (PFC) in rank and two Australian pounds was the equivalent of $6.44, a tenth of his monthly salary. But he was eager to claim the dog as his own, especially if she'd rallied as much as Dare claimed.

The deal was struck, and Wynne could hardly wait to fetch the odd little creature and lavish upon her the kind of care and attention he just knew she craved.

Just as soon as he had signed off duty Wynne hurried down to the motor pool. The reception he received from Smokums – Smoky now she was his – was everything that he'd been hoping for. She bounded about at the end of her lead, clearly overjoyed to see him again. Sure enough she seemed to have a new lease of life and was bubbling with energy and spirit. Wynne had to accept that Dare's assessment had been right: she had made a miraculous recovery.

He bent to inspect her for a second time, a little more

thoroughly now that the deal was done. He worked his thumb and forefinger around her back, just around her hips, and he could feel that she was bony still, but not as bad as the day before. Her eyes sparkled, her stubby little tail – docked at the first joint – flicked back and forth in a high-speed blur, and her ears pricked up excitedly. The look on her face seemed to be all about what adventures the two of them might have together.

Their very first adventure, which was hardly likely to be overly pleasant, lay right before them. Wynne whisked her up and made his way towards the tent that he shared with Downey. He soon realized that Smoky wanted a run around. He set her on the ground and she fizzed and buzzed around his feet. She was a real firework of energy, and Wynne made sure to scoop her up and tuck her securely under his arm again, as he ducked through the flap of his tent. There was nothing for it: he'd have to face down the dog-hater.

Downey was resting on his cot. He took one look at Smoky and his face darkened. 'I don't want that mutt in my tent,' he yelled.

Wynne stood his ground. 'She's staying,' he countered firmly, his voice calm but low.

There was a long beat of silence, a moment in which these two good friends might have come to blows. But finally, Downey seemed to back down. He gave a dismissive gesture, before adding, vehemently: 'Well, just keep the thing away from me.'

That was exactly what Wynne, the little dog's saviour, intended. He set Smoky down and she scampered over to his cot, making a beeline for the patch of drab olive material that served as a cover. It was spread out at the bottom end, and Smoky clearly had found her chosen spot. Under Wynne's careful gaze she circled a couple of times, before settling down for a nap. Smoky, at least, seemed very much at home.

Wynne let her rest, knowing this was very likely the first sleep in relative comfort and security that she'd had for some time. The crazed haircut made it look as if she'd been in some kind of savage fight, and he tried to imagine what her coat might look like when it grew back and was properly groomed. He could see why Sergeant Dare had chosen the name Smokums for her. Even shorn as it was, her hair had a gingery-brown tone with lighter, smoky tips at the ends.

Downey remained an issue, so this was hardly the perfect home for her, but it sure was a damn sight better than an abandoned foxhole in the jungle. What struck him most, now that he had her in his custody, was the responsibility that he'd just taken upon himself. Tiny she might be, but already he had a feeling that this was a little dog with a giant personality. He had no idea what breed she might be, but there was a fine elegance to her bearing that hinted at a real pedigree.

Smoky was something special, Wynne felt certain, and he was determined to discover her story. He wondered if she might be some kind of Japanese breed. There was an interpreter on camp who spoke fluent Japanese, and he decided to take Smoky to see him just as soon as she'd settled. If she responded to commands issued in Japanese – sit, stay, come – then that might go some way to solving the enigma that she embodied.

But for now, it was all about more prosaic issues. The first was food. Wynne and the rest of the 26th were fed on GI – Government Issue – rations, served in the squadron's mess tent and eaten at ranks of rough hewn wooden benches and tables. The food consisted mostly of dehydrated potatoes, powdered egg, bully beef (canned corned meat), canned Australian mutton (which had a terrible taste and smell to it), spam, plus citric acid to drink (which occurs naturally in citric fruits like lemons and oranges, and was taken to prevent scurvy).

There was a joke among the men of the 26th regarding the chow: 'Throw it in the mess tin, then go outside and throw it one way or another.' Fresh meat was a rarity, but fortunately canned fruit was in abundance and highly popular, though it would be no meal for a dog. Wynne worried that the kind of food available at Nadzab might kill a little animal like Smoky, causing pancreatic or kidney failure in a matter of months.

But there was little else to hand.

When Smoky woke from her nap he tried her on some bully beef. He opened a can and emptied half of it into his mess tin. Famished from her sojourn in the foxhole it seemed to go down a treat. Wynne figured that the key to keeping her safe and secure in the camp was going to lie in training. Between his duties at the photo lab and diving into the nearest shelter during air raids, he reckoned he could find the time to act as her instructor. He suspected that she was sharp-minded and would prove a quick learner.

The sooner that he could get her to understand the rules and constraints of such a place, the better. If he could teach her tricks, like he'd done with Pal and his other dogs, so much the better. She could entertain the men of the squadron, which should endear her to their number. A popular dog was far less likely to be on the receiving end of any ill treatment, or to fall foul of military rules or regulations. Even someone like Downey would have to rein in his antipathy if Smoky somehow became indispensable to the 26th.

Wynne knew a good deal about training champs. On the Parmadale orphanage's baseball field he'd learned how no-hopers could be melded into winners. In his teens he'd gone to Cleveland's West Technical High School, which had 5,600 students on its books. It was at West Tech that he'd first studied photography, which in time had led him to his role in the 26th. He'd also indulged his love of football, making it onto the high school first team, which was no small achievement in a school of West Tech's size and standing.

Torn ligaments in his right knee had put a premature end to his footballing career, but he'd learned a great deal about top-notch teams and their training regimes. A great coach-player partnership relied upon a combination of natural ability, the will to win, and trust. Sporting greatness didn't come easily. You had to have the drive to be the best, no matter what. His football coaches had called that quality 'intestinal fortitude', or the 'willingness to pay the price'.

Likewise, in a canine pupil-trainer team, each would only ever be as good as the other. He and Smoky would have to strive to be the very best, for the odds were stacked against them. Wynne knew instinctively that training, and forging an unbeatable partnership, would be the key to their survival.

He'd settled upon shortening Smokum's name to 'Smoky', in part because it rolled more easily off the tongue. It was smooth and quick for calls and recalls. Once he was certain she was fully fed and rested, he grabbed Smoky's DIY collar and parachute cord lead and took her for her first training session. He began by teaching her the basics: 'Heel! Sit! Stand-stay!' At that last command she had to remain exactly where she was, as he walked away from her and then returned to her side.

He sensed from the get-go that this was a dog who'd been trained before. She took to the commands so easily. He made sure to encourage her with an abundance of praise and play, as he'd been taught to do during the Cleveland Dogs for Defense classes. You never used physical punishment or harsh words with a dog. If you did, your aggression would tend to be transferred to the animal. A dog apes its owner. You had to use positive reinforcement to get the very best out of your dog.

At the Cleveland All Breed Training School they'd advised using a choke collar, a silver chain threaded through itself that would close tight and choke the dog if ever he or she tried to pull away. (It's something that many experts now advise is neither humane nor conducive to getting the desired results.) Here in Nadzab Wynne had only the makeshift leather belt that was threaded around Smoky's delicate neck.

Smoky loved the training, but she loved the breaks too. She seemed to have a massive drive for action and play. She thrilled to being taken for a run around the camp or playing tug-of-war with one of Wynne's socks, making throaty little growls as she tried to wrestle it from his hands.

For a moment, as they play-fought in this way, Wynne felt like a little kid again, though he was in the middle of the jungle and the wail of the air-raid siren might start up at any moment, signalling the need to dive for the nearest shelter. This was the beauty of owning a dog, even at war.

The obedience lessons would establish limits for the dog, allowing Smoky to settle into the more relaxed and calm animal that she doubtless naturally was. She seemed exceptionally eager to please, which made her a pleasure to work with. Bonds were forming quickly between the dog and her new master, and ironically, bearing in mind Wynne's concern for Smoky and her diminutive size, she seemed to be growing keenly protective over him.

Wynne decided to try her on a few choice tricks. One of the simplest and most effective acts that Wynne knew of was the 'play dead'. He taught Smoky to 'drop dead', the signal being him holding out his finger and thumb like a pistol and miming taking a shot: *Bang!* Right on cue Smoky had to fall down. She had to lie on her back, legs in the air and paws curled over, unmoving. She'd stay like that no matter what Wynne might say or do.

Then he'd give her the call: 'Smoky, okay! Okay!'

At the sound of his voice she'd spring back to life, jumping onto all fours and taking a bow. It was a simple enough trick but a compelling one, and Wynne felt certain they'd have audiences gripped in the palms of their hands (paws). Smoky also had a big voice for such a small dog, and she seemed to have an innate love of 'singing', or rather howling along to her master as he played his favourite tunes on the harmonica.

When Wynne blew a few exploratory notes, Smoky threw her head back and responded with a long, drawn-out 'Owoooooo'. Soon she'd learned to throw her head back in conjunction with her master, howling for all she was worth as he whistled along. But Smoky's singing was not without risk: it attracted the wrath off her chief detractor.

'When a dog cries someone's gonna die,' he growled, menacingly.

The threat was made in all seriousness, and for now at least Wynne decided to exercise Smoky's choral talents only when she was well out of anyone's earshot.

Very quickly, Wynne – still just twenty years of age – realized that Smoky had much to teach him. As man and dog trained together, so they appeared to be maturing alongside each other. Wynne felt ever more certain that this tiny bundle of mystery had been cared for, schooled and nurtured by whoever her previous owners might have been. It was more than a little intriguing.

As they got to know each other better, Wynne felt his earlier concerns about owning a dog once more gradually seeping away. After months soldiering in the loneliness and isolation of the New Guinea jungle and beset on all sides by dangers as they were, life could be incredibly stressful, and Smoky was proving a tremendous morale-booster.

As had happened so many times in Wynne's life, at the point of greatest need a dog had come to his rescue.

CHAPTER 5

After several days training squeezed between lab shifts, Wynne decided that Smoky was ready for her great unveiling. More to the point, he reckoned she might have a role to play within the finely tuned outfit that was the 26th Photo Reconnaissance Squadron. The capturing, processing, analysis and dissemination of photo intelligence were conducted round the clock. The labs, the drying machines, the analysis desks and the communications centre were never less than busy and they never closed.

Whenever an aircraft landed from a successful mission the images it carried were required by senior commanders as a matter of urgency. Combat missions were in the final stages of planning. Targets were being confirmed and apportioned to fighter and bomber squadrons. Beaches were being scoped for amphibious landings, caves and thick jungle probed for hidden enemy positions.

Usually, the first sign that a recce flight was in-bound came via the radio: maybe a P-38 had been detected on the base's radar, or the pilot had called in with an ETA. Once the landing time was known, the ground crew would head for the flight line to ease the half-frozen flier out of his cockpit. Once that was done, he'd report the basics of what he'd filmed to the squadron's intelligence officer.

The photo magazines would be removed and rushed by jeep to the lab. There the team – including Wynne if it was his shift – would develop the negatives in the darkroom, immersing them in pools of chemicals. They would be dried and viewed on a special light table. Prints were made of the most promising images, which were washed and run through drying machines that looked like giant industrial hair-driers. The finished images were sorted again, before being rushed to whoever had requested them. Often, they were packed aboard a light aircraft to be flown direct to the relevant headquarters.

It was intense, relentless work. The men found it hard to stay focused amid such a whirlwind of activity, especially as it was interspersed with long periods of simply waiting for something to happen, of hoping against hope that the recce squadron's Lightnings would come back safely. All too often there was the dark stress and strain of a flight going missing; of pilots simply not returning at all.

A few days after making her his own, Wynne took Smoky with him for her first shift at the photo lab. The laboratory was so hot – with gallons of chemicals being mixed by hand in vats, prints being washed in the steaming sinks and the oven-like driers whirring away – that the men tended to work shirtless and bare-headed. It lent an informal edge to the lab's otherwise intense and frenetic atmosphere.

Generators thudded in the background, for the photo lab – the driers especially – consumed huge amounts of electricity. Indeed, with the amount of power available Sergeant Waggoner, one of the 26th's engineers, had decided to form his own 'Power & Light Company'. He'd got men shimmying up palm trees, stringing cables from trunk to trunk as makeshift telegraph poles, providing electric lighting to those facilities that kept turning and burning day and night.

Nowhere burned the midnight oil like the photo lab, and Smoky's appearance there proved an instant hit. Most had already heard about the mystery dog, but few had managed to get sight of her up close. Smoky did a meet and greet with each of the lab team, starting with the lab chief Master Sergeant Irving 'Irv' Green, and she loved being the centre of attention.

Man and dog proceeded to demonstrate their first trick. Wynne pointed his finger at Smoky, forming a pistol shape. 'Boom!' he cried. Bang on cue she fell 'dead'. She lay rock-still, no matter what Wynne might do to her. He poked and prodded her several times, all to no avail. Squatting, he picked her up by her hind legs and rolled her over from hand to hand. She remained limp and lifeless as a ragdoll.

Wynne placed her on the ground, gently. He prodded her a few more times, as if doing a final check for any signs of life. Nothing. Then he turned and walked away, disconsolately, as if giving up on the little tyke. He waited a few seconds, before calling out: 'Okay!' At the sound of his voice the little bundle of shapeless fur exploded into life, jumping onto all fours and charging after her master.

The lab crew went wild.

Irv Green seemed more taken than anyone with his newest crew member. He had sandy hair cut longish and semi-quiffed at the front, and a quiet, pensive air. The demands of the photo lab could be all-consuming, the pressures debilitating. Methodical, calm, a little introspective – Green was the ideal kind of individual to run the place.

It was Green who came up with the concept of how Smoky might best serve on his team. Much of the work was endlessly repetitive, but the stakes were incredibly high. One wrong move, one moment of lapsed concentration, could ruin an entire roll of film and its irreplaceable images. The consequences of that were unthinkable. Smoky was the answer to livening things up a little, and to helping the lab crews stay focused.

In the shadows of the darkroom – it was lit only by dim, red-filtered bulbs, to protect the negatives – Wynne and Green got the tiny dog to squat in a tray of freshly developed film, ready to be passed through the 'light-trap', a hatchway sealed by thick curtains leading to the outside. Once all was ready, the tray was posted across complete with a tufty-haired, sparkly-eyed dog – for make no mistake, Smoky was loving this new adventure.

The crew outside, who were responsible for washing the freshly developed film, plucked her off the tray as she blinked in the bright sunlight. They caressed and cooed over the dog, the banter flying back and forth as they passed her around. Shortly, the tray was posted back, with Smoky taking pride of place once more. Irv Green declared himself delighted with the procedure. Smoky had found her niche in the laboratory: she was on Tray Duty. This was to become a regular procedure, one that helped the lab teams pass the interminable hours.

Shifts were long, hot and testing: twelve hours at a time. Mostly, the men of the 26th worked seven-day weeks, with no breaks. Nights, menaced as they were by air raids, were fraught with danger. Occasionally, there was a movie in the mess tent, whenever a new release managed to make it out to the wilds of New Guinea. Other than that, the pastimes for the GIs were writing letters to loved ones, listening to the radio or playing endless card games.

Isolated so far from home, it was an eternal struggle to keep morale high, one in which Wynne hoped Smoky could play a significant role. Though the Allies had started to turn the tide of the war in the Pacific, it didn't necessarily feel like that to the men on the ground, operating deep in the jungle facing a fanatical enemy, assailed by air raids and starved of news. Realizing this, the Japanese had started their own wily form of propaganda, which was beamed into Nadzab every day.

The squadron's typed Monthly Intelligence Summaries – stamped CONFIDENTIAL – listed the main issues affecting the unit, under such headings as 'RUMORS', 'PROPAGANDA ACTIVITY' and 'MORALE'. Alarmingly, that March 1944 – the month of Smoky's discovery – the morale of the 26th was listed as 'unusually low'. Much of the disquiet was due to the squadron's rumour mill, which seemed to have gone into overdrive, and one of the key reasons for this was Radio Tokyo.

In November 1941 Japan's national broadcaster – NHK, their equivalent to the BBC – had been nationalized by the Imperial Japanese Army. In fact, all news, whether newspaper or radio, was now to be regarded as an official pronouncement of the Imperial Army General Headquarters, in Tokyo. The 'Tokyo Rose' programmes had become the foremost weapon in the Japanese propaganda arsenal.

Those broadcasts were made by fluent English speakers, all of whom were female and whose identities remained a tantalizing mystery. They consisted of a clever blend of music, comedy and entertainment, interspersed with 'news flashes' that accentuated the privations and the losses suffered by the Allies. They aimed to demoralize Allied troops, who were already facing tough and testing conditions.

Marooned amid the mountainous jungles of Nadzab, those Tokyo Rose broadcasts became compelling listening to the men of the 26th. With carefully crafted disinformation slipped into genuine news stories, such propaganda proved remarkably effective, especially as the newscasters were fluent and soft-voiced young women, who the lonely soldiers couldn't help but imagine as pretty and alluring.

That March an extraordinary rumour swept through the squadron: President Roosevelt's wife, Eleanor, was demanding that all soldiers returning from the southwest Pacific theatre be sent to an island lying off the coast of the mainland USA, where they would be subjected to as much as eighteen months' quarantine. If true, it would mean a year or more of miserable isolation.

Troops would be screened for malaria, lice and other diseases endemic to the Pacific area. New Guinea was plagued by such ills, so much so that the skin of GIs took on an unhealthy yellow pallor, due to all the anti-malarial drugs they had to take, first and foremost the notorious Atabrine. So significant was the threat from malaria, that at the entrance to New Guinea's main field hospital was a sign that read: 'These men DIDN'T take their ATABRINE'. On top of the sign were perched two empty-eyed human skulls.

Eleanor Roosevelt played a very prominent role in the political and social life of the nation, so the story appeared to have credibility. The Allies had declared their first priority in the war was to defeat Nazi Germany, with Japan coming second. Accordingly, troops in the Pacific tended to worry that they were the 'poor cousins' in the conflict. That fear was now being exacerbated by outrageous and unsettling rumours of long months of quarantine.

In short, the Radio Tokyo story was a masterpiece of propaganda. It had taken the soldiers' deepest fears – of exotic diseases, of isolation and of being forgotten by those at home – and apparently made them a chilling reality. There was no truth at all to the story, of course, but that didn't stop the men talking among themselves.

The squadron's spring '44 Intelligence Summaries stressed the efforts made to quash such morale-sapping loose talk. They concluded that the story was 'obviously a malicious rumour intended to damage the character of the First Lady; it was pointed out to the men as such.' But the novelty of the shows and the allure of the mystery female hosts ensured that Radio Tokyo continued to draw listeners.

An even wilder report began to do the rounds. 'Rumoured also was the belief that "Madame Tojo" of Radio Tokyo is Amelia Earhart,' the Intelligence Summaries noted. 'Rumour is not generally believed.' Whether or not the men believed it, the very idea that one of America's most famous and heroic figures might be pumping out enemy propaganda was hugely disheartening. It sowed the seeds of doubt – doubt that could become corrosive if left to fester.

In 1932 Amelia Earhart had become the first woman to fly across the Atlantic. Blessed with fresh-faced, tomboyish good looks, there was a swashbuckling side to her character that played well with the public on both sides of the Atlantic. Upon touching down at Culmore, in Northern Ireland, after her fourteen hour fifty-six minute trans-Atlantic journey, Earhart had been asked by a curious local if she had come far? 'From America,' was her teasing reply.

In 1937 she'd set out with a male pilot to circumnavigate the globe. They'd completed 22,000 miles of the trip, before going missing in the southwest Pacific. What made the Tokyo Rose rumour all the more credible, at least to the men of the squadron, was that Earhart and her fellow pilot, Fred Noonan, had taken off for their fateful last flight from Lae, the port adjacent to Nadzab itself.

In spite of extensive searches made along their flightpath, no sign was ever found of the missing aircraft. Earhart and her co-pilot had disappeared seemingly without trace. But now, according to the Tokyo Rose broadcasts, Earhart had resurfaced as a female propagandist for the Imperial Japanese Army. It was said she'd been captured by the Japanese when her plane crash-landed, and now was being forced to help spread their gospel of lies.

Because they were a photo reconnaissance squadron, the men of the 26th were allowed to undertake a 'limited amount' of personal photography. In his spring '44 intelligence reports the 26th's intelligence officer stressed how he had 'enforced a rigid censorship of all photos . . . the lab chief is responsible for a check on all negatives developed.' By doing so he hoped that the flow of damaging images that might be mailed home, or fall into enemy hands, would be 'considerably reduced'.

But the real challenge remained to limit the damage caused by the Japanese radio broadcasts, which were beaming daily into the soldiers' tents. Faced with such sophisticated propaganda, could the squadron's newest and smallest member help turn the tide of demoralizing disinformation? Could Smoky do something to help lift the men's spirits? As it happened, yes, she could.

Sport is one of the great morale-boosters. Trouble was, in New Guinea there weren't many football stadiums or baseball fields to hand. Finding enough flat, clear ground to build the Nadzab airstrips had been enough of a challenge. But all work and no play makes Jack a dull boy; a strip of land was bulldozed out of the jungle that fringed the Markham River so that an inter-squadron softball series could be started.

It made sense to play softball here, as opposed to regular baseball – its need for a smaller field and a larger ball was more suited to the terrain. Excitement mounted quickly ahead of the first game, one in which Smoky was about to demonstrate just what a huge spirit-lifter such a tiny dog could be. As the teams warmed up, tossing the ball into the outfield, runners dashed about 'shagging flies' – catching balls thrown wide.

By now Smoky, the dog who had appeared from out of the blue, was pretty much known to everyone around the camp, and she was in the thick of it, chasing every ball that came in her direction. As the softball was the best part of four inches in diameter, and Smoky barely stood that high off the ground, it was as if the tiny dog was chasing after a massive boulder, ears flapping and hair streaming as she dashed from pillar to post.

Warm-ups completed, the competition got underway. The 26th was playing a game against a team from the headquarters of the 5th Air Force Wing, their parent unit. A quick ball left the bat and skittered along the ground. Before anyone could stop her Smoky was after it like a bullet from a gun. The player on third base bent to scoop up the ball, just as a careering canine hairball overtook it.

Smoky leapt to seize the ball and was flipped head over heels by the fast-spinning projectile, landing in the startled baseman's glove. The ball itself powered onwards, smoking past between the guy's legs. He didn't know what had hit him, but at least he managed to refrain from hurling what he'd caught – *a dog* – to fourth base.

Predictably, the doggie stunt provoked a great deal of hilarity. All around the field figures were clutching their sides laughing. Smoky, meanwhile, had returned to the sidelines a little chastised, and noticeably shaken and stirred.

Days later the news bulletin printed by the 5th Air Force declared of the match: 'O'Hara went to second on an effort by Havel and Smoky, Lightning Dog Mascot.' In a sense they'd hit the nail on the head: the little dog *was* becoming an invaluable mascot to the 26th, those who flew the unarmed P-38 Lightnings into hostile skies.

Smoky's value lay in humour, in her ability to bring light amid the darkness of war. Under the stresses and strains of combat and in such an environment, Smoky constituted a rare slice of fun. And, crucially, she was a reminder of a distant and much longed-for place: home. She served as a symbol of the simple freedoms and pleasures of life that all here were fighting to preserve.

Indeed, the more the men of the 26th got to know her, the more it seemed that spreading fun and laughter and light was the very essence of Smoky's being. Tiny though she was, Smoky just seemed to be the gift that never stopped giving.

And she was about to reveal her powers in the most unexpected way.

CHAPTER 6

Yank Magazine was a US military weekly founded in June 1942, with a view to boosting the morale of soldiers, sailors and airmen deployed overseas. The idea for the publication was inspired by the *Stars and Stripes* newspaper, which served a similar purpose during the wars. Written by enlisted ranks, the debut June '42 issue of *Yank* had the US actress Jane Randolph, one of the GI's favourite chocolate-box pin-ups, gracing the cover.

A few weeks after Smoky had been discovered in the jungle, *Yank Magazine* launched a competition to find the best mascots in the southwest Pacific theatre of operations. When Bill Wynne heard of it he was determined that he and Smoky would give it their best shot. It was an inspired idea guaranteed to occupy the minds of the troops, and Wynne sensed a real opportunity for him and his tiny dog to make a splash.

Soldiers mostly had to make their own entertainment at Nadzab, especially if they didn't fancy another night in with Tokyo Rose. Some made carefully crafted models of their trusty P-38s, using empty shell cases to form the body of the aircraft and the engine housings. Occasionally, a group of three or four might pay a sightseeing visit to a native village, and some had resorted to making collections of the giant butterflies that flitted through the jungle.

Indeed, Smoky herself found the huge, low-flying iridescent insects irresistible. Many a time Wynne had caught her bounding after a Queen Alexandra's birdwing, a butterfly whose wingspan could grow to twenty-five centimetres – enough to dwarf the dog's girth. There was something captivating about the way she pranced and danced and snapped beneath the giant creature; she looked like a crazed paratrooper desperately trying to recover a wayward parachute. But Bill Wynne was all too conscious of the dangers associated with such seemingly harmless fun.

Like a diminutive Pied Piper, the butterfly would flit and flap its way deeper into the jungle in an effort to escape its pursuer, drawing Smoky inexorably after. And that risked one of two outcomes. In the first, Smoky might lose her way once more – and there was no guarantee that this time she would be found. In the second, she might stumble into the path of one of the many predators that slithered and crawled through the dank shadows.

The ghastly thought of losing his new friend made Wynne intensify Smoky's obedience training, which he hoped might also give them an edge in the forthcoming *Yank Magazine* pageant. He was under no illusions as to how stiff the competition would likely prove. Indeed, one of their sister squadrons had a long-standing mascot who had already achieved a high profile. 'Colonel Turbo' had earned widespread infamy at Nadzab due to his wild, bad-tempered and downright destructive ways.

Colonel Turbo was a Rhesus Macaque – a monkey native to Asia, but not to the New Guinea region. Standing some twenty inches tall, and with brownish-grey fur and pink, hairless features, the Rhesus tends to look red-faced and angry at the best of times. There was no worse-tempered macaque than Colonel Turbo, though his tantrums were mostly tolerated because he had a fairly good excuse for such behaviour.

A pilot had acquired Turbo from a zoo in the States. Subsequently, that aviator had been killed in a plane crash. Feeling sorry for Turbo, his parent squadron had adopted him as their mascot. When they deployed from the US, Turbo had been dosed with sleeping tablets to keep him quiet during the long sea voyage. He'd been stuffed into a soldier's duffle bag to be smuggled aboard ship, and subsequently he was hung out of a convenient porthole on the end of a leash as a way of hiding him during ship's inspections.

By the time they reached New Guinea, Turbo's ways were pretty much ingrained. He took either an instant like or dislike to whoever he met. You'd know if it was the latter when he sunk his teeth – all thirty-two of them – into your arm or leg. Whenever he was free he'd race from tent to tent causing chaos and mayhem, ripping open cigarette cartons, shredding letters and parcels from home and eating whatever goodies he could find.

One of Turbo's chief sponsors at Nadzab had warned Wynne that Smoky would never get the better of their notorious mascot. 'Colonel Turbo can handle anything,' he'd boasted. Colonel Turbo, he'd bragged, would grab a tiny little thing like Smoky and eat her alive.

The monkey was known to have a wily way with dogs. He'd square up to any that he encountered with his head held low to the dirt, hips set high and hands reached back between his hind legs. When the dog approached – all ground-snuffling curiosity – those hands would shoot forward in a flash, grab the dog's front legs, and wrestle it to the ground, whereupon Turbo's jaws would clamp shut on the poor animal's ears. In no time the dog would be howling in pain and would beat a rapid retreat.

Wynne wasn't overly keen on Smoky fronting up to Colonel Turbo, but he sensed a certain inevitability about the showdown. There was only so long that these two larger-than-life animal characters could avoid running into each other in a place like Nadzab. He also had a sense of how big Smoky's attitude was, regardless of her size. There is an old saying: *it's not the size of the dog in the fight; it's the size of the fight in the dog.* It was to be more than borne out in the course of Smoky's first encounter with the infamous macaque.

Turbo was kept tied to a post most of the time. If not, he would run riot. He seemed to have little desire to escape into the jungle. Once or twice some of his less-forgiving victims had driven him deep into the forest, evicting him from their jeep and speeding away. But their efforts to free Turbo had always misfired. A while later he'd be seen sidling back into camp, moving with the side-swagger and crooked hop so typical of the species.

Upon first spying the monkey Smoky had been all perked-up ears and doggy curiosity. Bold as brass, she'd trotted over to check out this strange-smelling beast. Turbo had treated her well-meaning approach as he had that of a dozen dogs before her: in a flash he'd grabbed her by the nose, squeezing tighter and tighter until she was yelping in pain. Finally, Smoky had broken free and backed away in shock and surprise. But not for long.

Even as Turbo was basking in his apparent victory, she'd leapt forward on the counter-attack. Turbo tried to recover and nab her again, but she was too nimble and too quick. In an instant she'd darted beneath his arms and lunged for his face, snapping at and skinning his pink, protruding nose. It was Turbo's turn to yelp with pain. He'd jumped up into a tree above, and sat there rubbing his face and checking his hand for any sign of blood.

By now a crowd of curious onlookers had gathered. Sensing an audience, Smoky turned her back on the monkey. Believing his adversary was unsighted and vulnerable, Turbo dropped softly to the ground and lunged for her nether regions. But in a flash Smoky had whipped around and charged at him, barking in a wild, high-pitched yelp. It sounded as if the macaque had hold of some tufts of her hair and was ripping it out by the roots.

Nonplussed and panicked, Turbo fled, but Smoky was too fast for him. As he tried to leap for the safety of his tree again, she was upon him, snapping at his heels. Each time Turbo made a jump for the nearest limb of the tree, she would do the same again, putting him off his stride. Unable to reach the branch, the macaque was reduced to leaping repeatedly into the air to try to avoid the little dog's wrath. By now, the gang of onlookers was roaring with laughter.

Finally, Smoky allowed him space to swing into his tree. It was the first time a dog had got the better of Colonel Turbo, and from then on the two animals struck up a relationship based upon a measure of mutual respect. Whenever she tired of chasing butterflies Smoky would seek out Turbo for a runaround. He never forgot how feisty she could be and he never tried to bully her again. But as mascots went Turbo was still a legend and Smoky would have to go some to beat him.

Historically speaking, Smoky should have had the edge. The US military had a long tradition of keeping dogs as mascots. During the First World War the Germans were reputed to have referred to US Marines as the *Teufelshunden* – Devil Dogs – due to the ferocity with which they fought. The Marine Corps embraced the name, and before long a recruiting poster appeared showing a British bulldog snapping at the heels of a Dachshund. The iconography had taken root, with the Marines adopting both the name and a live British bulldog as their mascot.

As it turned out there were to be some 400 entries to the *Yank Magazine* mascot competition, most of which were dogs. Clearly, Smoky needed to find a way to stand out from the crowd. Fortunately, the 26th had two very strong cards to play: the dog's undeniably photogenic looks, and the fact that they were a photographic squadron. With this in mind, Wynne decided some truly creative images were called for, in combination with a little theatre.

First off he grabbed a camera from the 26th photo lab, and his GI helmet, with its distinctive bowl-like profile, jungle-green covering and canvas strap. From the moment Smoky had become such a seminal part of his life, he'd realized that grooming her was going to be of paramount importance, if her crudely shorn hair was to recover and if she were to survive the privations of jungle living. Searching around for a suitable bath he'd alighted upon his helmet.

It doubled as his daily wash-and-shave basin, so he could see no reason why it shouldn't serve a similar purpose for his dog. He filled it with water, placed Smoky inside, and it was perfect: deep enough for her to sit in, with her beady eyes peering over the side, hair shooting out like fireworks in all directions. As she gazed at him in excited curiosity, Wynne had proceeded to give Smoky her first proper bath and rub down since she'd been rescued from the jungle.

After treating her to a proper post-bathe grooming, he'd noticed that her hair seemed to have a natural parting stretching from the nape of her neck all the way to her tail. She'd shaken herself dry, and her hair had fallen straight down both sides of her body, from the ridgeline of her backbone. If he brushed it back again, with one shake it flopped into place once more, tumbling down from that natural parting. Smoky was full of surprises and again Wynne had been struck by a burning curiosity to find out what kind of breed she might be.

He readied his camera in preparation for the mascot competition photo, placing his helmet on the ground and knowing that Smoky would jump right in, as if taking a bath. Sure enough she did, and the shot he took served to emphasize her small size, for the helmet lent the photo a perfect sense of scale. Surely, no one at *Yank Magazine* could fail to be captivated by the image, or to be curious as to what kind of dog she might be.

But still he wasn't satisfied. Suddenly he had a flash of inspiration as to the type of dramatic image they could shoot for. It would need the assistance of a good number of the squadron, yet if they could pull it off it would surely be the clincher.

Wynne sought out Corporals Murphy and Piette, who were saddled with one of the unit's most onerous jobs. They were the 26th's parachute packers – charged with keeping the squadron's 'chutes in fine fettle. Murphy and Piette had to ensure that the parachutes were properly stowed, so if a pilot did have cause to bale out the expanse of life-saving silk would open on cue, blossoming in the skies above. The trigger system for this involved a small pilot 'chute that deployed once the rip-cord was pulled, which in turn would drag out the main parachute.

Wynne figured one of those pilot 'chutes was just about the right size to carry his dog. With his kindly, open features and receding hairline, Corporal Thomas Murphy was one of the old hands of the squadron, having joined in March 1943. He was the kind of guy who would do anything for anyone. His fellow parachute packer, Corporal Marion Piette, with his slicked-back hair and pencil-thin moustache, was the more sober of the two. But both men were noted for treating their craft with the seriousness that it demanded.

Fortunately, they were also big fans of Wynne's dog. In the parachute store-tent they tended to work bare-chested, but with a US military khaki field cap – similar in style to a baseball cap – jammed on their heads. They were surrounded by the tools of their trade: parachute harnesses, rigging, and shelves stacked high with bulging parachute packs, each about the size of your average day-sack. Just as soon as Wynne had explained his cunning plan, a pilot 'chute was quietly passed his way.

Normally, the pilot 'chute was attached to the main 'chute by rigging lines. But for Wynne's present purposes he had to fashion a parachute harness in which a seven-inch-high dog could hang suspended from those lines. He found the best material from which to do so was a bog-standard money belt. By lashing a couple together, he managed to form a cradle in which to strap his dog, which in turn was attached to the 'chute's rigging.

It was time to try Smoky out in her new apparatus. By now

man and dog were several weeks into their partnership, and it was almost beginning to feel as if they'd never been apart. In war, bonds tend to form far quicker than in peacetime. Extreme situations engender extreme emotions, extreme attachments. Already, Wynne and Smoky trusted each other implicitly. He fastened her into the DIY harness, tightened the straps and swung her about this way and that, aping the movements the 'chute was likely to make in an effort to get her accustomed to what was coming. Luckily, she seemed perfectly happy in her new rig.

That done, he went about recruiting his para-drop team. He needed a volunteer to cut the branches from the side of one of the trees that grew adjacent to the softball field; it would be from there that Smoky would make her first jump. Next, he needed someone to hold one side of the GI blanket in which they would catch Smoky as she fell. Wynne decided he needed to be one of the catcher-crew, and John Barnard, one of his buddies in the squadron, offered to hold the blanket's other side.

Finally, he gave the key role of official stunt photographer to Staff Sergeant Howard J. Kalt, a man whose thinning hair, protruding ears and self-effacing smile gave him something of a schoolmasterly appearance. A superlative organizer, Kalt helped run the squadron's movie nights, and he was forever taking stick for it.

However good or bad the film might promise to be, the tent was always packed, for a Hollywood release was a rare treat. But it was a major triumph to get through an evening's projection without something breaking down. The long-suffering Kalt had got used to all the catcalls and the jibes. How hard could it be capturing a parachuting Smoky on film, after facing countless movie nights at Nadzab, complete with their boisterous and disruptive audiences?

The man whom Wynne entrusted to release Smoky from the tree was Don Esmond, a fellow native of Cleveland. Esmond climbed into the branches, and Smoky was passed up to him with her parachute attached. Leaning out as far as he could, Esmond checked the reception committee was ready down below. He waited until the hot tropical wind that gusted down the valley had died down a little, and upon Wynne's yell to release her, he let Smoky and 'chute go free.

The silk blossomed above Smoky and she proceeded to float towards earth, her four legs splayed wide as if ready for a proper bail out and landing, her head peering forward and searching for the point to make touchdown. She landed right in the centre of the blanket, Wynne and Barnard breaking her fall, and the team let out a triumphant cheer. Smoky seemed to love the attention. She got to her feet and wagged her stumpy tail, gutsily. As she gazed at her team with a moist and shiny muzzle, tongue lolling out and eyes shining happily, they could have sworn she understood exactly what they were here for.

She seemed keen for more. Her para-drop team repeated the jump four further times, just to ensure that Kalt had it captured properly on film and from all possible angles. But when they sent her up again, drop number six was to prove a jump too far. The wind gusted fiercely across the softball field, just as Esmond set Smoky into motion. The blast hit the side of the 'chute, blowing it out of shape and collapsing it in an instant.

Moments later Smoky was falling, the 'chute balling up like a bundle of wet washing behind her. Wynne and Barnard rushed to reposition the blanket, but they were too late. Smoky tore past. As Wynne watched aghast, she arched her back, her four legs reaching wide, and disappeared into the foot-high grass. She bounced on impact, yelping with pain as she turned a somersault in the air, her head bent at an odd angle.

Moments later she hit the ground again and lay still.

Wynne raced to Smoky's side, feeling sick to the death at what he might have done. He was consumed with fear for his blameless companion. The others gathered in a stunned silence as Wynne held Smoky down, checking her for injuries. She continued to yelp and whine. Finally, he took her head in one hand and body in the other, and pulled gently. Something seemed to snap back into place, and Smoky stopped the agonized whimpers. She convulsed several times and vomited up the canned sausages that she'd eaten for lunch.

Wynne felt furious at himself, cursing his own stupidity for risking the life of the animal that he loved. Sure, there would be no better way to raise the morale of his squadron than to win the *Yank Magazine* competition, but that didn't mean it had to require a life-threatening stunt such as this. If Smoky died, or was left disabled, who knew what effect it would have on the spirits of the 26th?

Shamefaced, the team wrapped Smoky in the blanket and carried her back to her tent. By the time they reached it, she seemed to have recovered her spirits a little. She was still uncharacteristically quiet and inactive, but at least the pained whining was over.

Wynne sat up all night, watching over his dog. He didn't

DAMIEN LEWIS

know quite what he would do if she took a turn for the worse. All he could imagine was that he'd take her to the Nadzab Quartermaster Corps – the unit that oversaw administration for all military supplies routed via the base. If he was lucky there might just be a veterinarian within their ranks, or at least someone with that kind of experience.

Fortunately, he had no need to throw himself on the mercy of the Quartermaster Corps. Come morning, Smoky seemed almost back to her old self.

Kalt suggested they take a photo of her in a far less life-threatening role – fifty-five standing astride a 55-gallon steel drum. They would be extra careful with her this time. Once that image was developed, Kalt cut it out and pasted it onto a picture of a cloud, with Smoky's ears and her hair flying in the breeze. It was Smoky's version of the 26th's Donald Duck patch: all that seemed to be missing was the flying helmet.

That became her official *Yank Magazine* entry photo. Beside it Wynne wrote that her key responsibility within the squadron was morale. Whenever the men of the 26th had had a particularly bad day, all anyone needed to see was Smoky chasing after a giant butterfly, captivated by its every move, and they would find the heaviness lift from their shoulders. In no time they would be smiling and laughing again.

The *Yank Magazine* entry was submitted, the plucky little dog having survived her para-jumps apparently none the worse for wear. But little did Wynne realize how Smoky's para-training would prepare her for the rigours of what was coming.

For soon, she would be called upon to take to the skies.

CHAPTER 7

Throughout March and April 1944, the high-flying P-38 Lightnings flitted through the skies above Hollandia in an effort to capture images of the Japanese forces based there. Hollandia was the site of the single greatest concentration of enemy warplanes south of the equator, as well as being a vital staging post in the region for men, materiel and supplies. General MacArthur was determined to wrest those bases from enemy hands, and to do so he needed up-to-date recce photos. But the weather continued to be abysmal, which made securing those crucial high-altitude images a huge challenge.

Finally, a brief weather window opened and the fliers of the 26th were able to get airborne. They were able to buzz Hollandia fast and at 20,000 feet, capturing the images that senior Allied commanders hungered for. The negatives were rushed through the Nadzab photo lab, with Smoky performing her Tray Duty with admirable poise. The pictures so secured revealed hundreds of enemy fighters and bombers parked in serried ranks upon Hollandia's three airstrips, making for incredibly juicy targets.

Of course, the Japanese defenders had detected those lone recce flights sizing up their positions. But their commanders – foremost, General Hatazo Adachi – made the fatal error of underestimating their adversary. Assuming that Hollandia lay beyond the reach of any Allied air-attack squadrons, they had presumed that no airborne assault was possible. It was a mistake that would cost them dear.

Under Operation Cartwheel – MacArthur's grand strategy in the region – key enemy bases were to be subjected to 'Air Blockade', which had the following objectives: to destroy the enemy's air force on the ground; to destroy his airstrips and air defences, so no reinforcements or supplies could be flown in; to destroy the enemy's living quarters; and to destroy all stores and related installations.

The other key element of Air Blockade was surprise. As the official US Air Force journal from the time declared: 'Surprise is to air attack what mustard is to a hot dog. You can do without it, but it makes a big difference.' Following an Air Blockade, General George Churchill Kenney, overall commander of Allied air forces in the region, aimed 'to land troops with rifles on their backs and to have the enemy so thoroughly demoralized that the rifles are kept there as long as possible'.

Two factors would prove essential when it came to securing the element of surprise at Hollandia. The first was capturing those high-level recce photos: they confirmed that the Japanese had done little to make their warplanes any more difficult to target, which had to mean that they believed no attack was coming. Hundreds of aircraft were lined up like ducks in a shooting gallery. Indeed, General Adachi kept adding to his squadrons – building up his air power, in keeping with his orders to hold the line in New Guinea and repulse any Allied assaults.

The second factor was a cunningly crafted deception. General

Adachi rightly presumed that no Allied commander would risk an attack by heavy bombers without fighters in escort. He wrongly presumed that no Allied fighters had the range to make the thousand-mile round trip from Nadzab to Hollandia and back again. A new 'long-legged' model of the P-38 had just been introduced to theatre. The P-38F possessed underwing racks for carrying 'drop-tanks' – external fuel tanks that could be jettisoned when empty – an innovation that vastly increased its range.

The P-38F was deliberately kept under wraps, never venturing more than 300 miles from Nadzab, which further lured the enemy into a false sense of security. The Japanese were led to believe that Hollandia was safe, because their adversaries had no fighters that could cover the kind of distances required to engage in combat and defend their bomber squadrons. It was to prove a catastrophic oversight.

On 30 March 1944 the massed ranks of Allied warplanes took to the skies. The air above Nadzab darkened with the forms of hundreds of Consolidated B24 Liberators, the valley echoing to the roar of the heavy bomber's turbo-supercharged Pratt and Whitney radial engines. The Liberators formed up with their 'long-legged' P-38F escorts, and set a course for Hollandia, some three hours flying time to the northwest. It was the first time the Lightnings would venture that far from base.

The air armada reached Hollandia to find that surprise was almost complete. Of the 150 fighter aircraft that General Adachi had on the ground, only forty managed to get airborne in an attempt to intercept the Allied warplanes. They were scrambled in a disorganized and piecemeal fashion and they faced a perilous climb to the B24's cruise altitude. Long before they reached it the P-38F Lightnings fell on them with a vengeance, and half the Japanese fighters were blasted from the skies.

The Liberators, meanwhile, unleashed their payloads. Each heavy bomber was packed with 5,000 pounds of incendiaries, which were highly effective against the aircraft lined up on the ground. The closely packed Japanese warplanes – mostly prized Mitsubishi G4M high-speed, long-range bombers – were caught in long strings of blasts. In short order the aerodromes at Hollandia were wreathed in thick and billowing clouds of smoke and flames.

The following day the airborne raiders returned, wreaking further devastation. By the end of those forty-eight hours of action, 219 enemy warplanes had been destroyed in the air and on the ground, for the loss of only a handful of P-38s. Follow-up airstrikes pounded Hollandia's air-defences with 1,000-pound demolitions bombs, and ripped apart the stores and barracks areas that serviced them. By the end of the second week of April, 352 enemy aircraft had been destroyed, while Allied losses remained meagre.

But the Allies were not to have things all their own way: soon they would learn that they too could be taken by surprise.

On Sunday 16 April 1944 the weather turned. That day, which would become known as 'Black Sunday', a towering tropical storm darkened the skies above Nadzab, blocking out all sunlight. Out of the two hundred Allied warplanes that had set out earlier to raid Hollandia, scores would fail to make it back again.

Some three-dozen aircraft – Liberators, plus Douglas A-20

Havocs and their Lightning escorts – returned from the raids over Hollandia running short of fuel, only to find Nadzab Airbase blanketed in thick cloud.

On the ground, Bill Wynne and Smoky could hear the airplanes desperately circling in the dark skies. Some aircrew chose to bail out before their aircraft ran out of juice completely. Others flew on until all their fuel was exhausted, waiting for a weather window that never opened. Dozens of warplanes went down among the jungle-clad mountains that towered to either side of the Markham River Valley.

Black Sunday had delivered one of the worst blows the US air force suffered during the war in the Pacific, with the weather proving to be a more fearsome enemy than the Japanese. But all things told, the Hollandia operation was still regarded as a runaway success. 'The enemy's air strength, which he had been building for weeks, was wiped out as thoroughly as a janitor clearing a blackboard with a wet rag,' the US Army Air Force trumpeted in their report on the raids.

On the coat tails of the blistering air offensive, ground forces set sail for Hollandia, executing a 500-mile advance and catching many enemy garrisons by almost total surprise. With General Adachi's air power practically wiped out, he'd had little means to scour the seas for any approaching Allied ships. Less than a hundred hours after the amphibious landings had gone in, and after a series of intense and fierce ground battles, all three airstrips at Hollandia lay in Allied hands.

In some of the Japanese barracks breakfasts lay uneaten on mess hall tables. General Adachi himself was said to have evacuated his quarters leaving a pair of trousers in a clothes press.

The general had been caught with his 'pants down', the Air Force wrote gleefully, and 'must have made an incongruous sight tearing through the jungle dressed as a general only from the waist up'.

Indeed, Adachi had slipped into the thick tree cover that lay inland of Hollandia, taking 200,000 of his troops with him. On paper his options were limited. At his back lay the impenetrable New Guinea jungle. To his front lay the open sea. As they'd intended, Allied forces now dominated the airspace, and he could expect little relief or reinforcement from that direction.

But Adachi was far from done. He planned to lead his men through seemingly impossible swamp and jungle, in an effort to launch a counter-attack from where General MacArthur would least expect it. Leaving some of his forces to harass the new Allied positions, Adachi set out on a forced march through utterly punishing terrain, leading, as always, from the front.

With Hollandia lost, his army was isolated thousands of miles from home and effectively cut off from the rest of the Imperial Japanese Army. But by his example, Adachi intended to hold his men together and to strike a decisive blow. Putting himself on the same short rations as his troops, and disdaining old war injuries, he set out to fight a do-or-die battle.

As for MacArthur, he was already eyeing the next objective on his Operation Cartwheel shopping list: Biak Island, lying some 350 miles beyond Hollandia. Heavily garrisoned by Japanese troops, MacArthur needed his eyes in the sky to get airborne over Biak Island, to bring him the crucial intelligence he required. That meant the 26th had to get their aircraft up to Hollandia, just as soon as the runways could be made serviceable. But as the squadron began its move north, its man-and-dog team were struck down by one of the many mystery ills that stalked the New Guinea jungle.

Growing up before the war, Bill Wynne had been a big fan of the hugely successful movie *Bring 'Em Back Alive*, featuring the American adventurer Frank Buck. Filmed in the Malaysian jungle, it showed dramatic scenes of a giant python fighting a crocodile, and of a 'street brawl' between a tiger and a black panther. But what Wynne remembered most, now that he had Smoky to care for, was the scene of a python swallowing a pig, and the bulge the animal made in the snake's stomach.

He was determined that Smoky wouldn't suffer a similar fate here in Nadzab, and at night he kept her firmly tethered to the foot of his bed. But during daytime she loved to chase the helmeted guineafowl that ran wild around their tented camp. About the size of a chicken, the guineafowl has a grey-blue plumage spangled with white, and bright aquamarine and red colouring to its head.

Congregating in flocks of twenty-odd birds, the guineafowl were quite happy to fend off the occasional inquisitive cat. But not Smoky. Whenever she disappeared, Wynne knew exactly where to look. He'd follow the excited yelps, only to find his dog thrashing her way through the dense jungle to the rear of their camp, with a flock of portly guineafowl trotting along in front on spindly legs, issuing harsh calls of alarm.

It was obvious why Smoky found it such fun chasing the birds, but the bush was full of dangers. The worst were actually the invisible threats – first and foremost of which was Scrub Typhus, a disease caused by an intracellular parasite, carried by the mites that infested the jungle's thick vegetation. The bite of the mites – commonly known as 'chiggers' – caused a characteristic black welt on a human's skin. But not on a dog. And dogs were known to carry the disease, transmitting it to humans.

Scrub Typhus plagued those who were sent to fight in the New Guinea jungle. In some areas it had caused more casualties than combat. Symptoms included high fever, headaches, aching muscles, liver failure and haemorrhaging. Left untreated, it normally proved fatal. The way to avoid catching the disease was to avoid close contact with the vegetation on which the chiggers lurked, which was why Wynne called Smoky back whenever she went chasing the guineafowl.

He'd grab a low bush and start to shake it, enticingly, shouting: 'Here they are! Here they are!' Curious, Smoky would weave a path back towards him. They'd play that game for a while, before Smoky would wag her tail and cock her head to one side, eyeing Wynne knowingly.

Her expression seemed to say: 'Come on! Let's go! I know where loads of them are!'

But each episode chasing Smoky in the bush exposed Wynne to hidden diseases like Scrub Typhus. One evening shortly before the Hollandia raids, he had to work late in the lab. He returned to his tent, only to find that Smoky had disappeared. He figured he could hear her yapping in the distance. He searched high and low, but could find no sign of her. Horrible visions of bulging snakes filled his head.

Finally, he spotted some locals wandering along a path. In pidgin English – an English-based dialect used by the New Guinea tribes – he explained to them that his dog had gone missing. Using hand gestures he indicated her size, and pointing at his own hair he gave an impression of what her coat looked like. The locals nodded and grinned and disappeared into the bush. A few minutes later one of them was back, bursting through a thick curtain of vines. In his arms he held a squirming dog.

'Yah!' Wynne yelled; *you've done it!*

Before handing Smoky back, the villager turned her over and inspected her underside. He smiled. 'Smoky – Mary dog!' In pidgin all females were referred to as 'Mary'. Wynne nodded in agreement. Smoky was indeed a Mary dog. He had her execute a couple of tricks and the locals were amazed that she seemed to understand every word that he was saying.

Word must have spread about this amazing little dog. A short while later Smoky went missing again. In desperation, Wynne headed down to the nearest village to ask if his dog had been seen there. The locals had the reputation of being cannibals, at least in the remoter parts of New Guinea, but Wynne was less worried about himself being eaten and far more concerned about the fate of his dog. She'd make a tasty snack for any famished villager.

His first efforts in pidgin didn't seem to cut it. There were blank, uncomprehending stares all around. He resorted to a form of charades, miming a dog barking, raising one paw and standing on her hind legs. Eventually, it dawned on the villagers what he was after. They beckoned for him to follow and threaded their way deeper into the bush. Wynne had no idea where this magical mystery tour was taking him, but he hoped to discover his dog alive and well at the end of it.

Finally, they came to a clearing. He heard a familiar sound – a dog's yapping. It made his heart leap. It was Smoky all right. He found her surrounded by village children and running through her repertoire of tricks. Smoky was clearly in her element. The kids were laughing, cheering and egging her on to do more. The more she captured their attention, the more she wanted to captivate them all.

Wynne watched for a while, feeling torn. On the one hand he was overjoyed to have found her, and just wanted her back in his arms. On the other he was reluctant to break the magic of the moment. Finally, Smoky spotted him and came running. She looked proud as punch at her solo performances. He scooped her up and there were smiles all around from the children.

Wynne carried Smoky back along the path that meandered through the bush, jungle giants towering high above their heads, their trunks thick with vines. Finding Smoky here had been a surreal moment and a magical one, but each exposure to the wilds carried its own risks. Back at camp Wynne treated his dog to an extra-long soak in his helmet bathtub. Once her coat was thoroughly shampooed, rinsed and dried, they settled down to some serious grooming. Smoky's hair was growing back again, and it was getting longer, silkier and very much like that of a human.

Just like human hair tends to, Smoky's would get into knots if not regularly brushed. Repeated sojourns in the bush risked her picking up all kinds of parasites and pests, which could thrive in her coat. Caring for his dog – taking the time to properly bathe and groom her – was one of the means by which Wynne tried to counter such threats. But who was taking care of him?

When the sickness came, it hit like a whirlwind. Overnight almost, Wynne developed a raging fever. The alarm was raised, he was loaded into a field ambulance and rushed across camp to the 233rd Station Hospital. This was a tented field facility, which constituted the first line of care for front-line troops evacuated from battle all over New Guinea.

Wynne's fever was raging at 105 degrees, the level at which you start becoming delirious and hallucinating. High fever is a symptom of malaria, but the blood tests came back negative. If it wasn't malaria, it was most likely dengue fever, the doctors decided – another mosquito-borne disease, but this one caused by a virus. The symptoms of dengue are largely similar to Scrub Typhus: high fever, headache, vomiting, muscle and joint pains, plus a telltale skin rash. Again, if not treated properly dengue could kill.

While Wynne battled fever in the hospital tent, the medics ran more tests. As for Smoky, this was the first time that she'd been separated from her saviour for any length of time. The way Wynne was feeling, he had no idea how long he might be hospitalized, or when he might see Smoky again. He'd left her in the care of Francis 'Frank' Petrilak, a fellow dog-lover. With his fresh-faced looks, eager gaze and glasses, Petrilak appeared far too young to have been sent to war. But Wynne knew how fond he was of man's four-legged friend. He felt confident that Petrilak would care for Smoky, no matter how long they might be parted.

During the first night Bill Wynne spent in hospital, a casualty from the fighting around Hollandia was brought into the tent. Squadron Sergeant James M. Craig had been in the thick of battle for days, rescuing his buddies from a fearsome enemy mortar barrage. Eventually, he'd been evacuated, complaining of stabbing chest pains, but the doctors had concluded that Craig's problem was more mental than it was physical.

Craig wasn't alone in suffering in such a way. Hundreds of troops were arriving from the front plagued by 'combat fatigue'. Known as 'shell shock' in earlier conflicts, combat fatigue constitutes a severe loss of 'normal' human functions due to the trauma of war. It was characterized by the 'thousand-yard stare', an unfocused, weary, lifeless gaze. Sometimes called 'battle neurosis', it was often the precursor to what we today recognize as post-traumatic stress disorder (PTSD).

Back in civilian life the blond, tousle-headed Craig had been a real live wire. He had a thick New Jersey accent, a ready smile, and an easy-going manner and was a perfect potential roommate for Wynne. He'd been moved to Nadzab so the medics could keep a close eye on him. Like so many others in that hospital, at the first hint of a distant explosion he'd dive out of bed and scrabble for cover.

Panic, extreme anxiety and depression are common symptoms of combat fatigue. This was the first real exposure that Wynne had ever had to it. Craig was a war hero: he'd earned a high-valour medal for his efforts at Hollandia. But his nerves were shot to shreds. For Wynne, more accustomed to the loss of aircrew at a distance, this was a hugely sobering experience. Having contracted this mystery illness, all of a sudden he found himself face-to-face with the debilitating effects of front-line fighting.

Wynne was hugely fortunate to have ended up in this particular hospital. It was commanded by Colonel Charles William

Mayo, a surgeon in the United States Medical Corps who happened to hail from the family who had founded the famous Mayo Clinic. Colonel Mayo had served on the Mayo Clinic's board since 1933 and he remained a powerful advocate of the Mayo's core philosophies, of which the most important was that the needs of the patient had to take priority.

On his third day in the hospital Wynne had visitors. Frank Petrilak and Staff Sergeant Kalt – Smoky's photographer for the *Yank Magazine* competition – came to see him. As a bonus they'd brought Smoky with them. Upon explaining to the nursing staff how inseparable were patient and dog, Wynne was permitted to have his canine visitor, which was all in keeping with the Mayo's core values of putting the patient's needs first.

Upon spying Wynne, Smoky became a veritable tornado of excitement, whirling around and yelping happily. She was clearly as overjoyed to see him as he was her. Wynne tried to get her to settle upon his bed, as Petrilak and Kalt handed him a bundle of mail. In pride of place sat a large brown envelope stamped with the logo of *Yank Magazine*. Despite his sickness Wynne felt his pulse quicken.

He ripped open the parcel, eager for news of the mascot competition. He ran his eye over the first line of the enclosed letter. 'Dear PFC Wynne, I am enclosing herewith . . .' The letter announced the delivery of his first copy of *Yank Magazine*, which would be mailed to him weekly from now on, free of charge. It had to mean that they had been successful.

'Wow!' he declared. 'We must've won!'

He grabbed the magazine and flicked through its pages, stopping at the one entitled 'Smoky – FIRST PRIZE.' Next to the headline was the photo of his dog peering impishly from an upturned GI helmet.

'First prize!' Wynne cried triumphantly, as he flashed the others the fantastic news.

Yank Magazine had even posted Wynne a silver 'loving cup' – a two-handled drinking cup, for ceremonial occasions – to commemorate their win. It was engraved: 'SMOKY. First Prize Yank Mascot. Australia 1944'. When it arrived, that cup would stand as high as Smoky was tall.

Word of the news quickly spread, and shortly Smoky was being acclaimed as the hero of the 233rd Field Hospital. Wynne couldn't help but notice how just as soon as Smoky had made an appearance the eyes of the war-wounded were drawn towards his dog. Their vacant, thousand-yard stares seemed to soften slightly, regaining their spark and focus whenever she was within their sight.

Some of the nurses must have noticed as well. They approached Wynne with an unusual request: might they be allowed to seek permission from the Field Hospital's commander for Smoky to accompany them on their rounds? It seemed appropriate, especially as she was now the champion mascot of the southwest Pacific area.

'The wounded fellows are flooding in,' they told him, 'and they're sure to love her.'

Amid all the surprise and the high spirits Wynne was feeling markedly better, which he figured was just the kind of thing the *Yank Magazine* editors had hoped to achieve with their competition. He didn't doubt that having Smoky pay the wounded a visit would lift their spirits. He told the nurses that he could think of no better way for his dog to serve.

The nurses went to speak with Colonel Mayo and they were back a few minutes later. They'd won his absolute blessing. Not only that, but Wynne was to be allowed to have Smoky sleep on his bed for as long as he was in hospital.

As Smoky began to make the rounds, Wynne was amazed at the effect she seemed to have. There was a total change whenever she entered a ward. A soldier lying glassy-eyed would perk up at her appearance, as if he couldn't believe what he was seeing. The looks on their faces were of surprise mixed with sheer delight. Seeing a dog like her in a place such as this was so utterly unexpected. Seeing her standing duty at their bedside was even better. If such a tiny, gutsy dog could be happy in the midst of this war, so for sure could they.

Wynne was hospitalised for several days, for all of which time Smoky was allowed to sleep on his bed. She was collected at seven o'clock in the morning to accompany the medical teams on their rounds, and returned to his care each evening. Casualties were flooding in from the front lines and there was much work to be done. Best of all was when James Craig cradled Smoky, his cap pushed back on his unruly mop of blond hair, his eyes sparkling and his face grinning ear to ear. Petrilak managed to grab a photo of the smiling war hero posing with the champion mascot in his arms.

Whatever breed she might be, Smoky seemed particularly suited to this role. She was six pounds of pure tomboy attitude. Her confidence and sparky personality rubbed off on all those she visited, and her love of being the centre of attention meant that she was always game for more. She never seemed to tire of the ward rounds.

It was amazing to see how much care and attention such a small dog seemed to lavish on each and every one of the war-wounded. When Wynne looked at her, he saw a dog that just radiated love. For him, Smoky truly was the gift that never stopped giving.

Unbeknown to Wynne – or anyone else for that matter – Smoky was performing a role now widely recognized: that of therapy dog. Nowadays it has become widely understood that the very presence of a dog can transform the heavy, oppressive atmosphere of a hospital. Caring for an animal helps individual soldiers focus on the dog's needs, rather than their recent traumatic experiences. It draws them out of their shadowed past – where they were trapped within a cycle of reliving the trauma – to socialize and play with another living being.

But in the spring of 1944, the idea that a dog might perform such a valuable therapeutic function for those wounded and traumatized by war had rarely been entertained. Using a dog to bolster the spirits of the injured – both in body and mind – was unprecedented. It was one of the many firsts that Smoky and Bill Wynne were to achieve together.

But all too soon their hospital interlude was over. In a matter of days Wynne had recovered from his illness. He was discharged, and with that Smoky's ward duties came to an end. Their time at Nadzab was over and the 26th was shipping out to Hollandia. The heavy vehicles and equipment were to travel by sea, but mostly the men and machines of the squadron were to be airlifted there by C47 transport planes.

Man and dog were heading north, into terrain freshly seized from a die-hard adversary that was hiding out in the hinterland.

The move to Hollandia would take them closer to the enemy than they'd ever been before, that was for certain. Or rather, it was for Bill Wynne. For all anyone knew, Smoky, the champion mascot of the 26th, might have made her first home with the enemy, as some kind of a Japanese dog of war.

Perhaps the move to Hollandia would reveal it, one way or the other.

CHAPTER 8

As soon as Adachi's forces had been driven out, the 26th Photo Reconnaissance Squadron began to ferry their P-38s north to the newly seized airbases. In short order the ragged bomb craters were filled in, and a series of hasty repairs implemented to make the runways functional once again. It was now crucial to get the Lightnings of the 26th on the ground and operational.

The key to MacArthur's Cartwheel strategy was never to allow the enemy a moment to rest or regroup. Allied forces had to keep pushing north at speed. But such a frenetic pace of operations brought its own challenges, and no unit seemed to have been left unscathed.

It was May 1944 by now, and the strength of the 26th lay at thirty-five officers, with 235 other ranks. The squadron was equipped with nine warplanes – all P-38 F5s, the reconnaissance variant of the standard combat aircraft. In the last month alone they'd flown seventy recce missions, and, perhaps inevitably, they'd suffered losses due to the hectic demands that were being placed on them.

On 20 May a P-38 flown by First Lieutenant McDaniels had ploughed into the sea at Madang Harbour, around two hundred miles north of Nadzab. McDaniels had been piloting a P-38 'piggy-back' – a modified version of the aircraft that allowed a passenger to crouch in a compartment set just to his rear. Both he and his passenger, Troop Sergeant Harry R. Rogers, had been killed.

The P-38 piggy-back was a configuration that never caught on, and the flawed design concept was soon dropped. But the 26th were two men the poorer for it, and two good men at that. The loss of the curly-haired, buck-toothed Rogers was keenly felt by the men. Forever with a smile on his face no matter what might be afoot, Rogers would do anything for his fellow soldiers. He and McDaniels would be sorely missed.

After his spell in hospital, Bill Wynne found that he was slated to make his way to Hollandia with the squadron rearguard, travelling by ship. He was reluctant to subject Smoky to a long and potentially storm-tossed voyage, so he asked one of his pilot buddies, Lieutenant William Bishop, if he might fly Smoky to their new base, as a special favour.

With his jet-black hair and dark, intense good looks, Bishop was a popular pilot and known as one of the real daredevils of the squadron. As photo recce fliers went there were few better. He agreed to Wynne's request, but he pointed out they'd need someone on the ground to care for the dog once she got there. With the best will in the world a guy like him tasked with executing daily recce flights couldn't keep tabs on a dog. Wynne got one of the ground staff to agree to look after Smoky during his absence.

As Smoky boarded Bishop's aircraft, her para-jump crew wondered if they should remind her of the bail out drills they'd taught her, when leaping from the tree on the edge of the Nadzab softball field. But on balance the dangers of the coming flight seemed slight. After seizing Hollandia, the skies above New Guinea were largely free of enemy warplanes. The battle had moved on.

Indeed, it was to be those left on the ground who would face the biggest dangers, and from unexpected quarters. Shortly after Lieutenant Bishop had flown Smoky safely to Hollandia, Wynne and the rest of those travelling by ship moved to the nearby port of Lae. Barely had they got there when the heavens opened. The storm was like nothing any of them had ever seen. They set camp as best they could in the tempestuous conditions, the nearby Markham River swelling to a raging torrent.

That night the river burst her banks. Wynne and his fellows awoke to find the waters swirling around their cot-tops, their kit bags soaking wet and pairs of boots floating off downstream. The water just kept rising. By dawn it was as high as a man's thighs, and it had made quagmires out of the dirt roads. They had no option but to retreat to higher ground, carrying anything they could with them. The rows of heavy, sodden tents had to be collapsed and rescued from the rising waters, and re-erected on dry land.

They were forced to board the waiting vessel – a cargo ship called the *Joseph P. Bradley* – using small landing craft, which pitched and rolled terribly in the sea's wild waters. Each man had to take his chances and grab for the ship's ladder, weighed down as he was with his cot, rifle and barracks bag. No one could wait to get out of that flooded, blighted camp, but they would find little comfort or relief on the journey north.

Wynne was doubly glad that he'd got Smoky sent ahead by

air. Aboard the *Joseph P. Bradley* they had two choices of quarters: either they could roast below decks, or they could camp topside in crowded 'tents' improvised from tarpaulins. The nightly tropical downpours made short work of such shelters. Those on deck were soaked to the skin for the majority of the voyage. Anyone hoping they might find relief at the dinner table was to be sorely disappointed: the less said about the food on offer, the better.

They reached Hollandia a drenched and famished lot, to find operations in full swing, with reconnaissance flights roaring into the skies above a hot and dusty airstrip. Wynne's joy at being reunited with Smoky was tempered by some surprising news. During his absence she'd been left to run wild somewhat, and rumour had it that she'd found herself a boyfriend. Wynne tried to tell himself that it just couldn't be true. It was challenging enough looking after one dog in the midst of war, but what if Smoky had fallen pregnant? How would he cope with a litter of puppies on his hands?

He forced such worries from his mind. There were other, more pressing concerns to address. The squadron was based adjacent to the airstrip at Sentani, named after the nearby lake, which was ringed with thick jungle. Sentani lay on the edge of the city of Hollandia, but still it felt as if it were a million miles from civilization. A further move to Biak Island was on the cards, so little had been done to establish even the most basic of facilities.

They'd set up camp in an area of forest sandwiched between the lake and a nearby mountain. The kitchen store was a cave that the Japanese had tunnelled into the hillside, in an effort to shelter from Allied bombing. The cramped hospital tent doubled as the mess hall. There wasn't even a shower or any form of laundry facilities. The men were mostly camped along the riverbank. They had to wash both themselves and their uniforms in the stream, beating their khakis clean on boulders.

The water in the creek originated from a seven-thousand-foot peak, so at least it was cool and refreshing. But at night search-lights played a blinding light show across the skies above the Sentani strip, scouring the heavens for incoming warplanes. Around the airfield lay piles of wreckage – mostly bombed – and burned-out Mitsubishi G4Ms, bulldozed into twisted heaps. The cockpits of some of those aircraft were remarkably intact. The instruments looked strikingly – eerily – similar to those used in the squadron's own aircraft.

Located as it was in dense jungle, the camp at Sentani was besieged by crawling, stinging, swimming, biting, flying, venom-ous things. Swarms of mosquitoes flocked to the water's edge. The lake itself was home to huge sawfish – a ray boasting a long, narrow, bony nose extension that resembles a many-toothed sawblade – which grew up to three metres in length. The sawfish used their sawblades to slice up and impale their prey.

Any food left lying around camp was an invitation to an ant invasion. Table legs had to be inserted into tin cans filled with water, to keep the swarms of ants from crawling up them. The water had in turn to be sprinkled with engine oil, to prevent mosquitoes from hatching out their larvae. Huge venomous centipedes – *Ethmostigmus rubripes* – lurked in the shadows. Two men were hospitalized as a result of their agonizing bites. One had gone to put his shoe on, only to find one of the revolting critters hiding out in the toe.

Smoky reckoned she could take them on. After her victory over Colonel Turbo, the fearless dog presumed the six-inch-long insects would be a pushover. With its garish orange-yellow body and black bands, plus numerous wriggling legs sticking out the side, going after centipedes proved irresistible for Smoky. Having cornered one angry beast, she decided to do a back flip in an effort to confuse it. But she ended up with the swift-moving centipede beneath her, whereupon it whipped its head around and bit her on the thigh.

The modified claws that curve around its head allow *Ethmostigmus rubripes* to inject venom deep into its victims. That is how it hunts and kills its prey – normally small insects, snails and worms – but it also uses the venom to ward off larger would-be predators. Having been bitten, Smoky howled and wailed pitifully. The cries brought her protector, Wynne, running.

He gathered up his precious dog and tried his best to comfort her. He had no idea what the effect of the venom might be. Did the centipede pack enough punch to kill a six-pound pooch like her? Wynne just didn't know. First he'd been struck down by a mystery tropical disease. Now this. In the jungle, danger red in tooth and claw lurked on every side.

Not knowing what to expect, he waited anxiously for the outcome. Rest seemed to be the cure that Smoky craved. After a spell of nurturing care and relaxation she gradually recovered, although it looked as if the giant centipede's powerful poison was still going to leave its mark. Where Smoky had been bitten a patch of hair an inch or so across dropped out. The bare skin turned jet black. It was to be a permanent reminder to the little dog never to go chasing after venomous beasties again.

It was a huge relief to have Smoky well again, for the 26th was getting seriously busy, and the laboratory as much as any other part of the unit. Dozens of recce missions were flown over the Palau and Molucca islands, Biak itself, and even distant Ambon, which was a round flight of pushing 1,800 miles. That was right at the very limits of what the P-38s and their pilots were capable of, and everyone knew the risks of such ultra-long-distance solo sorties.

Four pilots – Captain John Brown, First Lieutenant Michael Koziupa, First Lieutenant Warner Buchanan and Second Lieutenant Ercel Powers – were awarded the Air Medal that June, for completing one-hundred hours of operational flying over enemy territory. The squadron also won its first ever high-valour medal, a Distinguished Flying Cross, which honours 'heroism or extraordinary achievement while participating in aerial flight.'

The citation for Captain Carl D. Lindberg's DFC read: 'for flying 1,450 miles to take the first aerial photographs of Manok-wari, Dutch New Guinea [now Indonesia]. He also sighted several large enemy naval vessels including a battleship, three destroyers and two cruisers.'

It was an epic flight that would have taken a minimum of five-and-a-half hours. With a top speed in excess of 414 mph, there was nothing that the enemy flew that could rival the Lightning. The ubiquitous Japanese fighter, the Mitsubishi A6M Zero, was some eighty mph slower. Even the Zero's replacement, the Nakajima Ki-84 *Hayate* – Storm – would be hard-pressed to catch a Lightning, but only if the P-38 pilot stayed totally focused. If he failed to spot an enemy aircraft's approach, he could do little to outfly or outpace it.

Pinpoint navigation was crucial on such missions, especially in a theatre that consisted largely of open ocean. On the Manokwari sortie, over half the flight had been executed across the Bismarck and Celebes seas – long tracts of water devoid of any landmarks. Managing the flow of aviation fuel was also critical. Throttling back the P-38's twin engines on those long and lonely stretches when sky and sea alike were empty was vital to husbanding fuel supplies.

By punching these high-altitude speed runs deep into enemy airspace, the pilots were earning a hard-won reputation. The risks and the hardships were extreme, so recognizing the gallantry exhibited by these unarmed recce fliers was crucial. It wasn't simply a question of helping to boost the pilots' morale. The secrecy of their work meant that their missions – their very existence – were rarely spoken of outside their own limited circles, so awards like Lindberg's Distinguished Flying Cross helped attract more recruits to the recce squadrons' ranks.

In the European theatre a handful of very high-profile reconnaissance flights had made it into the limelight. Most notable was the mission flown by RAF Pilot Officer Michael Suckling in May 1941. The fearsome German battleship *Bismarck* was reported to be lying at anchor in the shelter of the Norwegian fjords. If the 40,000-tonne behemoth – Germany's largest battleship – managed to break out she could wreak havoc among the Atlantic convoys, which were Britain's lifeline. The RAF were tasked to find her.

On 21 May Suckling had flown his Spitfire over the Grimstadfjord, south of Bergen, Norway's second city. It was 1.15 p.m. when he'd spotted what was possibly the elusive warship, nestling in a crook in the fjord. The photos he fired off from high altitude became known as 'the picture that sank a battleship'. From Grimstadfjord the *Bismarck* was tracked into the Atlantic, and eventually crippled by a Swordfish torpedo bomber, before being sent to the bottom by British warships.

More recently, the incredible high-altitude detective work executed by the recce squadrons in finding the V1 flying bombs and V2 rockets had also hit the headlines. One leading British specialist, the female photo-analyst Constance Babington Smith, would win glowing accolades in the US media: 'Connie Saves New York' ran one somewhat overblown headline. Babington Smith had played a key role in spotting the V1 launchers, at a time when German scientists had been developing rockets and missiles designed to hit the US eastern seaboard.

But those were the exceptions. Mostly, the high-risk, relentless and absolutely vital work of the reconnaissance squadrons was carried out wholly in the shadows. And at the 26th's new Sentani airbase it was beginning to take a heavy toll.

In the second week of July 1944, the Commanding Officer of the 26th himself was grounded by the base's medical staff, who cited combat fatigue. Barely five months earlier, the squadron's founding commander, First Lieutenant Shelton Hallett, had been lost in action. (Hallett's fate was known by now. He'd been shot down by enemy warplanes while executing a photo recce mission at sea.) Now his replacement, Captain Walter R. Hardee, had been pulled off flying duty, due to the cumulative stress of executing similar kinds of missions.

Hardee had once given a long-to-be-remembered speech to the men of the squadron, explaining how he'd been the valedictorian – the top student – at his high school, the one who delivered the final graduation speech. He expected nothing but the very best from those under his command.

It was in this spirit that he'd pushed himself to the edge, and perhaps beyond it, in New Guinea, flying more missions than most. Hardee – with his serious expression, swept back forehead and intense gaze – was finished in theatre. Just days after his grounding he was relieved of his command and sent back to the USA.

On 17 July 1944, Captain Orville L. Counselman took over command in Hardee's place. The squadron's new leader was cut from similar cloth to his predecessor. An archetypal recce pilot, he was a man whose kindly eyes and gentle smile belied the core of steel that lay within. Counselman would lead the squadron from the front, flying more often and further than just about any other pilot. He would push the risk envelope exponentially, and in time he too would reap the whirlwind.

But for now, it was to be Bill Wynne whose recent sacrifices were to gain him a little respite. After his severe bout of tropical fever and the rough sea voyage that had followed, Wynne was offered two weeks' 'recuperative leave' by the squadron's doctor. The 26th was scheduled to move to Biak Island any day now, and all knew they would need to muster their collective strength if they were to survive the trials and tribulations that lay ahead.

Allied commanders had sorely underestimated the numbers and tenacity of the enemy troops garrisoning Biak. They'd expected to face no more than 4,000 defenders: in truth, there were over twice that number. The island was a jumbled mass of mountainous coral, honeycombed with caves. Making maximum advantage of the terrain, the Japanese commander had refrained from opposing the amphibious landings in late May '44. Instead, he'd secreted his forces deep within the cover of the jungle-clad caves, overlooking key Allied objectives – including Biak's main airfield.

The enemy positions had been stockpiled with many months of water, food and ammunition. Within days of the Allied landings the battle for Biak Island had descended into a savage and bloody war of attrition. Air power could do little to help clear those entrenched cave positions. It took men on the ground to do so, and it had proved terrible, bloody work. But MacArthur needed Biak badly. It was a crucial stepping stone toward his overall objective: the Philippines.

Wynne, however, was heading in the opposite direction – to Brisbane, the capital city of Queensland, the state that lies on Australia's north-eastern coast. Sunny, semi-tropical and relatively untouched by war, it was a whole away from the hell of New Guinea. Still, the trip was not without its challenges. Reams of US military regulations forbade the taking of anything other than official war animals on military transports. But bearing in mind what he had been told about Smoky's amorous adventures at Sentani, Wynne was damned if he was going to leave her behind.

He managed to hitch a ride in a C47 with a crew who were heading south towards Brisbane. He'd taught Smoky to lie quietly and peacefully in his musette, an army-issue canvas haversack. Secreted away, she was rendered largely invisible to prying eyes. Fearful that she would be discovered by the authorities at some point en route, he'd taught her to keep still and silent just as soon as she'd scrambled inside.

Smoky might be a *Yank Magazine* champion mascot, but

that would cut little ice with the C47 crew, or, for that matter, the customs officers who would greet them upon arrival. Once he'd tucked her little body into the base of the bag and closed the flap over her head, tightening it gently with the straps, Smoky knew that she was not to move a muscle or to make the slightest sound.

By the time man and dog were ready to depart, the C47 – nicknamed the Gooney Bird by US forces, after a long-winged albatross known by the same name – was hopelessly overloaded. The aircrew had packed the hold with two radial engines still in their wooden crates, plus a dozen infantrymen in full combat gear.

It was pelting with rain by the time the pilot took to the airstrip. Straining to get airborne, the C47 seemed to be heading into a wall of water that blocked out all visibility. Even as the aircraft thundered down the runway the crew chief hurried aft and asked Wynne to move up to the cockpit, as the C47 was too rear-end heavy. Wynne grabbed his musette bag and its precious canine cargo and did as asked, the dozen-odd infantrymen crowding forward with him.

The sight that met his eyes as he entered the cockpit was hardly an encouraging one. Through the C47's rain-lashed split windscreen he could just make out the wall of ragged trees that edged the Sentani strip. It loomed out of the murk, looking frighteningly close. Wynne pulled Smoky's form tighter to him, as the Gooney Bird thundered ever nearer to that fringe of jungle. Right now, Australia seemed a whole world away.

It looked impossible that the C47 would even make it into the air, before smashing into that dark line of trees.

CHAPTER 9

With throttles pushed to the max and with her twin engines howling, the Gooney Bird seemed to shudder along her entire length as she heaved herself upwards through the torrential rain. Moments later, with her undercarriage kissing the treetops, she thundered over the highest of the forest giants, emerging on the far side miraculously unscathed.

The overloaded warplane was past the wall of thick jungle. The C47 skimmed across the roof of the forest, the storm-lashed waters of the Setani Lake opening out below her. For now at least, man and dog could sit back and enjoy the ride. Australia – and all its wartime wonders – were but hours away.

US troops serving in New Guinea had been given orientation briefings about Australia – the nearest nation where they could expect some R&R – and her people. America it was not. Everything in Australia was rationed, so they should expect the locals to be after all the freebies they could get. The tone of voice of an Aussie was something like a London 'cockney' accent, they'd been told. They were cautioned not to remark upon it.

American cigarettes were prized. 'You gotta smoke, Yank?' was to be an oft-heard 'cockney-toned' refrain. The GIs had learned all about the local brand, Craven A. 'After smoking one you'd still be Craven A cigarette,' the joke went. With beer in short supply, the bootleggers were doing a roaring trade, in what the Aussies referred to as their 'sly grog shops'. There were reports that the Aussie girls tended to warm to American service-men, because the 'Yanks' had what they termed real 'get up and go'.

But the first surprise for Bill Wynne and his dog upon touch-ing down in Australia was the climate. It might have been a balmy sixty degrees, but to a man and dog accustomed to the intense tropical heat of New Guinea, it felt positively frosty. Wynne was freezing, and he could only imagine what it was like for Smoky, still hidden away in his haversack. Despite her thick coat of hair, he feared that a small dog like her would be sensitive to the cold.

Once he'd managed to smuggle her through customs, Wynne and Smoky spent their first night in Australia huddled beneath a heap of US Army issue blankets. Man and dog shivered all through the dark hours. After eight months in New Guinea, Wynne craved fresh milk and fresh meat, but clearly their first priority had to be to find some way to keep themselves warm, for the military-issue blankets just didn't seem to cut it.

The following morning Wynne made his way to a local 'hobby shop', an emporium that specialized in hobbies, including all sorts of games. He managed to find a green woollen tablecloth made for a card table. Fringed with beads, it looked about the right size, shape and thickness from which to fashion the kind of DIY coat needed to keep a small, shivering dog toasty warm.

Having purchased the tablecloth, Wynne headed for the local Red Cross office. Scores of volunteers were busy at banks of sewing machines, stitching rank stripes and unit insignia onto new sets of uniform to be issued to those fresh out of the jungle, so they could look dapper during their leave. Producing his dog, Wynne explained just who Smoky was, and that she too had completed many months of war service in New Guinea.

Then he outlined the little dog's requirements. Unsurprisingly, there was no shortage of volunteers to get stitching for Smoky. The Red Cross ladies fitted the little dog by cutting the tablecloth so that it would cover her from neck to tail and almost to her ankles. Straps to the front and beneath fastened the blanket to her chest and underside, while the beads would lie around the fringes to weigh it down.

Wynne himself had recently been promoted to corporal, and he figured the 26th's champion mascot should at least carry the same rank. Warming to their task, the Red Cross volunteers sewed a corporal's stripes to the front left side of the blanket, the same place where a soldier would wear them. Behind the stripes they added the shield of the 5th Air Force – the 26th's parent unit – consisting of a star-spangled comet bursting through a golden '5'. A Good Conduct Ribbon – rewarding honourable and faithful service – plus one or two other badges completed the eye-catching spread.

Smoky now had her coat of many colours, which served both to parade her credentials and honours and to keep her warm. Wynne decided to billet himself with the American Red Cross in Brisbane, for they offered free accommodation and first-class food. After months in the New Guinea jungle this was heavenly. Barbara Wood Smith, an American Red Cross worker, seemed particularly taken with Smoky. She asked if they were willing to pay a visit to the city's hospitals, so the champion mascot might do the rounds of the wounded.

Wynne was in something of a quandary. Fearful of the rules and regulations, he'd had to smuggle Smoky into the country. After much deliberation he agreed that she could visit the hospital wards, but only if there was a publicity blackout. The fact that *Yank Mag*'s champion mascot was there would have to be kept under wraps. Wood Smith agreed, and so the deal was cut: Smoky would do her tour and everyone would keep schtum.

This time, there was to be another major difference from their time in the Nadzab hospital. As Wynne was healthy, he could accompany his dog, and that meant they could employ their full repertoire of tricks. After all their practice and training, Wynne decided they were more than ready to give the war-wounded a special treat.

They began at Brisbane's US 109th Fleet Naval Hospital. In the stifling heat of New Guinea, wounds tended to fester, injuries taking an age to heal. Here in Brisbane the long-suffering casualties of the war faced a far better chance of recovery. But long enforced stints in hospital weren't good for anyone's spirits, least of all sailors who had steamed halfway around the world to fight.

Man and dog did the rounds of the injured sailors, covering around eight wards that first day. In each they ran through their whole box of tricks. First, Smoky dashed through some obedience trials, just to show how strict and soldierly this champion mascot could be. Then it was on to the highlights – Smoky's playing dead had the wounded rolling with laughter. But if anything, her singing duet with Wynne was even more of a show-stopper. As man and dog threw their heads back and crooned, there were tears running down the cheeks of men who hadn't had a great deal to laugh about of late. Wynne and Smoky rounded it off with a new trick – the 'grapevine' – leaving the ward with him stepping quickly and her weaving a figure-of-eight around his feet as he went.

Upon seeing Smoky's sterling performance, one of the Red Cross workers decided to claim her as their own: she pinned an American Red Cross badge to Smoky's coat. Two days later, a lady from the Women's Auxiliary Corps (WAC) – the women's branch of the US Armed Services – noticed the Red Cross badge and figured that she would have to top that.

'If Smoky's a female in the US Army, then she has to be a WAC,' she declared. She removed her own lapel badge and fastened it to Smoky's coat.

While it wasn't exactly what man and dog had come to Australia for – Wynne was supposed to be here enjoying some recuperative leave – their hospital visits certainly went down a storm. Barbara Wood Smith asked if they might be willing to do a repeat performance at the 42nd General Army Hospital. There, Wynne regaled the wounded with tales of Smoky's adventures in New Guinea, relating the miraculous way in which she'd first been discovered, and how she'd gone on to win the *Yank Mag* contest against such stiff competition.

The wounded were enraptured. Starved of any form of entertainment or light relief, the tales had them gripped. Man and dog received a euphoric reception, with Smoky's antics invariably earning wild applause. So captivated were some of the injured soldiers that they took to accompanying the performers from ward to ward, carrying Smoky in their wheelchairs with her diminutive form perched on their laps.

That was what was really so special about such a visit: in the midst of all the trauma and pain of war, it was an incredible treat simply to be able to hold and to cherish a dog like Smoky. Just as had been the case in New Guinea, the hospitalized soldiers noticed how she somehow reminded them of their homes, and of what they were all fighting for. The wounded soldiers kept firing curious questions at Wynne, most commonly: what did he feed her on in the midst of the jungle?

'Regular mess hall chow,' he explained, proudly. Smoky got no more or less than he did: spam, bully beef and canned mutton, plus the occasional vitamin pill.

Their tour of the hospitals complete, Barbara Wood Smith wrote Smoky a personal letter of thanks. In it she addressed the little dog as 'a lady artiste without temperament'.

Being so busy and in such high demand, Wynne and Smoky's two weeks recuperation leave seemed to flash by. In short order it was time to head north once more, back to war. It was late spring 1944, and the Gooney Bird that man and dog boarded would fly them into the heart of the hell that was the battle for Biak Island.

Flights into Biak made their approach across Cenderawasih Bay – Bird of Paradise Bay, in the local language. From an aircraft's window the scene below might indeed look paradisiacal: the humped folds of verdant green stretched to the horizon, towering volcanic peaks plunging into stunning aquamarine waters. But as the flight carrying man and dog neared the Biak Island landing beaches, they revealed a very different story.

Biak Island sits just four degrees south of the equator, and blinding white coral sands fringe the brilliant ocean waters. But crammed into the dense jungle of an island just forty miles long and twenty square were several thousand Japanese troops, well dug-in and ready to die for their emperor. The terrain testified to the ferocity of the combat: the fighting during the landings had been so intense that the palm trees had been stripped bare of their fronds. Ranks of battered trunks stood sentinel over the beaches, their skeletal tops reaching forlornly into the hot skies.

The camp of the 26th lay just to the rear of the main landing beach, looking out over shredded stands of palms and with views beyond to the white breakers of Bird of Paradise Bay. But here, even the sea itself had become a battleground: every day, platoons of Marines would chug across the bay in their General Motors 'Ducks' – the distinctive DUKW amphibious truck-cum-landing-craft – to flush die-hard enemy forces out of the jungle.

With little tree cover remaining to shield the squadron's quarters, the camp lay on the open grassy hinterland to the rear of the beach. Huge shell craters pock marked the terrain. One of the largest had been adapted to form the squadron's shower facilities: a spring bubbled up from the depths of the crater, and a rough screen of sacking had been erected around it.

When the tide came in, it washed right over the floor of the shower, which was fortunate, for it briefly cleansed its terrible smell. For whatever reason, the spring-water reeked of rotten eggs. It was possible to get passably clean, but only if you could stomach the stench for long enough to do so.

Unfortunately, the squadron's camp lay directly under the

flight path used by Japanese warplanes. It was sandwiched between the beach and Biak's main airstrip, at Mokmer Air-base, and the open bay provided the line of attack for avenging Japanese aircrew. Whenever the Japanese bombardiers aimed short of the Mokmer strip, their payloads tore into the beach or the camp itself. It was hardly an ideal homecoming for Wynne and Smoky.

The Mokmer airstrip had been seized by US forces at dawn on 7 June 1944. Surprisingly they'd faced little resistance. In truth, they'd been lured into a carefully set trap. At 9.45 a.m. the Japanese guns – concealed in caves and bunkers on ridge-lines overlooking the strip – had opened fire, unleashing a savage barrage. For four hours the shells had rained down on the airbase. The US forces had held out, but the airfield itself remained unusable.

So desperate was the ensuing battle that it wasn't until 22 June – two weeks later – that the Mokmer airstrip was finally able to receive its first Allied warplanes. In the intervening days US troops had resorted to pouring drums of fuel into the caves in which the Japanese were holding out, in an effort to burn them out. Where that didn't work 'satchel charges' – powerful explosives, held in a military-issue satchel – were detonated in the caves' entrances. Invariably, that would bring down an avalanche of rocks, trapping the cave's occupants inside.

Several times the besieged Japanese forces tried to break out, by battling their way through the encircling US lines. Each attempt was thwarted, but there were still thousands of Japanese soldiers holding out in the island's hinterland. Their commander, Colonel Kuzume Naoy, had vowed to fight until the last man. Hundreds of American troops had already lost their lives in brutal close-quarter battles. US casualties on Biak would eventually top three thousand killed and wounded. Ten thousand Japanese soldiers would die.

The move to Biak Island hadn't exactly been viewed with relish by the men of the 26th. Tokyo Rose broadcasts had beamed stark warnings into their Hollandia camp: American forces faced thousands of Japanese warriors who had vowed to fight to the death in the defence of Biak Island. In many ways those broadcasts weren't so far off the mark.

Once again, the squadron's gossip-mill had gone into over-drive, and the senior officers of the 26th had found themselves struggling to quash 'dangerous and damaging rumour'. The loose talk and speculation had reached such a level that punishment was even mooted: 'violators have been informed that they may be subjected to disciplinary action.'

The squadron's arrival on Biak Island hadn't been accomplished without loss, either. A pair of P-38s had been hit on the ground by enemy warplanes. Yet there was to be no let-up in the demands being placed upon the unit. The incredibly testing conditions meant that requests for photo reconnaissance flights were running at an all-time high.

The squadron flew sixty missions during the first days of June alone. On one such sortie, First Lieutenant Warner M. Buchanan had 'completed a photo run with one engine dead and the other ready to quit at any time', the squadron's monthly war diary recorded. For that daring flight Buchanan would be awarded the Silver Star, the US military's third-highest decoration for gallantry in the line of duty.

As the days progressed the pilots of the 26th would punch out as far as the Philippines, flying a mission over Mindanao, which was approaching 1,500 miles away. There they would secure vital images of the Japanese naval bases, plus their key airfields, in preparation for what had been dubbed as 'MacArthur's Return'.

Two years earlier President Roosevelt had ordered General MacArthur to abandon his spirited defence of the Philippines. On 12 March 1942, MacArthur had acceded to that order, flying out on a B17 Flying Fortress. Upon landing in Australia, he had made his famous speech: 'I shall return.' Behind him, some 11,500 Allied troops had been forced to surrender. What followed were the horrors of the 'Bataan Death March', in which thousands of Allied and Filipino prisoners were forced to cross the jungle on foot and in utterly brutal conditions. Thousands had died.

MacArthur's promise to return was in part to avenge the inhumanity of the Bataan Death March and all those who had lost their lives. But in order to make that promise a reality he desperately needed intelligence, and for that the Lightnings of the 26th had to keep running the gauntlet, time after time after time.

During August 1944 the pilots of the 26th flew ninety-six recce missions. Every time they went out, they knew they were dicing with death. During the course of one of those sorties over the Philippines, Captain John B. Brown realized that more than an hour's fuel supply had been lost due to a break in his main fuel line. He'd switched to the wing tanks, only to find they too had malfunctioned. Regardless, he'd pushed on with his mission, out-flying enemy warplanes and securing photos of key enemy installations and shipping. He was awarded the Distinguished Service Order (DSO) for 'outstanding courage and devotion to duty'.

On the same day, 20 August 1944, another of the 26th's pilots, First Lieutenant Orin C. Darling, was in action over the Philippines. In spite of his radio dying on him, Darling had pressed ahead with his mission, though he was deprived of all communications. He'd managed to shake off three enemy warplanes and secure 'photographs of great value in our operations against the enemy'. He too would be awarded the DSO.

Such derring-do in the air was mirrored on the ground on Biak Island. Though few high-valour medals were handed out to the ground crew of the 26th, it wasn't for want of heroics on their part.

Upon arrival at Biak, First Sergeant Joyce B. Howell, the renegade Texan joker of the squadron, had decided it was time to dispense with his cowboy boots. Instead, he donned some suitable jungle wear and volunteered to join an infantry patrol going after the enemy. His plan was simple: if he made it through okay, he would forge the way for others from the 26th to do likewise. Strictly speaking, of course, it wasn't the role of the 26th to send men out to fight like infantry, but that didn't stop them wanting to go.

Three days after he'd set out, 'JB', as he was known to the men, returned with six notches carved into the wooden butt of his M1 Garand semi-automatic rifle, the standard US service weapon of the Second World War. He also brought back harrowing tales of deep jungle combat. At one stage he'd been pinned behind a fallen tree for hours as he waited for the rest of his patrol to fight their way forward and rescue him.

As soon as he learned of JB's near-death experience at the hands of the enemy, First Lieutenant – now Captain – Hartwell McCullough called the men of the squadron together. Custodian of the Squadron's classified Documents, McCullough feared that he'd heard in Howell's death-defying tales a threat to the unit's future and its fortunes.

'Men, there will be no more from the 26th permitted to go on infantry patrols,' he began, in his thick Louisiana drawl. 'If we lost anyone it'd be damn difficult to explain to Headquarters . . . Besides, I'm not sure y'all are as tough as Howell is. Squadron dismissed.' McCullough had a point. The 26th were a photo recce unit, and they needed to keep focused on the utterly vital task at hand. There was danger enough involved in executing their daring missions on the ground and in the air, without going looking for trouble.

And at the centre of the squadron's heroics here would be one man and his fearless dog.

CHAPTER 10

On Biak Island Wynne and Smoky's tent was an eight-by-ten-foot affair, and thankfully their new room-mate was a far cry from their first – notoriously dog-hating – companion. It was Frank Petrilak, the fresh-faced dog-lover who'd cared for Smoky during the time that Wynne had been in hospital with dengue fever back at Nadzab. That was the good news. The bad news was the fearsome bombing.

Their tent lay some fifty feet from the squadron's photo laboratory, which here on Biak Island was an operation that was busier than ever before. They could hear the night shifts going about their business and chatting away all through the dark hours as they processed incoming rolls of film. But they had to keep one ear open for the air-raid siren warning them that another flight of Japanese warplanes was inbound across Bird of Paradise Bay.

When the siren began its eerie wail, man and dog alike would make a mad dash for the nearest caves, which the Japanese had used as air-raid shelters before them. As they crouched in the dank and fearful darkness, they could hear the hollow whump of bombs exploding outside. As the ground shook and the air inside the cave contracted horribly with the pressure of the explosions, Wynne would do his best to comfort his dog.

They'd set up camp upon a war-blasted chunk of bare white coral that roasted under a remorseless tropical sun. Temperatures regularly climbed above one-hundred degrees. In the tents it was even hotter, sometimes topping 130. Biak was a baking-hot, blinding white, dusty, unrelenting trial of a posting, but none of that alone would kill. It was the Japanese air attacks that were the real risk to life and limb. If the warplanes came during the heat of the day, by the time the men had dashed for the caves they'd be soaked in sweat.

Smoky had already proven how smart she was on Biak. In the centre of the camp lay a barrel of drinking water. Any passing soldier was welcome to pause and slake his thirst. Smoky soon learned what it was for. If Wynne wasn't around, she'd linger by the barrel. When she spied someone approaching, she'd run up to it, bark, dash over to the passerby and bark again, before skipping back to the barrel to bark some more. The guy soon got the message. He'd bend over the barrel with cupped hands, then crouch down so she could lap thirstily.

Similarly, Smoky had shown how quick-thinking she was in her efforts to get away from her master whenever she fancied doing a little exploring, though this kind of unlicensed adventure could prove fatal, especially if she were caught in the open during an air raid. Smoky would locate Wynne in a crowd by sniffing around everyone's ankles. Once she'd detected the right scent she'd dash around and around his feet, excitedly. But if she wanted to get away, she'd execute ever widening circles, waiting for the moment when her master seemed distracted by conversation. Then, when the circuit took her directly behind him, she'd make a dash for the nearest patch of bush.

Wynne had soon got wise to this. He'd pretend not to be looking, but have her pinned out of the corner of his eye. When she made a run for it he'd yell: 'Stand! Stay!' Smoky would freeze in her tracks. He'd call her back with the standard instruction: 'Smoky, come!' She'd return to his side, acting for all the world as if she'd had no intention of going anywhere in particular.

A smart dog is forever on the ball, its mind forever busy. Smoky was the epitome of that. It took a smart master to stay one step ahead of her. But here on Biak, there were times when it made perfect sense to let the little dog have her head.

Before being sent to the front line, the professional war dogs of the Second World War were given intensive training to get them accustomed to explosions and gunfire. That was one of the key lessons learned by US and British K9 units: an animal deployed without any such acclimatization could well become a liability. Of course, Smoky had had none of that. A relative veteran these days, her capacity to deal with gunfire and bombing had had to be learned on the job.

Her reaction to the blistering air raids on Biak was telling. Just as soon as the siren's first blast was heard, she'd tense up along the entire length of her body. She'd start barking in alarm, and keep up the refrain during the mad dash for the cave shelter, as boots – and paws – tore across the coral. Yet there were times when she seemed almost to start barking *before* the air-raid sirens had raised the alarm. The knack she appeared to have for sensing things – threats especially – before they became obvious to humans was uncanny, but no one on Biak was about to question her early-warning abilities.

Could a dog like Smoky really sense the presence of incoming warplanes before they became visible or audible to humans? Possibly she could. A dog's hearing is infinitely more sensitive than our own. Dogs possess eighteen separate muscles with which to raise, lower or swivel their ears, ensuring they can determine exactly from which direction a sound emanates. Tiny though Smoky was, she could twitch her ears this way and that, using them to track distant sounds, and she could pinpoint the source of such a noise in one-six-hundredth of a second – pretty much instantaneously.

But clearly her ability to detect those incoming Japanese warplanes and the threat they embodied went beyond the purely physical. Somehow, she sensed that this thunderous noise on the distant horizon equated to danger. Smoky seemed able to sense *danger itself*, and quite possibly dogs have evolved to do just that over the millennia.

All dogs, no matter what breed or size, are descended from *Canis lupus*, the grey wolf. Dogs share 99.96 per cent of the wolf's DNA. Of course, their wolf-like ancestry has been overlain with thousands of years of selective breeding, as humans and dogs have forged the most long-lived and enduring man-animal part-nership of all. The dog was the first animal to be domesticated, and today they possess an ability to bond and form relationships with humans that no other creature can rival.

Prior to domestication dogs used their acute sense of hearing to track prey and predators. They are able to hear a far greater range of frequencies than humans, and they can do so over far longer distances. In fact, a dog's hearing is around ten times more efficient than our own: a sound a human might hear at ten metres they can hear at a hundred or more. Had there been a snake living on Biak's coral, Smoky would have been able to hear its slithering from a considerable distance away.

One thing was for sure on Biak Island: if Smoky started yelping her signature bark, her fine head tilted out towards Bird of Paradise Bay, it was time to run hell for leather for the shelters.

The hectic pace of operations that August 1944 rarely faltered. Breaks came only when the squadron found itself grounded due to bad weather. Whenever that happened the men of the 26th took the rare chance to unwind. Biak's white sandy beaches were undeniably glorious. In another time, this would have been the archetypal tropical paradise island. The crystal-blue waves rolled in throatily, boasting curling white crests that dashed themselves to exhaustion on the battle-scarred sands.

In time someone discovered that discarded P-38 drop-tanks made passable surfboards, and even better hulls for fashioning DIY sailing boats. With a cockpit cut into the topside, the right amount of ballast inserted, a lone mast and sail raised above the cylindrical hull, plus a rudimentary rudder, a drop-tank could accommodate two fully grown men at sea quite comfortably. But some of the 26th's crew went one better: they adapted an old generator to serve as an inboard motor on their drop-tank craft, powering a screw.

The heat was soporific and cooling off in the sea heavenly. Sergeant Gilbert J. Frankhuizen, one of the squadron mechanics, decided the beach-goers needed some chilled drinks. Taking an unused fuel tank from a B24 bomber plus an old generator, Frankhuizen – big-boned and rangy, with an open-faced honesty about him – set about building the squadron an ice machine.

More normally, Frankhuizen, a sheet-metal specialist, would

be working on the Lightnings' fuselage and cowlings, repairing stress fractures or battle damage caused by enemy fire. The ice machine, a truly ingenious feat of improvisation, provided welcome relief. With an outer skin filled with a thick layer of compressed sawdust that acted as insulation, it was able to produce eight blocks of ice per day, each about the size and shape of a concrete slab.

A net was erected, with posts lashed to old oil drums, so the men could play beach volleyball. It too provided a real boost to spirits. As the squadron's Monthly Intelligence Summaries reported, 'Individuals lured by aquatics spend leisure hours swimming and sunbathing on the beach.' Yet despite such leisurely pursuits, the war was never far away and neither was the enemy.

One day some of the squadron's more intrepid seamen were out testing their motor-powered drop-tank yacht, when they spotted a low-lying object on the far horizon. Thinking it might be a downed airman or ship's crew on a life raft, they grabbed a small rowing dinghy, lashed it to the rear of their craft and motored out to investigate. They found what they had least expected – a makeshift raft crowded with Japanese soldiers.

Mindful of the reports of Japanese troops fighting to the last man, those crewing the 'USS Drop-Tank' decided they would take no chances. Holding off a distance, they ordered the enemy to strip. Once they were sure they had no hidden grenades or pistols secreted on their persons, they motored in and took the enemy party captive. The prisoners were loaded aboard the dinghy and a course was set for land. But en route the improvised motor conked out, so everyone had to put their backs to the oars, to beat the tide back to shore.

Unsurprisingly, a crowd of onlookers had gathered. This was the closest most of them had ever got to the dreaded enemy. But the Japanese soldiers seemed cowed and subservient, not at all the fanatical die-hards most had been expecting. They were clearly half-starved. Sitting cross-legged on the bare coral, they wolfed down the stale crusts of bread they were given and downed gallons of water between them.

It turned out that these enemy troops had become isolated from their unit, and had held out in the jungle for two hellish months. Finally, they'd run out of food completely. Taking to the raft had been a last gamble to save themselves. Those emaciated Japanese soldiers quickly became the most photographed men on Biak Island. Their clothes were in rags, their faces thickly bearded, their limbs skeletal.

More than anything, the men of the 26th couldn't help but pity them. As with most forces embroiled in this terrible conflict – the enemy included – the majority of the troops were conscripts. They had been ordered to fight by their governments or rulers and they'd had little choice but to obey. Here on Biak Island – as had happened with so many of the Japanese positions – they had been told to fight to the last. This handful of Japanese troops had decided they wanted to live and they had made a desperate bid to do so.

Getting into the beach spirit, Wynne found Smoky an excellent, sheltered swimming pool. Dogs of her size needed to be careful in rough water. The powerful surf could dash a dog like Smoky on a reef, or the tide could drag her out to sea. Wynne found a novel solution to the problem: he discovered a particular bomb crater on the beach that was just right for his dog. The breakers rolled gently into it, filling it to a depth of about four feet with calm, balmy water. It was perfect.

Smoky loved it. Her favourite pastime became chasing flocks of small birds across the beach, in the direction of the swimming pool. When they took flight to cross it, she'd dive in, doggie-paddle over, and leap out the far side to resume the hunt. The birds seemed to learn that by luring their pursuer into the crater-cum-swimming-pool they could gain themselves some short respite. They took to flying back around, knowing they'd be able to dunk her in the crater time after time.

Of course, the repeated immersions in salt water, combined with the harsh, dry nature of the bare coral, weren't exactly conducive to Smoky keeping her fine coat of hair in top order. Wynne ensured she got a daily fresh-water bath. A full helmet was used to soap and to scrub her, a half to rinse her thoroughly thereafter. Somehow, Smoky seemed to master the tough, challenging conditions. She'd yet to fall sick, unlike her master.

Fortunately, the accommodation tents were pitched upon one of the few patches of grass in the area. It helped cushion the velvety-soft pads of Smoky's feet from the sharp coral, at least when she was resting. Those pads were covered in minute, fingerprint-like tracing marks, like the tiny spreading branches of a tree. They were beautiful, and delicate, and so very easy for a dog to tear, especially when moving fast over rough, dry terrain, or running from enemy warplanes.

Smoky took to sleeping right underneath Wynne's army cot. He figured she sensed an extra layer of protection there. Or maybe it was simply all down to the smell. The scent of the familiar. She might have had her own bed – the strip of khaki material that served as the cot's cover – but it wasn't a patch on where Wynne slept. Not in Smoky's eyes or, rather, not according to her nose.

A dog's nose is up to a million times more sensitive than a human's. We might poke our nose into a cup of tea to smell if it's been sweetened with a spoonful of sugar, and even then we might not be entirely sure. But a dog can detect the scent of a teaspoon of sugar in a million gallons of water – enough to fill two Olympic-sized swimming pools to the brim.

As far as Smoky was concerned, the cot cover smelled of her. By contrast, Wynne's cot itself was crammed full of the scent of her best buddy snoozing through the heat of the New Guinea night. It resonated with his smell, the one that she adored.

Like all dogs, Smoky's sense of smell represented her universe; she was a creature of the nose. For her, the world was an incredibly rich and exciting tapestry of smells. More often than not, that was how a dog experienced a new scene – via a scent carried on the breeze. We humans see the world. A dog smells it. And, somehow, Smoky seemed able to smell trouble, too.

One fine morning Frank Petrilak invited his tent buddies for a sail on the bay. There was no flying, so it would be a welcome diversion. Petrilak was no sailor, but his friend, Jack Tankersley, was. Tankersley's first name was actually Rholan, but he preferred being known simply as 'Jack'. A corporal like Wynne, he had fine-boned, delicate features and the demeanour of a scholar. He'd spent a good deal of his youth crewing yachts, and that gave the two landlubbers – three, if Smoky were included – the confidence that they could master the coming voyage.

Theirs was a drop-tank craft, but a slightly more ambitious

model than the mono-hulled vessels. By lashing two drop-tanks together, set a few feet apart, they'd managed to form a makeshift catamaran. The whole affair was topped by a wooden platform, on which the intrepid sailors could perch. Cut into each of the drop-tanks was a cockpit, in case those crewing her needed to take shelter from wind or spray. The sail that was hoisted above was fashioned from a discarded parachute, boasting a wide expanse of the US Army's finest silk.

Tankersley proposed a cruise across the bay to visit one Biak's native settlements. The Biak Islanders tended to live in so-called 'water villages' or 'floating villages', where entire neighbourhoods were constructed over the sea. The wooden huts were suspended on stilts and linked by a labyrinth of bamboo walkways. There was little flat ground upon which to build among the island's dramatic, hilly terrain, plus the water villages took full advantage of the cooling sea breeze.

Popping Smoky into one of the drop-tank cockpits, the three men pushed off. The early-morning bay was as smooth as glass, and at first each of them had to help paddle. But shortly the wind picked up a little, the sail snapped and billowed, and they began to gather speed. But all of a sudden Smoky leapt out of the drop-tank cockpit where she was riding, and with zero warning launched herself into the water. The boat was at least half a mile out by now, and Wynne had no idea what could have got into his dog.

As the tiny dog paddled for all she was worth for shore, his biggest fear was the sharks. The outer reaches of the bay were infested with them, and while they'd yet to see any V-shaped fins cutting through the surrounding water, the sharks were sure to be lurking somewhere close by. Throwing caution to the wind Wynne dived in. He caught up with Smoky when she was about twenty-five yards from the boat. Holding her up out of the water and away from any hungry jaws he side-crabbed his way back to the vessel.

Handing Smoky up to Petrilak, he heaved himself hurriedly aboard. The sea was wonderfully warm and Smoky seemed unharmed. Puzzled as Wynne was, he was relieved that no real damage had been done. After that brief and unexpected interlude, the crew set a course for the nearest floating village, which was perched on the very tip of a distant headland.

As the drop-tank catamaran ploughed onwards, those aboard began to wonder why Smoky had taken flight. It wasn't like this dog to go running scared of anything. She was always up for any adventure. Most dog lovers have at one time or another experienced the uncanny sixth sense of their canine companions. Had Smoky detected something, danger perhaps, in the bay? The sky remained clear and the sea calm, but for whatever reason she'd seemed reluctant to journey with them. In fact, she'd seemed desperate to abandon ship. What on earth could have spooked her?

A while later Tankersley steered the craft towards shore, navigating a course around the outcroppings of a coral reef. Locals waved a welcome from the nearest stilted hut and the three men and their dog were invited in. Everything in these villages seemed to be made of bamboo, which grew to a great height and breadth in thick stands in the surrounding jungle. The hut had a split bamboo floor, the walls were of split bamboo, and even the beds themselves were made out of solid bamboo frames.

As the villagers welcomed the three visitors, Smoky dashed outside to entertain the local kids, crab-chasing on the beach. She'd pounce on an unfortunate crustacean, growl menacingly, spin around a few times in a wild blur, then let the beast go. The crab, hardly believing its luck, would rise on its legs and scuttle off, whereupon Smoky would give chase again.

But after a while the sky above the bay began to darken. Out of nowhere heavy clouds appeared on the horizon. Alert to how changeable the tropical weather could be, the three adventurers decided it was time to head back to camp. They pushed the catamaran back out to sea, paddled past the reef and set a course for home. The craft picked up speed as the wind began to gust more strongly. A particularly powerful blast drove the boat forward, the conical noses of the drop-tanks digging into the waves.

Seawater sloshed into the open cockpits. The wind grew stronger, the sharp, double-prow of the craft repeatedly being driven underwater. Petrilak started bailing, as Wynne moved to the stern of the boat, in an effort to use his weight to lift the bows. The wind stiffened. The swell to left and right became ever more ominous. Tankersley began to tack back and forth, as he tried to navigate the cumbersome vessel through the rough seas. Worryingly, he announced that he'd never had to cope with anything quite like this back home in the States.

Had they been crewing a proper yacht, they would have been able to furl the sail, drop the anchor and ride out the storm. Not in their drop-tank catamaran. The open nature of the twin steel hulls meant that she was in danger of being swamped. If that happened, their weight would drag them down to the depths.

There were no air tanks or flotation aids to keep her afloat, and if she shipped too much water she'd go down like a stone.

As they fought against the conditions and bailed frantically, all of a sudden the boat's steel double-prow ploughed into a submerged obstruction. They had struck a reef lying just below the surface and they were stuck. Wedged fast, the waves kept pounding the drop-tanks against the sharp rocks, punching dents in them. More water washed inside the open cockpits and the vessel groaned alarmingly as she twisted and slewed with each wave, but still she remained trapped.

The makeshift catamaran sounded as if she was in danger of breaking up and being torn in two. Aware that they were in desperate straits, Wynne did the only thing that he could think of: he jumped overboard, floundered around until he'd found reasonably firm footing on the reef and began to shove for all he was worth.

Straining with the effort, he managed to heave the craft back into the sea. That done he dived for her twin steel hulls, and with aching muscles managed to drag himself back aboard. The wind propelled them onwards at speed now, driving all before its blast. The only option was to keep sailing and to keep bailing for all they were worth.

They would have to try to ride out the storm.

CHAPTER 11

The battle to keep the catamaran afloat lasted for two perilous hours, and for all of that time the crew were continuously bailing out the drop-tank hulls in a bid to stay afloat. When finally their exhausted, sodden party neared the beach, they could see a group of fellow soldiers standing on the shoreline, scrutinizing their every move with binoculars. Caught up in their struggle to navigate the vessel home, Wynne and his fellows had been oblivious to how dire a predicament they had been in. It had been crystal clear to the watchers ashore.

They made landfall, and Wynne's first concern now was for his dog. Smoky was soaked to the skin and had plainly swallowed a good deal of seawater. The wind howled around them still, the storm blustery, cold and dark. So powerful were the blasts that several tents had been blown down. Luckily, Wynne and Petrilak's was still standing. It was to be a long, cold night, but at least the men and their dog had come through that sea voyage alive.

As they reflected upon the day just gone, the intrepid seamen wondered about the smallest sailor among them, Smoky. One thing stuck in their minds – the moment when she had leapt overboard. Had she somehow sensed that the storm was coming, and thus taken the desperate measure of trying to jump ship and swim to shore? Had she tried to head for land before it was too late, hoping to communicate to her fellow sailors the coming danger?

They could remember occasions before when Smoky had appeared to sense an incoming storm long before it had struck. For no apparent reason she would go very quiet and sniff the air, before starting to whimper and head for her sanctuary – invariably, the space beneath Bill Wynne's cot. A while later the storm would hit. Maybe that was what had driven her actions today?

Perhaps Smoky had demonstrated one of the most unusual and extraordinary aspects of canine behaviour: 'intelligent diso-bedience', the ability to hear and understand a human's order or command, but to disobey it for the simple reason that the dog knew better. She'd known that morning that she was supposed to sail to some mystery destination, but had she also sensed the approaching storm, and done her level best to force an abandonment of the voyage?

Some animal behaviourists and scientists argue that dogs can sense a change in the weather. They claim dogs are able to detect a drop in the barometric pressure that presages a storm. They also may detect changes in the atmosphere's static electrical field, which alters at the approach of a thunderstorm. Lightning ionizes the air forming ozone, which has a sharp metallic scent, so they may even be able to smell an approach-ing storm. In a similar way dogs and other animals may sense a coming earthquake, by detecting electrical signals produced by the movements of tectonic plates beneath the earth's crust.

Whatever the truth, there was no doubt that Smoky had been utterly determined to get off the 'Good Ship Drop-Tank' that morning, risking a long swim through shark-infested waters to do so. What breed of dog possessed such refined senses, her fellow sailors wondered? What kind of pedigree produced such a seemingly extraordinary set of instincts and an innate sixth sense? As luck would have it, they were about to find out.

It was during those long hot weeks on Biak Island that a major part of the mystery surrounding Smoky would be solved. An excited Staff Sergeant Kalt – Smoky's photographer during her *Yank Mag* parachute jumps – came to seek out man and dog. He knew what breed Smoky was, Kalt declared, breathlessly.

One of the squadron had just received his April '44 issue of the *National Geographic Magazine*. (It had taken several months for it to make it out to New Guinea.) By chance, along with features entitled 'Japan and the Pacific' and 'Jungle War: Bougainville and New Caledonia', there was one called 'Toy Dogs, Pets of Kings and Commoners', and another entitled 'Dogs In Toyland'.

'They prove she's a Yorkshire Terrier,' Kalt announced, excitedly, pointing to the magazine's dog-related features.

'A what?' Wynne queried.

'A Yorkshire Terrier,' Kalt repeated. There was a photograph of one of the breed illustrating the article, he explained. It was the spitting image of Smoky.

Wynne got his hands on the magazine and flicked through the pages. There were the adverts for 'US War Savings Bonds', and Coca-Cola and one that boasted about how 'America's fighters move in with GM Diesels', plus a stunning photo of Japan's snow-capped Mount Fuji, 'an outstanding guidepost to

Allied Bombers', the magazine declared, looking ahead to the bombing of the Japanese homeland.

The article entitled 'Jungle War: Bougainville and New Caledonia' was richly illustrated with oil paintings by an official US Army war artist. They captured the grit and fire of combat in New Guinea. One was captioned, '"H" Hour of Bougainville – Marines of the First Wave Swarm into Landing Boats'. 'Jap planes attack!' read another. 'Into Empress August Bay falls a flaming Mitsubishi Dive Bomber'. Then: 'First wave! A Jap mortar shell blasts a landing boat. Casualties are heavy, but the fighting marines gain the beachhead'. A final painting showed marines standing by a thickly tangled wall of vegetation: 'At jungle's edge Marines watch for Japs and dig foxholes'.

But what Wynne hungered to see most were the articles about the toy dogs. The first, by British writer Freeman Lloyd, lay seventy pages into the magazine. The piece warned about the threat of such small dogs being stolen to order, and how no one was immune. 'Being easily caught and carried away, toy dogs have always been a special prey for professional dog thieves,' Lloyd wrote. 'Charles II expressed . . . his concern over the loss of some of his dogs, and actually begged the thieves to leave his pets alone.'

The professional dog thieves were 'shrewd rascals who kept up to the minute on breeds and values', the author wrote, describing the Sunday morning black market for such stolen dogs, in Shoreditch, east London. Lloyd was eighty-four years old, and he'd been an editor of *Field and Stream* magazine for a quarter of a century. He was pictured at a field trial for spaniels, dressed in a feathered derby (a kind of bowler hat), formal black coat, stock necktie, corduroy breeches, heavy stockings and short gaiters. That, apparently, was what any self-respecting canine expert should be seen in at such an event.

He was certainly an authority on his subject. Several pages into the article there was the first mention of the Yorkshire Terrier. It concerned the starring role that one such dog had assumed on the stage. 'The increasing popularity of the Yorkshire Terrier (Plate V) may have been heightened ... by the appearance of one of that breed as "protector" of the leading lady in *The Enemies* – Lillie Langtry. The little dog growled or barked at the approach of the villain in the play.'

Protecting the leading lady from the bad guys – now that sounded like Smoky all right.

There were further features on the Toy Poodle, Affenpinscher, Pug, English Toy Spaniels, Chihuahua and Pekinese. The section on the Japanese Spaniel – 'the toy dog of the Orient' – drew the eye, but the description didn't sound like Smoky at all. 'The profusely haired plume or tail carried over a side of the back proclaims the Jap to be of an ancestry different from that of ... the toy spaniels of Europe.' That was definitely *not* Smoky.

The 'Plate V' referenced by Lloyd related to the Dogs in Toyland section – a gallery of colour photos that followed the main article. There were two pictures in Plate V. The top showed a Yorkshire Terrier which – though thoroughly beribboned, primped and prettied-up – was the spitting image of Smoky. 'Silken-haired "Suprema" is a Champion Yorkshire Terrier,' announced the caption. 'Yorkshires are excellent mousers and when not on show this one gives the family cat stiff competition.'

The image was transfixing. It was a dead ringer for Smoky.

In early March 1944 a tiny dog was discovered by Allied troops, abandoned in a jungle foxhole. A total mystery – was she a Japanese military mascot that had somehow got left behind? – she was named 'Smoky' by Corporal William 'Bill' Wynne, the soldier who adopted her, due to her distinctive colouring. Though he was unsure even of what breed she might be, Smoky would go on to forge one of the most extraordinary records of any dog that served with Allied forces.

Facing suicidal resistance from Japanese troops, and fighting across horrendous terrain, Allied troops – and their diminutive canine mascot – were stalked by venomous jungle critters and exotic killer diseases, but it was then that Smoky really came into her own. When Bill Wynne was struck down with suspected dengue fever, Smoky was allowed to sleep in the field hospital on his bed. Overnight she became an informal therapy dog, comforting those traumatised on the frontline of war, and bringing light into shattered lives.

After many months of taking it, the anti-malarial drug, Atabrine, turned troops' skin a signature yellow. This sign, at the entrance to one of the main field hospitals, left little doubt as to what fate awaited those who missed their pills.

Smoky became the prize-winning mascot of the 26th Photo Reconnaissance Squadron. Pilots flew their lone, unarmed aircraft fast and at high altitude deep behind enemy lines to capture crucial photographs on film. Their distinctive aircraft, the P38 Lightning, was nicknamed the Fork-tailed Devil by the enemy, due to its distinctive twin tailplanes. Soon, Smoky too would take to the skies on a series of daring sorties.

Moments of downtime were rare, both for the men and their diminutive canine mascot. Smoky was determined to get involved, more than once being mistaken for the ball in the rough and tumble.

Colonel Turbo was a Rhesus Macaque, and a mascot of a rival squadron. But Smoky got the better of him, both in their first and only fight, and when she beat him to first place in a mascot competition.

Allied forces swept through the Islands of the Southwest Pacific, often moving so swiftly that they bypassed Japanese garrisons. But in the spring and summer months of 1944, enemy forces were found to have fortified deep caves on Biak Island, drawing Allied troops into a series of brutal close-quarter battles. Many suffered terrible shell-shock or combat fatigue, which meant that Smoky's healing powers were in even greater need.

Advancing towards the Philippines in convoy, for the Lingayen Gulf
Landings, Bill Wynne found that Smoky's powers of forewarning would
save him in the most miraculous of ways. In desperation, the Japanese
military had resorted to using kamikazes – suicide pilots – in an effort
to sink the Allied fleets and slow their advance. Wearing ceremonial
belts and headscarves, the Kamikaze pilots took off on their one-way
trips, blessed with flowers … Waves of such aircraft swept into attack
the landing craft on which Bill Wynne and Smoky were riding, as ships
were hit and sunk in terrifying kamikaze strikes. After she saved his life,
Bill Wynne would nickname Smoky 'The Angel from a Foxhole.'

British serviceman Rouse Voisey would be captured by the Japanese, and forced to work as slave labour clearing airstrips from the jungle and on the notorious Sumatran 'hell railroad'. Worse still, when loaded aboard the Japanese hellship *Junyo Maru*, Rouse found the ship hit by torpedoes. Packed into bamboo cages in the hold, few escaped before the *Junyo Maru* went down. Those who did suffered terrible vengeance at the hands of their captors, but amazingly Rouse lived to tell the tale. When Bill Wynne and Smoky took to the war-torn skies, part of their mission was to scour the seas for such shipwrecked Allied survivors.

Incredibly, Smoky survived the long months at war on the ground, at sea and in the air, becoming one of the most famous mascots and therapy dogs of the Second World War. Bill Wynne, an amateur magician, taught her a raft of tricks with which to entertain war-weary and homesick troops. After the war, they forged a show-business career together in the USA, with their wartime exploits taking centre stage.

So was the description of the breed and its distinctive coat. 'A bright, golden tan, is the desired light colour that contrasts so beautifully with the bright steel-blue hair that extends from the back of the head to the root of the tail . . . The dog should have a cushion to lie upon; hay, straw or shavings may otherwise become entangled with the coat.'

A cushion to lie upon: some hopes of that here on Biak Island!

Yorkshire Terriers – known colloquially as 'Yorkies' – were bred in the 1800s, the article explained, to hunt for rats in the woollen mills of the north of England. In the 1850s weavers in Lancashire and Yorkshire had crossed Halifax Terriers with other terrier breeds – most likely the Skye Terrier, the Paisley Terrier and the Maltese. They had produced an incredibly tenacious and courageous dog.

Their small size was actually crucial to the role for which they were bred: it enabled the Yorkie to pursue vermin down drains and tunnels. Yorkshire Terriers were born hunters, which would go some way to explaining Smoky's acute territoriality, her fearlessness – the epic battle with Colonel Turbo being just one example – and her fierce protective instincts over those that she loved.

The Yorkie was a breed still practically unknown in America, which explained why Wynne and the rest of her fan club in the 26th had failed to recognize her. But wonderful though it was, discovering her breed – that she was of English ratting origin – had done little to explain how she'd come into Bill Wynne's hands.

How on earth had a dog bred to hunt vermin in Yorkshire in the 1800s ended up abandoned in a foxhole in New Guinea at the height of the war? Her presence here in New Guinea remained an enigma, and there was not much that anyone could do to solve that right now. There was, after all, a war to be fought.

General Krueger, the American commander charged with wresting Biak Island from the grip of the enemy, had his hands full clearing Japanese troops from Biak's thick jungle, labyrinthine peaks, valleys and caves. A veteran of the First World War, Krueger had turned sixty-three in January '44 and he'd believed himself too old to be given front-line command. But MacArthur had expressed himself 'particularly anxious' to have Krueger with him.

MacArthur appreciated Krueger's hard-charging attitude. He was too good and aggressive a commander to stand by and wait for a Japanese attack, even when – as at Biak Island – estimates of Japanese strengths had turned out to be way off the mark. In the protracted and bitter fighting that had followed, Krueger had gone head to head against Adachi, the Japanese general in overall command of the enemy's New Guinea campaign.

Horribly cut off, and with his own forces plagued by disease and hunger, Adachi feared it was a campaign in which the Allies had the upper hand. Even so, he would never give in. In an effort to relieve the besieged forces at Biak Island, as well as his own encircled troops, a powerful Japanese task force was ordered to set sail for New Guinea. It consisted of the Imperial Japanese Navy's foremost carrier fleet, which would launch a massive air assault against US positions. Ground offensives would follow, intended to seize back the initiative and stabilize the Japanese lines.

As it transpired, the Japanese warships were intercepted by the

US Navy's Fifth Fleet in the waters around the Mariana Islands, which lay to the north of New Guinea in the Philippine Sea. The F6F Hellcat, the US military's leading carrier-based fighter plane, had recently arrived in the Pacific. Rugged, super-efficient and deadly, boasting superior speed, armour and armaments, it could outperform and outfight the Japanese Zero.

As the two fleets converged, the Japanese carriers sent up four massive waves of aircraft, boasting 373 warplanes. Only 130 would return. The rest were intercepted by the Hellcats and blasted out of the skies. By day two of the onslaught, which became known as the 'Great Marianas Turkey Shoot', three of the Japanese carriers had been sunk and they'd lost a total of 633 planes. The American air losses were less than a sixth of that number.

In forty-eight hours the Japanese Navy had lost ninety per cent of their carrier-based aircraft, most of their highly trained pilots and three of their most valuable warships, rendering their surviving carriers largely useless. The Battle of the Philippine Sea – the largest carrier battle in history – was a blow from which the Japanese military would struggle to recover.

The Japanese task force had failed to relieve Biak Island. They had failed to link up with General Adachi's dwindling band of fighters, marooned in the New Guinea jungle to the south of Hollandia. By late August 1944 General Krueger was able to declare the Battle for Biak Island won. There were small pockets of enemy troops stubbornly holding out, deep in the island's interior, but the key areas lay in Allied hands. Though it had not been without heavy sacrifice, it constituted a huge step forward for the Allies.

Krueger's victory at Biak, and his outfighting Adachi, would lead to him being hailed as a hero at home, his photo gracing the cover of *Time Magazine*. Such defeats left the Japanese increasingly desperate, prompting their senior commanders to seize upon a wholly new means of waging warfare, one designed to slow up the American advance and to sink as many of their warships as humanly possible. It would call for the ultimate sacrifice from their remaining pilots, who would strike first in the defence of the Philippines.

Vice Admiral Takijiro Onishi, one of the most senior Japanese commanders in the region, feared that with so few aircraft and pilots remaining to call on, the battle for the Philippines could not be won. In late August 1944 he conceived of the concept of the kamikaze, which he christened *tokubetsu kogeki tai* – the 'divine wind special attack teams'. The more familiar name of kamikaze, which usually translates as 'god-wind', would come into usage in October of that year.

Under Vice Admiral Onishi's purview, land-based squadrons would be trained for kamikaze missions, in a last-ditch effort to prevent the Americans from reaching the shores of the Imperial Japanese homeland. The Japanese hoped that such suicide attacks would make the war so costly to the US, that the Allies would be forced to offer peace terms.

The concepts underpinning the kamikazes were rooted in the Japanese samurai tradition and its sense of duty and obedience, and the importance of achieving an honourable death. As part of Japanese bushido – the martial tradition dating to the Middle Ages – *giri* (obligation) meant that the true warrior should be willing to sacrifice his own life, and of his own free will, due to his beliefs and his love of homeland, which were paramount.

Onishi organized the first kamikaze flights into four units, each named after a patriotic Japanese poem: *Shikishima* (Spirit of Japan); *Yamato* (True Japan), *Yamazakura* (Mountain Cherry) and *Asahi* (Rising Sun). He decreed that a ceremony would be held to speed each kamikaze pilot on his way. Dressed in a headband adorned with the rising sun, and with a *sennibari* – a belt of one thousand stitches made by one thousand Japanese women – strung around his waist, the pilot would eat a last ball of rice and drink sake, before climbing into the cockpit of his aircraft.

The *tokkotai* – the manual drawn up for the kamikaze – exhorted those flying to their deaths never to close their eyes, not even in the moment of their own annihilation. If they did, they might miss their way and fail to strike their target. In the final few seconds they were to shout at the top of their voices *Banzai* (an ancient Japanese war cry) and *Hissatsu* (critical strike).

By late summer 1944, General MacArthur was readying his next push northwards towards the Philippines. Once the US general had, as he'd famously promised, *returned* to that war-torn archipelago, Allied forces would be able to starve Japan of oil supplies. Deprived of fuel, she would be a defeated nation in all but name. The Japanese commanders, well aware of the danger, readied the divine wind special attack teams for what was coming.

The 26th Photo Reconnaissance Squadron would sail into the heart of the coming storm, and when they did they would have a new, and wholly unexpected, addition to their number. Yet before all that could happen there was flying to be done – both for Bill Wynne and the squadron's champion mascot.

Man and dog were about to take to the skies.

CHAPTER 12

In late August Bill Wynne decided it was time that he got airborne. He'd trained as an aerial photographer back in the US, but he'd never yet been able to indulge his craft. Of course, he couldn't do so with the 26th, for their P-38s were single-seater aircraft. The 3rd Air-Sea Rescue Squadron were also based at Biak, and they flew missions in multi-seater planes. They were eager for specialists with his kind of skill.

He and Troop Sergeant Lester E. Switzer, a fellow aerial photographer with the 26th, volunteered for air duties. Switzer, known to all as 'Les', was the 26th's camera repair chief. The device he and Wynne would be using was an Eastman-Kodak K24, which resembled a giant iron cauldron laid on its side. It was almost as big as a man's torso, and it had a pair of solid wooden shovel-like handle grips set vertically to the sides, for swinging the heavy camera around.

Wynne and Switzer had spent months working in cramped, baking-hot confines on the ground, at either the photo lab or the camera repair department. Both fancied a change of scenery and a spell in the air, but there was another powerful incentive for those who wished to get airborne. Any airman who completed 300 hours of 'combat flying' was eligible for return to the USA. In short, they could earn a permanent passage home.

Combat flying was defined as time over territory 'where enemy fire is probable and expected'. To survive *300 hours* of such high-risk operations was a tall order indeed. On average, that might equate to one hundred or more sorties, each of which pushed deep into enemy airspace. But still, it was a dream the aircrew could hold on to and nurture.

For Switzer it was a fairly easy decision to move onto flying status with the 3rd Air-Sea Rescue Squadron. For Wynne, slightly less so. Air-sea rescue patrols generally spent inordinately long stretches in the air. The very nature of the work – scouring vast tracts of jungle or ocean for downed pilots – demanded time, and Wynne worried what he was going to do with his dog during the hours that he would be airborne and away from camp.

Towards the end of the month a young lieutenant from the 3rd Air-Sea Rescue Squadron said he was keen to have a photographer accompany him on his next flight. A fighter pilot flying a P-38 had gone down behind enemy lines in the deep Biak jungle. If the 3rd Air-Sea Rescue Squadron could find and photograph his crash-site, they might be able to guide an infantry patrol to reach the downed airman. The enemy were thick on the ground, but rescue was still a possibility.

Wynne volunteered for this, his inaugural combat flight. It would take place in a Stinson L5 Sentinel, a diminutive military liaison and spotter aircraft. The Sentinel was only a little bigger than a Piper Cub, the ubiquitous single-engine light trainer that had been co-opted for wartime service. The Sentinel's simple, reliable design and good low-speed handling made it ideally suited for military purposes, including reconnaissance, message carrying and ground control.

The Sentinel's fuselage was made from steel tubing covered with cotton treated with dope, a liquid that both stiffened and waterproofed the fabric, while the wings were fashioned from wooden frames covered in the same way. Pilot and co-pilot/observer/photographer sat side-by-side in the cockpit. While the aircraft was easy enough to fly, it barely topped 150 mph at full speed and it offered zero protection from enemy fire. The prospect of passing 300 combat hours in such an aircraft wasn't exactly enticing.

Wynne gathered together his leather flight helmet and goggles, his summer flying overalls, plus his .45 calibre M1911 semi-automatic pistol – standard US military issue – grabbing a few spare magazines of rounds, including some packed with rat-shot. When armed with that type of ammunition the pistol was basically converted into a low-power shotgun. The rat-shot was ideal for taking out snakes and any other nasties that might appear at close quarters. Lastly, he strapped on his bowie knife, a large military-issue combat blade that could be put to a wide variety of uses in the jungle.

Long before he'd climbed into the Sentinel's cockpit, Wynne had made the decision to leave Smoky in the hands of some of the squadron's old faithfuls, with his tentmate, Frank Petrilak being given special responsibility. With Petrilak keeping a watchful eye, there shouldn't be a great deal of harm that could come to her. The tiny, twenty-four-foot-long aircraft bumped and rumbled its way down the airstrip and clawed its way into the hot air. Shimmering thermals rising from the coral shook and buffeted the aircraft like a kite as the pilot fought to gain altitude.

The Sentinel climbed above the ridge that lay to the rear of the airbase, levelling off at 800 feet over what was no-man's-land. This was terrain over which US and Japanese forces had fought horrendous close-quarter battles and in which hundreds had died. Here and there pockets of the enemy were holding out, stubbornly refusing to lay down their arms.

The pilot steered a course over a series of stark ridges and valleys, the high ground marked by bare expanses of glistening white coral, the valleys tight with verdant jungle. Finally, the Sentinel reached a relatively flat section of terrain lying towards the centre of the landmass, one overshadowed by the island's rugged volcanic spine. He began to lose altitude, swooping down until he was flying around fifty feet above the ground.

With the Sentinel's fixed undercarriage almost skimming the tree-tops, the pilot began to fly search transects across the terrain, eyes searching the ground for any sign of the missing warplane. Almost immediately, Wynne noticed several holes in the ground, each of around five feet across. The caverns were equipped with crude palm-thatched roofs, though most looked as if they had been torn and blasted askew.

The pilot jabbed a thumb at the nearest. 'See those damn things?' he yelled above the engine noise.

'Yeah.'

'Those're Jap foxholes.'

Wynne had sudden visions of the enemy popping their heads and their gun-barrels out of the nearest and opening fire at less than one hundred yards. With no armour to protect the Sentinel's crew, he suggested that the pilot get them out of there pronto.

The pilot grinned. There was nothing to worry about, he assured his nervous flight companion. They'd bombed the enemy out of those very positions the previous day.

'Bombed them out like how?' Wynne queried.

The pilot's smile widened. 'We flew over and dropped hand-grenades into 'em.'

They continued their low-level search until they reached an area scattered with wreckage. A crater marked what looked like the epicentre of a crash-site. A large chunk of debris lay at its centre. It was the scorched and mangled remains of a distinctive Allison V-1710 twelve-cylindre liquid-cooled engine. The only one of its kind to see service during the war, the Allison V-1710 was fitted almost exclusively to P-38 Lightnings.

There was a long and scorched skid-mark leading up to the crater. The dark scar that had been torn through the vegetation and rock suggested that it was unlikely that the plane's pilot had made anything like a safe crash-landing. The impression was heightened by the mangled fragments of the aircraft's aluminium fuselage that were scattered to either side. While the Sentinel circled the wreckage, Wynne took a series of photos with his K24 camera. It was impossible that anyone could have survived such a violent impact, but there was always the possibility that the pilot might have bailed out while still in the air.

The Sentinel's pilot jabbed a thumb over one shoulder. He'd spotted the wreckage of a second P-38 not so far away. They flew over to check it out. At first it looked as if the aircraft was more or less intact, but as the Sentinel drew closer they could make out where a low-hanging tree had ripped open the cockpit. The pilot wouldn't have stood a chance. The poor devil had been torn to pieces by the branches.

There was little point lingering above either crash-site. The Sentinel climbed to altitude and the pilot set a course for base. As they came in across the bay and began their final approach to the Mokmer airstrip, the distinctive form of an enemy fighter – a Japanese Zero – could be seen lying in the ocean shallows. It looked largely undamaged, its marking – the red sun symbol surrounded by a thin band of white – standing out clearly on the upper side of the wings.

That pilot had more than likely survived his crash-landing. Such were the vagaries of war.

Once the Sentinel was safely down and Wynne had delivered his photographs to the lab, he went to seek out his dog. After a joyful reunion with Smoky, Petrilak and some of the others gathered, eager to hear news of Wynne's first such flight. He and the Sentinel's pilot had logged barely thirty-five minutes of 'combat flying' – that was the extent of the time they'd spent over the enemy positions. It sure would take many such flight missions to clock up the required 300 hours, so as to earn him a ticket back to the USA.

After listening to his tale, the guys forming Wynne's audience seemed more interested in his dog, and what would happen to her if Wynne took a bullet on any future such sorties.

'Hey, Wynne, if you get knocked off can I have Smoky?' one piped up, eagerly.

'No way,' Petrilak countered. 'I get her. She's mine!'

Other voices chipped in, each laying a claim to the prize-winning mascot of the 26th. As they bickered over Smoky's fate, not a man among them seemed particularly worried for Bill Wynne's welfare. It stuck him that they didn't appear to be that concerned for the well-being of his dog, either. It angered and discomfited him. He ended the debate by telling them all in no uncertain terms that if the aircraft in which he was flying went down, then Smoky would go down too.

From now on, she would be flying with him.

The dangers involved in undertaking any kind of air missions were ratcheting up all the time. Now that MacArthur had his eyes firmly on the Philippines, nearly all photo-reconnaissance flights were operating over vast distances, where for the most part the threat of enemy action was very real. And wherever those airmen flew and went missing in action, the air-sea rescue aircraft had to follow.

As the summer months turned to autumn (at least in the US or UK; there were no such seasons in the tropics), the 26th would win another DFC, for a sortie flown by Captain Herbert A. Curran, over Leyte Island, General MacArthur's intended landing point on the Philippines. Curran's daring mission had involved spending nine and a half hours in the air, during which 'heavy weather en route caused an hour's delay and consumed dangerously large amounts of carefully measured fuel'. Though well aware of this perilous state of affairs, Curran had continued with his sortie, landing back at Biak with 'only ten minutes' supply of gasoline' remaining.

The 26th pushed the limits still further. Flights were executed over Balikpapan Bay, a key Japanese harbour in Borneo (part of modern-day Indonesia), through which was shipped more than eighty per cent of their war materiel. The flights to the Philippines involved a 2,200-mile round-trip; those to Borneo a total journey of well over 2,500 miles. Typically, such sorties were led by Captain Orville Counselman, who'd taken over command of the 26th.

On one such October 1944 flight to Balikpapan Bay, a P-38 made several passes over the harbour at 28,600 feet, trying to stay above the level of enemy flak, which was clawing up as high as 23,000 feet. The pilot fired off seventy-odd exposures spread across three strips of film, capturing an armada of Japanese warships lying at anchor. Those vessels included one massive 12,000-tonne merchant ship, five 'Sugar Charlies' (2,300-tonne freighters), seven 4,000-tonne fuel tankers, plus countless smaller ships.

With all of that captured so clearly on film, Balikpapan Bay represented an incredibly tempting target. But such photos alone rarely revealed everything. Even after the closest of studies by the squadron's analysts, the actual nature of the ship's cargo might still elude discovery.

Just three weeks earlier, a Japanese merchant vessel of 5,000 tonnes had been sunk by the Allies, only for it to be discovered that she had been packed full of thousands of Dutch, British, American and Australian prisoners of war, as well as locals requisitioned as slave labour.

On 18 September 1944, the *Junyo Maru* had been steaming north up the coast of Sumatra, part of present-day Indonesia. Originally the British cargo ship the SS *Ardgorm*, she'd been renamed the *Junyo Maru* after being sold to a Japanese company in 1926. On the outbreak of war the *Junyo Maru* had been converted into a so-called 'hell ship', with extra decks fitted into her hold made from bamboo, and lined with bamboo cages, for carrying thousands of Allied POWs.

In early September the *Junyo Maru* had picked up more than 6,000, many of whom had already slaved away in inhuman conditions, hacking airstrips out of the thick jungle and levelling coral runways. They were to be shipped northwards to the 'hell railroad', a railway line being forced through the impossible jungle terrain of Sumatra. The railway line was to be used to transport coal out of Sumatra, to help fuel the Japanese war effort. Thousands were to die during the utterly nightmarish months of its construction, but on that September morning many more were to perish at sea.

The *Junyo Maru* was spotted by a British submarine, the HMS *Tradewind*, off the coast of Sumatra. Her captain, Lieutenant-Commander Lynch Maydon, was unaware that she was carrying such a desperate human cargo. He fired his torpedoes. Barely six hundred would survive what followed, as the *Tradewind*'s salvo slammed into the *Junyo Maru*'s hull. The ship went down in a matter of minutes, thousands of Allied POWs trying to fight their way out of the bamboo cages and reach the deck above.

Even those who did manage to abandon ship by leaping into the sea were far from being saved. Armed trawlers formed the *Junyo Maru*'s escort, but the Japanese sailors crewing them beat off any who tried to clamber aboard, using iron bars. Hundreds of POWs were forced to hold out for forty-eight hours in the sea, clinging onto wreckage, as one by one their fellows lost their grip and drowned, or were picked off by the sharks.

At the time, the sinking of the *Junyo Maru* – in which some 5,620 POW and local slave-labourers perished – represented the single largest loss of life in a sea disaster ever. Determining the nature of a ship's cargo via photos taken at 28,000 feet was never going to be easy, yet it was critical to do so, hence the fliers of the 26th returning again and again to locations such as Balikpapan Bay, for each set of images was sure to yield fresh clues.

That October the squadron executed 122 reconnaissance sorties, shooting 6,776 photos from which 94,707 prints would be made. The ratio of photos developed to prints made – over 10:1 – demonstrated the very high demand for such images. That month one of the squadron's top pilots would win an Air Medal with Oak Leaf Cluster for completing 200 hours of combat flying, and the CO himself, Captain Counselman, would win a Bronze Oak Leaf Cluster to his Air Medal, for executing 100 hours of sorties.

But inevitably, such extreme risk-taking and heroics would prove costly. On 24 October 1944, a pilot from the 26th would fail to return to base.

This time the loss would be deeply personal, for Bill Wynne and his dog.

CHAPTER 13

The pilot listed as MIA was First Lieutenant Clair J. Bardsley, a good buddy of Bill Wynne's. They'd forged a friendship over sport, and particularly their great rivalry over basketball.

When based at Nadzab, they'd held a hoop-shooting contest to see who was the most skilful player. One by one all of the competitors had been eliminated, until only Wynne and Bardsley – a fiercely competitive, bull-necked redhead who wore a wispy moustache below a focused, level gaze – remained. The sun was well below the horizon by the time Bardsley had shot at and missed the basketball hoop, leaving Wynne the overall winner. The two men had remained good friends ever since.

On 24 October, Bardsley had taken off from the Mokmer airstrip at 0615 hours, heading for Ceram Island in the eastern Moluccas (part of modern-day Indonesia), another significant hub for Japanese shipping. The flight ahead of him had consisted of a round trip of over 1,000 miles, during which he'd have to climb above the New Guinea landmass and head west across the Ceram Sea. The Casualty Report penned after Bardsley went missing stated the bare, bald facts: he had encountered 'extreme adverse weather conditions . . . No further information is available.'

All anyone had to go on in terms of mounting a search was the flight plan and bearings that Bardsley had logged before taking to the skies. Clearly, no Sentinel light aircraft was capable of even attempting to track and trace such a long flight. Instead, the task would fall to the workhorses of the Air-Sea Rescue squadrons – namely the Consolidated PBY-5A Catalina flying boats.

One of the most widely used seaplanes of the war, the Catalina – 'Cat' for short – was a stalwart of anti-submarine work, convoy escorts, cargo transport and air-sea rescue missions. Wide of wing and seemingly ungainly, yet somehow hugely evocative and graceful once she took to the air, the Cat was known affectionately as 'Dumbo' to the crews that flew her. Some 3,000 were serving with the US military, and they'd been particularly effective in the southwest Pacific theatre, operating over the vast stretches of ocean that lay between the myriad scattered islands.

Indeed, Cats had played a leading role in bottling up the enemy shipping discovered at Balikpapan, by laying mines across the mouth of the bay. Those missions – executed at night – had involved over twenty hours of flying, culminating in the mines being released from 200 feet above the water. The Cats had also earned a certain infamy among Japanese ground forces for carrying out 'terror bombing' at night – dropping empty bottles with razor-blades inserted into their necks, which emitted an unearthly screaming as they fell, thus terrorizing the enemy.

Bardsley had gone missing just three weeks after he'd won his promotion to first lieutenant, something that he'd long been hoping for. Wynne was determined to be the photographer on this search and rescue flight; finding the missing airman was personal. He was equally determined that Smoky was going to accompany him.

The Catalina had a crew of ten, including a pilot and co-pilot, navigator, radio operator, radar technician and four gunners. For this late-October search and rescue sortie their crew would also include an aerial photographer, plus of course one four-legged flier.

It was 0200 by the time Wynne had grabbed his flying gear and his dog, left his tent and climbed into a jeep to drive the short distance to the camp of the 3rd Air-Sea Rescue Squadron. The night was comparatively chilly, and it would be far colder at the Cat's cruise altitude of 15,000 feet. He'd made sure to wrap Smoky snugly in her special coat of many colours.

For Wynne, flying in a Catalina had the great advantage that the aircraft's 15,000-foot flight ceiling was low enough to take a dog on board without needing any oxygen.

Wynne set off keeping the jeep's lights doused, just in case there were any enemy night-fighters prowling the skies. At first he wondered if he were seeing things, for in the faint moonlight the road ahead seemed to be alive, writhing eerily. It turned out that a mass of bright-red crabs was moving across the island, heading from forest to beach in their seasonal migration.

Having made his way safely through the undulating mass of crustaceans, he arrived at the 3rd's base in time for a glorious breakfast of fried eggs and salty bacon. Smoky had to make do with eggs alone. The salt in the bacon would make her too thirsty to cope with the many hours she would spend suspended at altitude.

During the pre-mission briefing, the aircrew were reminded

of their duties and the drills. Catalinas had rescued thousands of Allied airmen and sailors during the war. Often, a lone Cat would stand off from a major air mission, waiting for a MAYDAY call, which signified that a warplane was going down. On those occasions when the Catalina had fighter cover, the pilot would put down in the sea as soon as they had located the aircrew they had been sent to rescue. If not, the Cat's aircrew would take their chances, swooping low to drop life rafts and other supplies.

US airmen had a dye dispenser attached to their life jackets. It would trigger upon contact with seawater, the dye staining the surrounding ocean a bright yellow-orange. It was supposed to serve a dual function. One, it would mark their position to friendly aircraft like the Cats. Two, it was believed to deter sharks. But by now Bardsley's dye would have dispersed long ago. What they would be scouring the seas for was most likely a lone life raft, in the hope of finding Bardsley still alive.

With a top speed of less than 200 mph the Catalina wasn't fast. It couldn't outrun the enemy – it could only rely upon its gunners to try to outfight them. If a plane were hit, the beauty of being able to land on water meant that they could ditch just about anywhere there was ocean. The downside was that not all the natives were known to be friendly. There were stories – quite possibly apocryphal – of US aircrew having survived being shot down, only to get taken captive and eaten by remote villagers.

Readying himself for the flight, Wynne slipped Smoky into his haversack, fastening down the straps with the buckles that held them tight. As she disappeared inside, the spirited dog flashed him an eager look, as if she knew they were going on their airborne adventures again. Only, of course, the diminutive dog couldn't know that this time it was going to be very different. They weren't heading to friendly Australia for some much-needed R&R; this was a flight into the teeth of the enemy.

By 0300 Wynne found himself scrambling onto a second jeep along with a bevy of fellow aircrew. There was only the one vehicle available, so they had all had to clamber aboard, laden down as they were with parachutes, personal kit, weapons and, in Wynne's case, a hidden dog. The mass of bodies meant that the driver couldn't actually see to navigate properly, so those sitting in front of him had to yell out directions.

Once safely at the aircraft, Wynne took up position in one of the gunner's 'blisters' – a man-sized bulge of clear Plexiglas that stuck out of the side of the aircraft, just aft of the wings. Each of the blisters had its own access ladder leading up from the ground, and each was crammed with a 50-calibre heavy machine gun, mounted on a pivot.

Although the 3rd was primarily a search and rescue squadron, their aircraft was painted up like any standard combat aircraft, with a bold single star and stripe running along either side of the blunt nose. The gunners doubled as medics, and it was their role to paddle a rubber raft to any downed aircrew found at sea, often dragging them into the Catalina through the side-blisters.

Wynne decided to wait until they were well and truly airborne before revealing the presence of their mystery stowaway. The pilot punched the starter buttons and there was a belch of black smoke as first one and then the other engine roared into life. The massive Catalina, with her 104-foot wingspan and two Pratt & Whitney radial engines mounted high on the wings, rumbled down the white coral runway, the surface glowing silver in the moonlight. She lifted off, clambering ponderously into the skies.

As they climbed to altitude, Wynne reached inside the haversack and eased Smoky into the open. She pricked up her ears and gazed all around the strange new environment that she found herself in. She was suspended in a see-through blister surrounded by the expanse of the dark but starlit heavens, and with the faint glow of the sea far below.

It wasn't long before the medics-cum-gunners discovered they had a surprise crew member aboard, riding shotgun. Once Wynne had explained why he'd felt compelled to bring Smoky along, they seemed to find the whole thing hugely amusing. The idea of having a flying dog join their crew as a gunner was just fine and dandy as far as they were concerned. They hung Smoky's haversack over a nearby bunk-like stretcher, making sure she was nicely settled.

If any enemy warplanes did appear, the gun turrets would soon be spewing hot brass, as the gunners met fire with fire, at which point Smoky would be right in the thick of it. But she was a veteran and had rarely shown herself fazed by anything. Wynne reckoned she should do just fine.

It was fortunate that Smoky had experienced a few training parachute jumps, back at Nadzab. If the Catalina did get badly hit, Wynne wasn't about to leave his beloved dog in the stricken aircraft. As he'd vowed to Petrilak and the others: 'We'll go down together.' He would fasten Smoky's haversack around his waist, and bale out with her strapped to his person. Then he'd pull the 'chute, hoping to ride the thermals and find his dog a safe landing.

The Catalina powered onwards through the night, the steady

beat of her twin radial engines allowing those inside into a comparative calm. Bardsley's last known position was just east of Ceram Island. He'd completed his recce flights and had turned for home by the time the storm had hit.

As dawn broke, the sun clawing above a horizon of burnished copper and gold, the pilot began to lose altitude. He dropped to a couple of thousand feet, throttling back to ninety miles per hour. As the Cat idled along Wynne found himself scanning the rumpled folds of the ocean below him with intense focus. Bardsley had been a good friend and he was determined to play his part in locating the missing airman.

The Catalina droned onwards. The sun rose higher, the light becoming flatter as the sea became awash with a fierce tropical glare. Downed airmen carried mirrors attached to their life-jackets. They were trained to point those mirrors at a passing friendly aircraft, to signal their whereabouts in the sea. Ten pairs of eyes scanned the waves for the slightest sign of any human presence.

There was none.

Indeed, there wasn't the barest suggestion of movement any-where on the entire expanse of water. They were flying over the Ceram Sea, a 12,000-square-kilometre stretch of ocean sandwiched between the islands of modern-day Indonesia. The war might have been raging all around them, but here there was nothing, not a single vessel of any description. Indeed, it was to be another thing altogether that drew the aircrews' gaze.

As if from nowhere a long bank of black cloud seemed to roll across the horizon, darkening all. The storm swept in towards the Cat, massive and menacing. The roiling bank of cloud towered above them, reaching thousands of feet into the skies. There was no way to fly around it: their base at Biak Island lay on the far side of the vast weather front. They couldn't race ahead of it, either: they didn't have the fuel to do so.

This was similar to what must have happened to their missing airman and friend: as the Casualty Report on Bardsley had concluded, he'd hit 'extreme adverse weather' over the Ceram Sea.

The Catalina was dwarfed by the on-rushing storm. There was no option but to abandon the search. The Cat turned for home, the pilot trying to climb above the darkening tempest. As the seaplane struggled to gain altitude, its airframe shook and juddered with the impact of the first squalls. The Cat reached 12,000 feet, Smoky's haversack swinging wildly as the aircraft was thrown about by intense gusts, but still there was no way over the storm.

The pilot was forced put the Cat into a dive. They dropped to around 100 feet of altitude, all the time searching for a break in the fearsome wall of cloud. It extended from sea level to the upmost reaches of the heavens – dark, boiling and angry, and lit here and there by flashes of lighting. There was no choice: they would have to try to fly right through the heart of the cyclone, for that way lay home.

This storm was a true monster: very closely packed cells of cumulonimbus – dense, towering, vertical columns of cloud – punched upwards to great heights. Hidden within those cloud cells were massive updrafts and downdrafts. An aircraft flying into those could get its wings ripped asunder, or the fuselage twisted and warped catastrophically.

They were swallowed into the storm. It felt as if a giant was smacking the top and bottom of the Catalina with a massive sledgehammer, powerful gusts slamming into the wings and fuselage. The aircrew had to try to blank their minds to the terrible noise. Using the Cat's radar reading, the pilot had to try to steer his way through the storm cells. The radar painted a picture of where the heaviest rainfall might be, and where the most powerful up- and downdrafts were to be located. If they could avoid the points of most intense activity then they might just stand a chance of making it through.

In a tropical storm such as this, one cell of air might be descending at 5,000 feet a minute, while the one adjacent to it was rising at the same speed. If the Catalina blundered into the border between the two, it could prove catastrophic. If one wing so much as strayed across the divide, it would be like placing it into a giant guillotine. And if that happened, there would be no grabbing Smoky in her haversack and bailing out with her strapped to anyone's person.

The crew and their stowaway dog would be vomited into the howling void of the storm.

CHAPTER 14

Wynne reached out to touch the haversack in which Smoky was riding. He had to resist the urge to reach in and retrieve her, for the wildly pitching warplane was no safe place for an unsecured dog. She was better off in her bag-cum-hammock, which served to cushion the Catalina's vicious lurches and rolls. Even so, he couldn't help but marvel at how she could retain such equanimity when they were in the grip of such unrelenting violence. Possessed by a preternatural calm, the little dog had barely moved a muscle.

For what seemed like an eternity the flying boat fought her way east through the howling, wind-whipped darkness. The Catalina was thrown around like a toy in a giant's hands, the airframe groaning and shrieking with the strain. Gripped as they were in the heart of the tempest, daylight, sunlight – the air itself, it seemed – had been banished. The storm front was a thing of the night, and it dragged darkness inchoate and screaming in its wake.

Occasionally Wynne sought out the aircraft's tortured wing-tips, but they were lost in the storm, and he was blinded by the rain that drenched the Plexiglas blister. The Catalina's extremities had been swallowed by the tempest. Visibility was limited to less than a few dozen yards, which would make the job of navigating nigh-on impossible.

Somehow, after four hours entombed within that terrifying force of nature, the Catalina finally shook herself free. Achieving something close to a miracle, the Catalina's navigator had steered them safely to New Guinea through several hundred miles of perilous skies.

As the aircraft thundered into the airspace above Biak Island, the weather before them cleared. Majestic and apparently unscathed, the Catalina touched down at Mokmer airstrip, to be welcomed by a sunlit calm. It was as if the storm had never taken place at all, such were the vagaries of the weather in this part of the world.

For several minutes the crew sat within their trusty plane, taking stock and calming their thoughts. After the trials of being trapped in that storm for hours on end they needed a moment to get their pulse rates back to a little more like normal. Eventually, Wynne reached over and unhooked the haversack that held his dog. He ran a hand along the underside, feeling the warm bulge of a living, breathing animal.

By the regular rise and fall of Smoky's chest, he could tell that she was fine. She seemed to have weathered the storm better than most of them. He shouldered the bag and clambered down the ladder, giving thanks that they'd come through alive. Sadly, they'd found no sign of his friend, Bardsley, but at least eleven other lives hadn't been lost while searching for the missing airman.

Four days after Bardsley disappeared another of the squadron's fliers was listed as MIA. First Lieutenant Lee G. Smith – the pilot who'd executed the abortive recce mission over Cape Gloucester, at the time of Smoky's discovery in the foxhole – was reported lost somewhere to the south of the Talaud Islands. Lying on the border of what is now Indonesia and the Philippines, the islands were some distance north of where Bardsley had gone down.

Smith, like Bardsley, had flown into a terrible weather front. He and his wingman, Captain Carl D. Lindberg – the pilot who'd won the 26th's first DFC – had wheeled about in the face of that storm, abandoning their mission. But as they'd turned for home Lindberg had lost radio contact with Smith's aircraft. Lindberg had reported Smith as missing and a Catalina had taken to the air, but their search – like so many others – had come to nothing.

In late October 1944 the weather appeared more dangerous to the men of the 26th than enemy warplanes or ground fire. As if to prove the point, by early November the searches for Smith and Bardsley were finally called off. It was a measure of how unforgiving was this conflict that a man of Smith's stature and popularity was to leave only a fleeting memory in the squadron. There was little time or space for sentiment. On 4 November 1944 an order was issued 'to inventory and dispose of the effects of First Lieutenant Lee G. Smith, 0743523, 26 Photo Rcn Sq, missing in action'.

Yet still the grim reaper wasn't satisfied. First Lieutenant Samuel Dunaway had been deployed with the 26th from their earliest days in New Guinea. Much admired for his 'skilful and intrepid flying' and well-liked due to his modesty and good spirits, Dunaway had been executing a sortie near Biak when he dived to investigate something at sea, misjudged the distance slightly, and his wing tip had hit the water. The P-38 crashed, killing Dunaway on impact.

At times like these the men of the squadron were in sore need of something – anything - to lift their spirits. Wynne figured that Smoky might just fit the bill, but he and his dog would need to develop something truly spectacular, if they were to deliver the morale boost that all hungered for. With this in mind, Wynne decided that they would embark upon their most ambitious training exercise yet, one inspired by something that he'd witnessed during his childhood, and which had always stuck in his mind.

He was eleven years old when he'd seen a show in a local Cleveland shopping mall. A department store had sought to draw in the crowds at Christmas by having a showman and his dog perform. That dog was able to walk a double-wire tightrope, blindfolded. The young Wynne had watched the performance transfixed. He'd tried to teach the dog he owned a similar trick, but with little success.

He wondered if he might have more luck with Smoky here on war-torn Biak Island. Just as with their parachute training at Nadzab, he reckoned he'd need a talented and enthusiastic support team. First he recruited Frankhuizen – the squadron's ice-machine wizard – to weld together a T-shaped metal bar. That done, Frankhuizen torch-cut two six-inch-square plates from a discarded steel drum. These were then mounted as platforms upon the narrow ends of the Ts, the cross-strokes serving as stands upon the ground.

The inverted Ts were wedged firmly into the coral rock. A pair of old aircraft control cables were stretched between the platforms, about three inches apart, and anchored at the far ends to spikes driven into the ground, like guy-ropes. The cables were further tightened using aircraft turnbuckles – stretching screws that resembled the kind that are commonly used to tighten the ropes of a boxing ring – attached to the uprights at each of the four corners.

The tightrope walk was built within reach of the photo lab, for ease of access. That way, Wynne, Smoky and the rest of the lab crew could do some training during breaks from shifts. For Smoky's first session, Wynne found he had a ready audience. Lab Chief Irv Green watched with tender concern as he set Smoky on the course for the first time. He began by placing her four paws on the wires, and allowing her to get a feel for her balance.

Once she'd got the hang of that, he urged her to walk slowly across from one side to the other, with one hand on her lead to guide her, and the other resting lightly on her back. Slowly, under his steadying hands she seemed to gain confidence, her tiny paws becoming accustomed to the unfamiliar feel of the wires. The second day he repeated the routine, finishing with Smoky completing a full lap off the lead and with no hands to steady her at all. She navigated the strange apparatus with real assurance. But then she had always possessed an uncanny knack for learning new tricks; it seemed that there was nothing she couldn't take in her stride.

On day three of the high-wire training Wynne decided it was time to try out the blindfold. He wrapped a length of cloth around Smoky's head, binding her trusting eyes, and set her upon the wires once more. Smoky put her front down low, so her nose was between the wires, and for a moment it looked as if she was too disorientated to continue. But after a few encouraging words from her master she began to inch ahead, and she felt her way to the far side. She seemed to master the feat of being a blindfold wire-walker with ease.

Frankhuizen made a ladder with inch-wide steps, and Smoky learned to climb that. She could sit atop her perch as the blindfold was applied, before shuffling across to the far side. She was ready to deliver a staggeringly accomplished performance, but learning it had been hard and physically challenging work. Wynne decided they would refine and polish her technique during the cooler hours of the evening.

To augment the tightrope walk, he decided Smoky should also learn to trot atop a barrel. Together, the two acts would be a showstopper. They practised with an empty fifty-five-gallon steel drum that had until recently held photo chemicals. Wynne pushed the drum onto its side, then perched Smoky on top of it. Next, with her lead gripped tight he began to roll it gently using his foot, encouraging Smoky to move her feet in unison. She was such a fast learner that in no time she could jump on and off the drum at the beginning and end of the trick.

Wynne reckoned they were almost ready for the big performance. To make the show go with a real bang they needed to cut the barrel down to size and to paint it in bright 'circus' colours. Although Wynne had a team help him prepare the show's accoutrements, he conducted the training strictly by himself. Smoky wasn't kept in purdah – during a rare movie night, he'd generally allow the entire gathering to pet and to cuddle his dog – but he knew that when it came to teaching her tricks or obedience lessons, she could only have one instructor, or she would be left confused.

He decided to give the barrel roll a few final turns, once the barrel had been cut down to Smoky's size, and they'd be ready. But oddly, she seemed reluctant to engage. Instead, she lay down and rolled onto her back, refusing to get moving. Again and again Wynne tried, but Smoky kept lolling onto her side. Wynne couldn't understand what was wrong with her. This was a dog who loved to learn and to perform. What on earth could be the matter?

Maybe it was the evening heat? He took her back to their tent for some rest, laying the tiny dog on his cot. She did not seem herself at all. As he studied her carefully, wondering if maybe she was sick, from out of nowhere she produced a tiny little ball of damp black fluff. For a moment Wynne stared at it in astonishment, before he realized with a shock what it was. Their Hollandia pigeons had finally come home to roost.

'Holy cats!' he declared in astonishment. 'It's a puppy!'

Petrilak and the others within earshot came running. By now Smoky was licking the puppy all over, cleaning it up so that it would be presentable for the gathering audience. Like any good mother she seemed proud as punch at what she had produced. Wynne darted outside. It occurred to him that she might have dropped another pup or two while on the barrel and without anyone noticing.

He searched the area but couldn't find a thing. He returned to discover the tent buzzing. The general consensus was that Smoky had just lost her good conduct medal. It would need to be removed from her coat, until she'd put in a spell of the kind of chaste behaviour that would earn her the right to wear it again. There was little doubt as to the identity of the father of the pup. John Hembury, one of Wynne's good friends in the

26th, had adopted a mixed-breed terrier that was a native of Nadzab. Duke was a dark-haired, cheeky-faced devil of a dog, and it was pretty obvious that it was Duke who'd managed to work his magic on Smoky.

Word of the new arrival spread like wildfire. From all over the base GIs congregated to see the puppy that had been born in some kind of miracle birth, from a dog which herself weighed only six pounds or so. One of those visitors was a very special guest for Bill Wynne. It was Jim Craig, the guy who'd occupied the bed next to Wynne at the Nadzab field hospital. Craig seemed to have shaken off his combat fatigue and he gave a good impression of being back to his old self.

He was overjoyed to meet Smoky's surprise offspring. The puppy was so tiny that you could lay him along your two forefingers and he wouldn't even reach the palm of your hand. As Craig held her puppy, Smoky gazed at it adoringly. Wynne invited Craig to the squadron's Enlisted Men's Club – a grand name for a bamboo-framed tin-sheet hut set to the rear-side of the beach.

There was one major draw to the Club, apart from the company. The 'barman' had acquired a quantity of Coca-Cola syrup – a paste which when mixed with water plus a burst of gas transformed itself into the popular drink. Its arrival on Biak Island was ingenuity itself. A handful of B25 Mitchell bombers had been stripped of all armour and guns, so pilots could practise flying on instruments only – navigating through darkness or minimal visibility – and those practice flights had often ended up doubling as supply runs.

The B25s were loaded up with cases of booze, crates of fresh meat and barrels of the much-coveted Coca-Cola syrup. In fact so much was crammed into the bomb bays that the bomb doors often couldn't be closed properly, and the aircraft flew with the cargo hanging out of their guts. This gave rise to an affectionate nickname for the planes: the 'Fat Cats'. On one such flight the aircrew had stuffed aboard a real taste of home – 550 crates of beer, all of which had been brewed in Minneapolis, Minnesota.

The Enlisted Men's Club had been founded so the squadron could hold the odd party there. Those shindigs gave 'the men something to look forwards to', the squadron's Monthly Intelligence Summary concluded. In the autumn of 1944 they'd had a major knees-up to celebrate the first anniversary of the unit's deployment. A Fat Cat had smuggled in a consignment of liquor and the partying had ended in a wild beach brawl. Come morning, other than their pounding headaches, no one seemed particularly the worse for wear and the punch-up was already long forgotten.

Behind the makeshift bar of the Club were mounted a couple of compressed-air bottles, like conventional beer pumps. When combined with some of Frankhuizen's crushed ice, and a burst of air to lend fizz, the Club's chilled cokes were a rare kind of treat in a place like Biak. Craig and Wynne toasted the squadron's new arrival with round after round of drinks. Smoky had come with them, of course, and at the first mention of her name – 'To Smoky!' – she'd issued a sharp little bark.

The puppy had been promised to Frank Petrilak, who seemed by far the most deserving candidate to be custodian of the newest member of the squadron. They'd decided to name the unexpected offspring 'Topper'. Smoky's performance giving birth from out of the blue had topped just about anything they'd seen from her so far. In the aftermath of the birth, Smoky's new repertoire of tricks were shelved. She had maternal duties to attend to and had earned a short reprieve.

As October bled into November 1944, the 26th was about to receive its greatest accolade yet, in the form of a Presidential Unit Citation from Franklin D. Roosevelt himself. The high-prestige award recognized the squadron's ground-breaking work flying over the Philippines, where the 26th had captured any number of images that were of critical import to the war. It was a story of success in which one small dog had played an unarguable part.

When Bill Wynne had lost his beloved Pal as a kid back in Cleveland, the trauma had been so great that he'd vowed never to get that close again to a dog. Smoky had torn those vows to shreds. She'd shared his dangers and hardships, both on the ground and in the air. She'd made Wynne and his buddies laugh and forget. She'd learned to respond to his every command, she'd earned his true friendship, and she – plus Topper too – had furnished him with a much-needed diversion from the dark realities of war.

They'd stayed safe so far, but Wynne knew that further dangerous missions lay ahead. Soon the Catalina crews would be airborne again, searching for the missing. The thought that their partnership might end so suddenly troubled Wynne, and he vowed to do everything in his power to protect Smoky. Yet if the war had taught him anything, it was that danger often lurked where you least expected it.

The squadron's diary for November 1944, stamped SECRET, makes crystal clear how the weather frustrated much of that month's planned recce flying. Indeed, in many ways the thick cloud cover proved the enemy's greatest friend. But that did little to stop the spirited fliers of the 26th from trying, and that in turn meant that the air-sea rescue Catalinas had to brave the skies, searching for those lost during the storms.

It wasn't just the recce flights that were plagued by the bad weather. At 3.00 a.m. on a black November night Wynne and Smoky took to the skies once more, their lumbering Catalina labouring to gain altitude. Their mission on that night was somewhat different from those that had gone before. They were the lead flight in several waves of warplanes, all of which were making for the enemy positions located to the west of Balikpapan Bay.

The Cat left first, for it was the slowest of this mighty air armada. At 5.00 a.m. a massive flight of bombers would take to the skies, followed by their quicker fighter escorts, which would get airborne only as dawn broke across the airfield. They would form up as one over Balikpapan Bay, with the intention of launching a devastating air raid. But things didn't go quite to plan. Unbeknown to the crew manning the Catalina, a storm descended upon Biak Island shortly after their take-off. Their aircraft was the only one that had managed to get airborne, and its crew flew on in blissful ignorance, unaware that the mission had been abandoned.

Wynne had slung Smoky in her 'accustomed' place – her haversack dangling from the Catalina's bunk. Today's flight promised to be a twenty-two-hour marathon and he'd need to keep a careful eye on his dog. He couldn't keep her bagged for that long, so he'd let her run around a little on the bunk. But it was a delicate balancing act – giving her the chance to stretch her little limbs, while also making sure that she didn't get so excited that she ended up having an unfortunate 'accident'.

Smoky invariably displayed such an insatiable appetite that unless her master watched her closely, she'd eat everything she could get her paws on. He was in the habit of feeling her back and stomach daily and adjusting her meals to match her waistline, to make sure she remained healthy. On air missions such as this, Smoky had to follow a strict diet, for the enforced inactivity cooped up on board a plane meant that there was always a chance that she would end up putting on too much weight. Wynne had allowed her just a single meal, which she'd scoffed early in the morning.

They'd been welcomed with open arms by the air-sea rescue crews. Most wanted a souvenir photo with the famous dog after completing a successful mission. On previous flights Wynne had realized that whenever he allowed her out of her haversack, Smoky provided a wonderful diversion for the crews manning the Cats. She had a gift for taking their minds away from the life-threatening reality of their missions. But pooping or peeing everywhere might quickly change all that.

Undertaking that long, solo flight deep into enemy airspace was a trial even for the champion mascot of the 26th. It was bitterly cold, and after a while Wynne noticed that Smoky was shivering. He wrapped her up tight in extra woollen blankets and popped her back into her snug haversack. The drone and vibration of the engines, set to either side of their position, could play havoc with the nerves. It had to be doubly tiresome for a dog blessed with sensitive hearing. At moments Smoky looked nervous, and he noticed her panting tongue had turned a deep red. Luckily he was on hand to comfort her as only he knew how.

After a ten-and-a-half-hour flight the Catalina arrived over the target, only to discover that she was the sole aircraft to have made it into the air that morning. They were many hours into enemy airspace and if they were spotted, the lone and ponderous flying boat was a sitting duck. If a flight of Japanese Zeros came tearing up to intercept her, she would be blasted from the skies.

Many times Wynne had noticed how attuned Smoky was to his comrades' stress levels and anxieties. She was so closely in tune with her human companions that she was able to sense their worries and their trauma. But what made her truly exceptional was her ability to make the stressed and the traumatized smile, even in situations when there was so little to smile about. This was most certainly one of those.

Yet for now, they had no option but to turn tail and run like the wind.

CHAPTER 15

A few weeks previously Smoky had demonstrated most power-fully what a talisman she had become to the Catalina's aircrew. It had been another 3.00 a.m. start, with another marathon flight looming. Wynne had let his little dog off the lead to relieve herself on the grass beside the airstrip. Instead of squatting down to do her business, Smoky had made a mad dash for the bush and within seconds she was lost from sight.

The airbase was busy with airplanes and vehicles roaring hither and thither. Her sprint across the runway into the night could so easily have ended in disaster. Wynne went after her. Although it was pitch dark, he found the little dog about five hundred yards away, safe and sound. Nevertheless, he gave her a piece of his mind. He wasn't angry with her for running free, so much as he was by the thought of what might have happened to her. She could have been crushed under a taxiing aircraft's wheels, or caught in a propeller's murderous backwash. He understood that she was a dog, and that dogs love to play in the bush, but there was a time and a place for everything.

He tucked her under his arm, protectively, and carried her back to the aircraft. He climbed the ladder into the blister, and went to place Smoky in her position as haversack gunner. But as he did so, he noticed that the Catalina's crew were eyeing him and his diminutive dog in an uneasy silence. The fuselage was thick with tension and unspoken questions. Had Smoky bolted for a reason, they wondered? Had she sensed something? Had her sixth sense told her to run?

As luck would have it, the flight went ahead without the slightest incident – not even any bad weather. But Wynne and the rest of the crew had been left to wonder. Had Smoky delayed their take-off for long enough for the aircraft to avoid some hidden danger lurking in the dark skies? Had the Grim Reaper waited, poised with his scythe to cut down the aircraft and her crew, only to be frustrated by the spirited disobedience of one small dog?

Aircrew are notoriously superstitious and the men based at Biak Island were no exception. They were always on the lookout for the kind of special talisman that they believed would protect them. Some pilots flew with a pair of their sweetheart's silk stockings wrapped around their neck. Others took to the skies with crucifixes or shamrocks, or a special photograph clutched to their chests. Every man would swear blind that it was his lucky charm that kept him safe in the skies.

In time the men of the 3rd Air-Sea Rescue Squadron had begun to view their haversack gunner-dog in a similar light. If she could brave such flights unscathed, so could they – especially with their lucky charm at their side. Smoky was one of the gang and she was cherished by all with whom she flew.

Smoky's magic certainly seemed to be working when the Catalina and her crew made it back from their lonely Balikpapan mission. They touched down at Biak Island unscathed and with a huge sense of relief: those of a superstitious nature could draw their own conclusions about the presence on that flight of their talismanic flying dog.

There were of course more concrete means to keep safe in the skies. On several sorties with the 3rd Air-Sea Rescue Squadron, Wynne and Smoky were blessed with having the very best of escorts. Two of the foremost American aces in the region, P-38 pilots Major Richard Bong and Major Thomas McGuire, flew alongside them. There was a fierce rivalry between the men. Each had over three-dozen kills to his name, but Bong always seemed to be just two or three ahead of McGuire. And while the Catalina's aircrew weren't too bothered about which of the two had downed the most Japanese warplanes, they certainly appreciated the protection they provided.

By the time they flew their thirteenth mission with the 3rd, Wynne and his dog had completed over seventy hours of combat flying – nearly a quarter of the total required to earn them a ticket back to America. It was during that thirteenth mission that they were to realize they were about to leapfrog north again, heading for the Philippines, and ever closer to Japan itself.

The Catalina was returning to their base on Biak Island, when through a momentary gap in the cloud Wynne spotted a vast armada spread out far below. One of the greatest invasion fleets ever assembled was on the move, steaming northwards towards the enemy. Wynne noticed battleships, aircraft carriers, cruisers, destroyers and a plethora of smaller craft, including troopships. They seemed to stretch from horizon to horizon.

It was obvious that the armada was friendly; if not a murderous barrage of fire would have torn them out of the skies. Even so, a pair of Navy F4U Corsairs – a carrier-based fighter aircraft as potent as the Hellcat – came roaring up to intercept the lone seaplane.

Those flying the Corsairs were right to be suspicious of the lone Catalina. In February 1942 the British stronghold of Singapore had fallen to Japanese forces. Fortress Singapore had been the key British base in southeast Asia and the cornerstone of her defences in the region. The battle had lasted a little more than a week, with 80,000 British and Allied troops falling captive to the enemy. It was a crushing blow, one that Churchill had lamented as being the 'worst disaster' and 'largest capitulation' in British military history.

But along with the troops, the Japanese had captured a treasure trove of Allied war machines, including at least one Consolidated flying boat. They'd likewise seized scores of Allied aircraft across the islands of the southwest Pacific, including Bristol Blenheims, Hawker Hurricanes, Boeing B-17s and P-51 Mustangs.

Repainted in Japanese colours those aircraft had been press-ganged into service with the enemy, which is why the Corsairs had raced up to challenge the Catalina. In spite of the large and prominent star and stripe – the recognition flash for a USAAF aircraft – painted on her nose, the Corsair pilots remained suspicious.

Reports were beginning to reach Allied aircrew of a new and terrifying weapon: the suicide bomber, or kamikaze. There was clearly no better aircraft in which to attempt to crash into an Allied warship than one of their own models. The Catalina's pilot dipped his right wing, the recognized signal for 'friendly', repeating the manoeuvre several times before the Corsair fliers eventually seemed satisfied, and peeled away.

The Catalina flew over that giant armada for approaching thirty minutes. It stretched across sixty miles of ocean. To those aboard the flying boat it was clear the ships had to be steaming for Leyte Gulf, where MacArthur intended to mark his return to the Philippines. And wherever the combat troops went the 26th were bound to follow, just as soon as those new airbases lay in friendly hands.

With the invasion fleet steaming for Leyte Gulf, the air recce missions of the 26th assumed even greater urgency. That November a record 115 photo reconnaissance sorties were flown, resulting in 32,796 9 x 10-inch photos being printed and distributed to those in high command. Daily courier flights were shuttling in rolls of film from outlying airbases, and shuttling out with the printed images. Three shifts were required at the Biak photo lab to keep it churning around the clock.

That November the squadron's CO, Counselman, would earn a second Bronze Oak Leaf Cluster, for completing yet another hundred hours of combat flying. The citation read: 'For meritorious achievement while participating in sustained operational flight missions . . . during which hostile contact was probable and expected.' But continuously pushing the envelope would prove life threatening for some among the 26th.

On 17 November 1944, Hartwell McCullough – Custodian of Squadron Classified Documents, and the 26th's heart and soul – suffered a perilously close brush with death. Returning from a special mission, his aircraft had suffered a total failure of its hydraulics, without which he couldn't lower his landing gear. He'd made a perfect crash-landing on the aircraft's belly.

While he'd walked away with barely a scratch, his plane was ruled 'a total loss'. Others weren't to be so fortunate.

The squadron's MIAs needed to be replaced urgently. One recent newcomer was Second Lieutenant James H. Morrison, fresh out of training. Just days after Morrison had arrived in Biak he was assigned his first combat sortie. At 1.35 p.m. on 22 November he had taken off from the Mokmer strip, but only managed to get three-quarters of a mile into the air. His P-38 ploughed into the coral at the far end of the runway, killing him outright. The accident and its causes were recorded in a squadron Casualty Report: 'Pilot took off with full flaps, causing the aircraft to stall at an altitude of 300 feet.'

Morrison had been killed on his very first combat sortie, which had taken place on the day before Thanksgiving. That year the men of the squadron were treated to a traditional Thanksgiving dinner of turkey and pumpkin pie. Despite losing Morrison, they made a point of trying to celebrate, knowing full well that this would be the last partying any would enjoy for some time to come.

Their move to the Philippines was imminent. 'We were, we knew, moving in with the troops making the invasion . . .' the section of the 26th's war diary titled 'History & Legend' recorded. 'We would be put ashore shortly after the combat troops . . . and before more than a beachhead could be established. Our mood . . . was of fatalistic anxiety.'

But for one man among the 26th, there would be no advance to the Philippines. For Captain John M. Brown, the war was pretty much over. Brown had just topped his 300th hour of combat flying, spread across sixty-five separate missions. He left the squadron, bound for America and home. Having completed only thirteen missions and seventy-three hours of combat flying, Bill Wynne was still some way from earning his ticket back to the US, but he was offered some December shore leave in Australia. It was now or never. He'd have to grab it before the advance north, for there would be little chance of taking such breaks once the squadron was on the move. Once more, he slipped Smoky into her covert travel bag and climbed aboard a C47 Gooney Bird. This time they were heading for the bright lights of Sydney.

This flight was a little less tortuous than their previous sortie aboard the overloaded C47. Upon reaching Sydney, man and dog billeted themselves with an elderly lady who tried to argue that as combatants they should take the room for free. Wynne insisted he pay her. She'd already bent over backwards for them, turning a blind eye to the house rules that said that no dogs were allowed. She'd taken an instant shine to Smoky, and as long as Wynne could keep the little dog hidden she assured them they'd be okay.

He managed to smuggle Smoky out for daily exercise in a local park. On one of their outings, Wynne decided to give Smoky some experience of walking to heel on Sydney's busy streets, but doing so off the lead. All was going well until he went to check her position and realized that she was gone. They were in the middle of Sydney on a street thronged with people and she could be just about anywhere.

His eyes scanned the crowd, desperately. Suddenly he spotted the distinctive form of the rear-end of his dog, stubby tail and hind quarters sticking out from under the arm of a woman who was hurrying away as quick as her legs would carry her. Just as he'd read about in that *National Geographic* article, someone was in the process of trying to steal his dog!

Wynne was having none of it. He gave chase. He caught the woman up, whereupon he took her firmly by the elbow. 'Excuse me, ma'am, but you've got my dog.'

The woman turned on him, bold as brass. 'No, he isn't, Yank,' she countered. 'He's my Silky, he is!'

The Silky is a breed of terrier closely related to the Yorkie. Developed in Australia, there is little to tell the two breeds apart. The woman kept a firm hold of Smoky, as she tried to argue that the dog was walking past freely, so she'd claimed her as her own.

Wynne raised his voice now, drawing the attention of the crowd. Smoky had been his for many months, in New Guinea, he explained. She was an acclaimed war veteran and a unit mascot. 'You'd better give her back, right now!'

Realizing that it didn't look good stealing a war veteran's dog, the woman handed 'her Silky' back to Wynne, but with little good grace. He took her, and got a happy little lick on the face as his reward for having rescued her. With Smoky tucked firmly under one arm, they continued on their way. He vowed that was the last time he'd walk Smoky off the lead in Australia.

In fact, his little dog was far safer staying in their kindly landlady's room. Smoky seemed happy enough to remain there as long as she had some item of clothing – a shirt or a hat of her master's – to lie close to. The smell was comforting and it served as a reminder that her companion was never far away or gone for long.

A little later Wynne was on one of his solo outings when he

ran into some aircrew from the 90th Bomber Group, the 'Jolly Rogers'. Fellow US airmen, they made for natural drinking companions, especially as the 90th had flown missions all across New Guinea and at the same time as the 26th. They'd earned their distinctive nickname due to the massive skull and crossbones they had painted on the tail-planes of their Consolidated B24 Liberator bombers.

The fliers got to swopping war stories. There were tales told of the greatest near-death experiences the Jolly Rogers had suffered. Wynne's closest brush with death had occurred before he'd even been deployed to New Guinea. He'd been in Brisbane, he explained, en route to join the squadron, when a powerful storm had hit. He and four others had huddled together in a shack to shelter from the rain. A massive gust of wind had blown down a tree, which had smashed onto the roof of their shelter, crushing it.

All five were thrown to the ground. Although all the others were seriously injured, Wynne had landed on his haunches with his hands between his knees and bounced up again pretty much unharmed. It was nothing short of miraculous. When Wynne finished telling his story, one of the Jolly Rogers, a tail-gunner, fixed him with a very direct look.

'You know what you're being saved for?' he announced, jabbing a finger at Wynne's chest. 'You're being saved for a bullet!'

The comment stuck in his mind, and a part of him believed it, too. If he were destined for a bullet, Leyte Gulf was most likely where he would find it.

And if he did, what then would happen to his beloved dog?

CHAPTER 16

The Japanese commander who had been charged with stopping the Allies from taking the Philippines was General Tomoyuki Yamashita, one of the masterminds of their February 1942 victory at Singapore. For his successes there he'd earned the nickname 'The Tiger of Malaya'. Yamashita had taken command of all Japanese ground forces in the Philippines, operating from his new base in the capital city, Manila. He was determined to harass, delay and confound MacArthur, and to ensure that his conquest of the Philippines would cost him dear.

It was December 1944 by now, and General Adachi was well out of the picture. Adachi had made a stand in New Guinea, as ordered. But spirited though his defence had proved, he'd been sidestepped by the breakneck speed of MacArthur's advance. Adachi would hold on in the New Guinea jungles until the very end of the war, but by then barely 10,000 of his original force would be left alive, with most dying from malnutrition and disease.

At the end of December Wynne and Smoky flew back into Biak Island. With the squadron's advance on the Philippines looming, preparations were well underway. All around the camp there were heaps of gear being crated up for the big move.

Christmas and New Year were imminent, but it was hard to get into the festive spirit. At one point Wynne's exasperation boiled over, and he found himself uttering the frustrated phrase 'Holy Christmas!' At the mention of those words Smoky had jumped up and down, excitedly.

It made an instant impression upon Wynne. Did she under-stand or recognize the word 'Christmas', he wondered? Was she familiar with the festive season? If so, that had to be a clue to her missing past. Surely, that had to mean she was of English-speaking origin. He repeated the word 'Christmas!' Sure enough, Smoky leapt about, her eyes shining with excitement. He tried another tack. 'Sport!' he exclaimed. He got the very same reac-tion, and the same when he cried 'Rover!' So much for his Christmas hypothesis. He was none the wiser.

Just prior to Christmas Day all reconnaissance flights were halted so the men could concentrate on readying themselves for the move. This was just as well for there was still a great deal to be done. Everything the photo recce squadron owned had to be crated up, all except the aircraft: they would be flown north to their new Filipino airbases, once they had been secured.

At 0400 hours on 1 January 1945, Hartwell McCullough called the entire squadron together, to brief them. He was typ-ically brief and to the point. They were going to be organized into twenty-one work parties, each consisting of ten men. This done they were to take down their tents and board the waiting ships. Two hulking great LSTs – Landing Ship, Tank; a giant, flat-bottomed vessel designed to disgorge heavy vehicles and troops directly onto almost any kind of beach – had pulled up on Biak's shoreline. Empty, they displaced around 3,600 tonnes. Fully loaded, they could carry approaching 2,000 tonnes of cargo.

Their giant bows, which split to enable loading, were swung aside and the ramps lowered, whereupon the men and machines of the 26th began to hustle aboard. Trucks loaded with kit were driven to the beach, backed up to the open ramps of the LSTs, and unloaded by hand, with their cargo being stacked in the shadowed bowels of the vessels. It was hot, thirsty and back-breaking work.

The dark and cavernous entrances to the ships dwarfed the convoys of Army trucks. Mounted on the bows of each 400-foot vessel was a circular gun-emplacement, boasting 40mm and 20mm anti-aircraft weapons, with similar gun-stations positioned at the rear. They served as stark reminders of the dangers of the coming voyage.

This was the first time the entire squadron had moved by ship since their arrival in New Guinea. It was decided to split the men and equipment between the two vessels – LST-927 and LST-706 – in case one of them was lost at sea. That way, there should still be enough skilled operators left aboard one of the ships to restart the squadron once they had reached the Philippines.

It turned out that the 26th weren't headed for Leyte Gulf after all. The Leyte landings had gone ahead, establishing MacArthur's foothold in the Philippines. The 26th were to head further north, making for the Lingayen Gulf, which lay some 500 miles beyond. They were to fight their way ashore and advance on Manila, spearheading MacArthur's bid to seize the nation's capital. Intelligence suggested that the Japanese believed an amphibious landing on the Lingayen Gulf beaches was beyond the means of US forces. The hope was that the shoreline would be only lightly defended.

But of equal, if not greater, worry than the landings was the 1,700-mile sea voyage that lay before them. The Leyte landings had cost MacArthur dear, with the kamikaze, the newest and most fearsome form of Japanese attack, responsible for the greatest part of the losses. Already, the very mention of that word struck fear into the hearts of Allied troops, and a fatalistic mood fell upon the men as they boarded those two waiting LSTs.

Wynne had been allotted to LST-706. As part of its hull camouflage it had a giant 'shark's mouth' painted on the prow. The ship exuded real power and menace, and with all who were crammed aboard she was chock-full. In theory there was supposed to be space below decks for 250 souls, but in practice it seemed as if it was standing-room only. Wynne chose to sleep topside. He figured the lack of crowding, coupled with the fresh air and sea breeze would be better for him and his dog. But the LST's deck was itself jammed with vehicles, and they would have to find a place wherever there was space.

Smoky seemed very particular about their billet. Eventually, they settled in a gap between a jeep and a ten-wheeler truck. They were on the ship's prow, just to the rear of the circular gun position, with its steel protective wall lying a few feet away. Between that and their billet was an armour-plated ventilator, which pumped air down to the decks below. It stood about three feet high, and when he was lying prone on his cot it pretty much formed Wynne's pillow. Nearby, a flight of steps ran below decks, to where a good number of the 26th had chosen to billet themselves.

A typhoon had just blown through and the convoy set sail into the tail end of the bad weather. The sea was rough. Wynne could feel the prow of the ship slamming into the twenty-five-foot swells, followed by the roll of the vessel as she slid along the wave, and then the leaden thumping of the propellers as the stern lifted clear of the water. The vehicles were strapped to the deck with thick chains that were turning orange with rust. They rattled and groaned with every shudder of the vessel's hull.

To either side dozens of ships were spread out across the sea. Their ship, LST-706, was second in line in a column of vessels lying on the right flank of the convoy. They were making no more than ten knots – the speed of the slowest vessel – so were bound to be a good week or more at sea. On their right the sleek form of a destroyer kept pace, her sharp bow cleaving a line through the sullen, stormy waters. It was good to see her there, standing guard.

Notices had been posted on the ship's bulletin boards. They warned of 'the possibility of pro-Japanese civilians and the effects of loose talk' when they hit the ground in the Philippines. After nearly three years of occupation some of the locals might be in league with the enemy. The men of the 26th would have to be vigilant once they'd set foot on hostile soil. But before that moment came, there would be dangers enough at sea to occupy the minds of the troops.

The convoy would steam east through the Celebes Sea, before swinging north through the Sulu Sea, which would take them past the Japanese stronghold of Mindoro Island, and finally into the more open expanses of the South China Sea. The passage would take them up the west coast of the Philippines, which was a labyrinth of inlets, islands and bays. There were any number of places for Japanese warplanes to conceal themselves as they lay in wait, ready to attack.

Men gathered on the deck in groups that first day, playing cards, chatting and swopping nervous gossip. The word on everyone's lips was the kamikazes. Apparently, the convoy ahead of their own, which was carrying the 175,000-strong force that was to form the first assault wave, had been hit by scores of suicide strikes. Indeed, the skipper of their vessel, LST-706, had adopted a strict drill to try to lessen the dangers of kamikaze attacks.

He was happy enough for those on deck to erect DIY canvas shelters for the night, but come daybreak they had to be cleared right away. If a kamikaze hit their ship, the skipper wanted the deck kept as free as possible of anything that might burn. But that pretty much ignored the chief fire hazard, which was the scores of vehicles cramming the deck, each of which was loaded with petrol.

Wynne had more prosaic issues to deal with: how to keep his dog well fed, groomed and watered. Although he'd slipped her aboard riding in his haversack, it was no longer a secret that Smoky was there. It was inconceivable that anyone might object to the 26th's champion mascot travelling north with her unit. After all, she'd braved hostile skies with her fellow pilots, and she'd comforted the troops during the worst of their trauma. But still, Wynne wasn't expecting anyone to extend any special favours to Smoky.

Meals aboard LST-706 were strictly Army rations – canned or dehydrated food. Smoky was back to living out of tins, mostly of mutton stew or the ubiquitous bully beef. Wynne set himself a strict pooper watch: whenever Smoky had to relieve herself, he made sure her waste was bundled up and dropped overboard. When she had to pee, the rains would clean it away in no time. The main challenge was fresh water: there were limited amounts to drink, and nowhere near enough for the daily helmet-wash that Smoky was accustomed to.

That first day at sea her coat became stiff with sea salt. Worse still, where she hurried about on deck and brushed against the ship's chains, it became thick with rust. Within hours, Smoky had turned a dull orange-red, her hair sticking out in all directions like a cartoon explosion. She quickly attracted a fan base. Once the servicemen realized who she was – the famed champion mascot who could perform the most incredible tricks – she had a daily audience. Once again, her very presence on that ship kept the minds of soldiers and sailors off the darkness that was coming.

She wasn't the only animal stowaway. Frank Petrilak had Smoky's puppy, Topper, to care for and another unit had smuggled a big Dalmatian – their own mascot – aboard. The two dogs struck up an unlikely friendship and the Yorkshire Terrier–Dalmatian pairing proved hilarious. Smoky's spotted friend towered over her. He wore a life-jacked strapped around his middle in case he tumbled overboard, which only served to make the two of them look even more incongruous. Soldiers on the lookout for a memorable souvenir photo kept accosting the two mascot-dogs.

As far as Wynne was aware, it was Smoky's first time aboard a ship. Remarkably, she didn't seem to suffer any sickness. The LST was full of new and fresh experiences for her, most notably the smells. There was the heady reek of fuel oil from the ship's smoke stacks; the tang of sea salt; the iron scent of rust; the sharp bite of the disinfectant used to sluice down the decks. Plus there was the growing smell from the soldiers and sailors crammed aboard ship – unwashed uniforms, sweat . . . and the barest hint of fear.

By the time LST-706 was approaching the Sulu Sea, Smoky had very much found her sea legs and was eating like the proverbial horse. She would need all of her strength and her fortitude for what was coming.

As the convoy neared Mindoro Island, and the Japanese air bases sited there, the captain of LST-706 gave the order that no canvas shelters were permitted on deck day or night. No matter if it rained or not, the men would have to sleep out under the stars, for his priority was to keep the decks as free of fire hazards as possible.

They were entering kamikaze alley.

Those riding aboard LST-706 became ever more businesslike. Before setting sail the men of the 26th had been given a refresher course on the use of their Browning .50-calibre machine guns, their heaviest weapons. With the salt-laden sea air it was a struggle to keep the guns rust-free. More time spent cleaning them meant less time for playing cards or gassing. Figures sat cross-legged on deck with a canvas sheet spread before them, the various working parts of a disassembled weapon being wiped over lovingly with an oiled rag. Every now and then the sharp *clatch-clatch* of a carbine's working parts being ratcheted back and forth rang out across the deck.

They were several days into their voyage by the time the men of the 26th had grown accustomed to the rigours of life aboard ship: showering in salt water; the nightly blackout; frequent and seemingly ill-timed drills and alerts, at which point everyone would have to sprint for their allotted stations. They'd also managed to pick up some of the sailor's slang. The key saying appeared to be: 'Pass the word.' That phrase seemed to round off all announcements over the ship's Tannoy system.

The word being passed right now was distinctly ominous. Scores of Allied vessels in the seas ahead had been hit by kamikaze strikes, and no ship, no matter how well-defended, seemed immune to such attack. One of the first vessels to be sunk was the aircraft carrier, the USS *St Lo*, hit by a Mitsubishi A6M Zero kamikaze. She had gone down within thirty minutes of being struck, some 150 men losing their lives.

In the first week of January 1945, Allied forces had gone ashore at Leyte Gulf. In the process, the cruiser USS *Louisville* was hit by three kamikaze strikes. The first caused little damage, and the second succeeded only in knocking out one of her main gun turrets. But the third tore into the starboard side of the bridge. Rear Admiral Theodore E. Chandler, senior Allied commander of the cruiser force, was killed. He died while trying to help others escape the resulting inferno.

Overall, forty-one sailors were killed and over one hundred injured as a result of the kamikaze attack. The USS *Louisville*, though burning fiercely, was saved, and she steamed to a repair depot. Incredibly, she would be struck by further kamikaze strikes in the months to come.

At the same time as the USS *Louisville* was being targeted so too was a humble cargo vessel, the SS *John Burke*, one of the so-called 'Liberty Ships' – mass-produced freighters designed for transporting Allied war supplies. Packed full of ammunition and lying low in the water, the *John Burke* had been sailing north as part of the convoy riding ahead of the armada of warships carrying the men of the 26th.

As the fleet had steamed north through the Sulu Sea a kamikaze squadron had attacked. One suicide pilot flying an Aichi D3A – a mass-produced Japanese dive-bomber that was now hopelessly obsolete – made it through the *John Burke*'s defences. Such outdated aircraft had been reduced to training duties, or, as now, reborn in the kamikaze role.

Screaming towards the *John Burke*'s deck in a steep dive, the Aichi, though damaged, succeeded in hitting her between cargo holds, which were packed full of munitions. There was a blinding flash as the plane disintegrated on impact, the fuel she was carrying and the explosives packed into her fuselage detonating violently. For several seconds thick smoke billowed out of the impact site, before an enormous pillar of flame erupted from the hold. Instants later, the ship dissolved into a massive fireball, which engulfed her completely.

A mushroom cloud of smoke punched above the horizon, several of the ships to either side of the *John Burke* being damaged in the blast. When the resulting cloud of smoke cleared, the *John Burke* was no more. Another, smaller, ship steaming nearby had also been sunk in the cataclysmic explosion. The shockwave caused by the *John Burke* being torn apart was so violent that neighbouring vessels reported being hit by torpedoes. Though ships searched the sea, there were no survivors.

No vessel was too insignificant to escape the attention of the kamikazes, especially the workhorses of the infantry, the LSTs. LST-749 formed part of the same convoy as the *John Burke*. On 21 December, as the fleet had steamed north through the Sulu Sea, the kamikazes swept in. A wave of forty aircraft attacked, with Allied fighters chasing them and blazing away on their tails. As the kamikazes neared the convoy every gun on every vessel had opened up, and the fighters had been forced to peel away.

One kamikaze had made it through to hit LST-749, ploughing into the ship's bridge and wreaking death and carnage across her deck. The survivors had abandoned ship, leaving her a burning wreck. Another LST had been hit, but just the wing of the kamikaze struck the vessel, the body of the aircraft cartwheeling into the water. Theirs was a lucky escape.

LST-460 was next to be targeted. The kamikaze that made for her flew straight and true. The aircraft hit her like a massive arrow, tearing through the bridge and penetrating the mess deck, killing all of its officers more or less instantly. Fire flashed through the vessel. Those who managed to abandon ship found themselves in the water, as other kamikazes pushed home their attacks. One hit a liberty ship in her open hold, which was fortunately only loaded with timber. The crew managed to extinguish the fire.

But LST-460 was burning fiercely and she was doomed. She was sunk by US warships to prevent her from acting as a beacon for further attacks. The *John Burke*, and the two LSTs that had been sunk, were the fourteenth, fifteenth and sixteenth Allied vessels lost to such suicide attacks. In late December 1944 and early January 1945 dozens of warships were damaged or sent to the bottom of the sea by kamikazes.

Into the heart of that storm would sail the 26th, including one man and his brave little dog.

CHAPTER 17

In light of their early successes, the Japanese had embraced the kamikaze concept with fanatical zeal. Around 2,000 pilots were being trained for suicide strikes, and hundreds of warplanes were being made ready.

With stocks of old or obsolete aircraft beginning to run low, the Japanese rushed through designs for a one-use kamikaze aircraft – the Nakajima Ki-115 Tsurungi (Sabre). Of simple, basic construction and made largely of wood, the Ki-115 was able to jettison its undercarriage. Made of crude steel tubing, the wheel-assembly would drop after take-off. After all, nobody expected the pilots to be coming back to land again.

The Ki-115 was designed to be able to use any engine that might be in storage, including those from old 1920s or '30s aircraft. It was fitted with an 1,800-pound bomb, which when combined with the impact of the aircraft strike was powerful enough to split a warship in two. The Japanese high command planned to build 8,000 of these kamikaze warplanes every month, in workshops spread all across Japan.

News of the kamikaze strikes spread fast. The chief value of the kamikaze had become fear. There was little the average soldier could do against an enemy who was determined to sacrifice his own life in order to claim as many of his adversaries as possible. You could blaze away all you liked with a ship's guns, but if a kamikaze was lucky enough to get through, your vessel was very likely doomed, and possibly all who sailed aboard her.

It was the first week of January 1945 when the convoy carrying the men of the 26th entered the waters of the Sulu Sea, south of Mindoro Island. Just prior to dusk the call to action stations was sounded. Aboard LST-706 Bill Wynne was playing pinochle – a trick-taking card game popular with the troops – together with three buddies from the 26th, Dom D'Angelo, Jim Everett and Donald Esmond. The four were seated on two cots facing each other, forming makeshift pews. The alarms had become so frequent by now that they were wearing their life jackets day and night.

To left and right the ship's crew dashed to their gun positions, dragging on their helmets as they ran. To starboard of the convoy, Wynne spotted a flight of in-bound warplanes. There were eight that he could count, though he could hear others crying warnings that there were as many as twelve. They were attacking from the east, powering in towards the convoy from out of a cloudy, overcast, brooding sky.

The ship's Tannoy ordered anybody who was not crewing the ship to take cover below. Boots clattered down the iron ship's ladders. Below-decks in the gloom the ship's crew ran through the hold slamming and bolting shut the bulkhead doors. The men of the 26th had been warned that it was an offence punishable by court martial to open any of those hatches once they had been sealed. If the ship were hit, keeping those hatches closed and the individual compartments air-tight might be the key to keeping her afloat.

The war diary of the 26th picks up the story of those first few minutes of the kamikaze attack: 'Enemy planes had been sighted . . . Some of us saw six, some saw twelve . . . The value of the drills was now apparent . . . we went to the stations below decks to which we had been assigned. Then the planes came over. We knew it only because the ack-ack guns had started to fire . . . we learned of the action concussion by concussion.'

As the ship reverberated to the drum-beat of the guns, keeping below decks became impossible for men who felt a burning urge to witness the unfolding battle. Many clambered top-side again. 'Flak burst into patches of black and ominous cloud above us, so thick that it seemed impossible for a plane to pass through unscathed . . .' the war diary recorded. 'A plane was hit and exploded in the air, as another crashed into the sea. But . . . one did come through. In the hands of one of the famous Kamikaze pilots, one of the Jap planes dove straight and sure through the fire . . .'

The lone aircraft screamed in. Spying the imminent threat Wynne grabbed Smoky, but he was momentarily frozen as to where to dash for cover. Should they make for below-decks, or was it too late? Then an urgent, irresistible impulse – one that Wynne could only say later was inspired by his dog – told him exactly where to go. He was to seek cover beside the wheel of the jeep adjacent to their sleeping quarters. He felt Smoky's presence guiding him, almost as if she had spoken the words in his ear.

Dog in his arms, he dived into the space between the armoured ventilator and the jeep's front wheel. Hitting the deck, Wynne pulled Smoky's form tight to his chest, trying to shield her as best he could, cupping one hand over her tiny ears to muffle the deafening sound of gunfire. He was utterly determined that no harm was going to come to his dog if he could help it. He'd shield her with his own body if he had to.

From just a few feet away the LST's gun-emplacement spat fire. The thick barrels of the cannons groped skywards, pumping rounds at the on-rushing aircraft. There was a 20mm gun positioned right behind Wynne and Smoky's place of hiding, and the crew kept reloading and firing repeatedly. The noise was all-consuming, and with each round Wynne could feel a judder of fear run along Smoky's entire frame.

He pulled her closer, whispering the words of reassurance that he hoped might calm her. 'It's okay, girl. It's okay. Don't worry, girl. Everything will be fine.'

Suddenly, there was the violent crash of something striking their ship. An instant later a wild cheering broke out all across the LST's deck. One of the enemy must have been shot down. Glancing skywards, Wynne saw two further aircraft making their approach, diving right out of the heavens.

One seemed to be headed directly for the guns that were belching fire next to where he and Smoky had taken cover. With Smoky tucked under one arm, Wynne began to crawl on hands and knees. His hands landed on something hot, jagged and sharp. It was shrapnel. Further slivers of razor-sharp metal were scattered over the deck. Somewhere close, LST-706 must have been hit.

Wynne clambered to his feet, trying to get his bearings. He watched transfixed as the LSTs gunners duelled with the on-coming warplanes. The sky was a mass of violent black explosions, as flak burst in the suicide pilots' path.

'Come on, get the bastards!' someone yelled. 'Get the lousy Japs!'

The cry was taken up by figures dotted all over the open deck. The dive of the nearest kamikaze aircraft seemed to veer off unnaturally, as if the pilot had lost all control. Moments later his warplane hit the sea, a geyser of white water erupting in its wake. A rousing cheer went up from the deck. That one at least had missed his target.

But the pilot of aircraft number two was not to be so easily brushed aside. He flew on, braving the murderous barrage of fire. To one side of LST-706 there sailed a liberty ship, heavily laden with cargo. The kamikaze chose her as his target. The aircraft bore down on the freighter, drawing ever closer. Finally, it slammed into her superstructure amidships. Within moments the liberty ship was billowing black smoke.

The guns on LST-706 were still firing, but gradually they petered out to nothing. In the comparative silence that followed, Wynne pulled Smoky close and tried his best to comfort her. She was shaking from nose to tail.

An eerie silence settled over the ship. Wynne noticed the two young gunners on the single-barrel 40mm cannon nearby, chewing gum and eyeing the sky, warily. They began to wind the cranks of the gun, swivelling it around, popping gum to the rhythm of the crank handles. The barrel swung across and lowered. They were tracking a distant target. Wynne followed the trajectory of the barrel and suddenly he could see it: yet another kamikaze was speeding towards them.

This one was trying a stealth approach, flying in only thirty feet above the wave crests. The nose of the approaching warplane was pointed directly at their ship. When it was about 500 yards out, the gunners opened fire. Boom! Boom! Boom! All it took were those three carefully aimed shots. The kamikaze did a half-spiral, before a wingtip ploughed into the sea, sending up another plume of white water.

A rousing cheer swept the deck of the LST.

The liberty ship that had been hit was the *Lewis L. Dyche*. Like the *John Burke* before her, she was packed full of a highly combustible cargo – bombs and fuses. The kamikaze had wreaked devastation, the plummeting aircraft breaking through to the ship's hold. The fire quickly spread. Eventually, it caught the first of her cargo of munitions. The ship disintegrated in a series of giant explosions. Debris from the blast damaged a nearby oil-tanker, plus a mine-laying ship, the 3,100-tonne USS *Monadnock*.

Like the *John Burke* before her, the *Lewis L. Dyche* was vaporized with all hands lost. The fate of that vessel, and the black pall of smoke she cast, was all too visible to those aboard LST-706. It served as a sobering reminder of how lucky they had been. Indeed, even aboard the LST there were those who had not escaped unscathed, and the injured included several of Bill Wynne's card-playing buddies.

In the aftermath of the attack, a dazed Dom D'Angelo approached Bill Wynne. He waved his bleeding hand. A shard of shrapnel had torn into it. Nearby, Norman Smith – a veteran of the squadron who'd just won his Asia-Pacific Campaign Medal and a Bronze Star for meritorious service in combat – was down and wounded.

Someone was kneeling over him and crying for a medic. Smith had taken a chunk of shrapnel to his side. Wynne's pinochle partner, Jim Everett, had also been hit, as had five others.

Incredibly, the only casualties aboard the ship had been within a ten-foot radius of Wynne and Smoky. Yet somehow, he and his little dog remained unscathed. One fragment of spinning shrapnel could have taken Smoky's head clean off, or eviscerated her. They had been so very lucky.

Smith's injuries were serious. The shrapnel had punctured his lung and he was bleeding heavily. He needed an urgent blood transfusion. His blood group was A Negative, and a call went out over the ship's Tannoy for a match. One of the 26th volunteered to give blood. That done, Smith was taken off the ship by a landing craft so he could get proper medical attention.

Smith had spent his entire war being utterly sanguine about the dangers of being hit. 'If it's going to happen, it's going to happen,' was his refrain, as he refused to dig yet another foxhole. Now it had happened.

Wynne remained curious as to how all those around him had been hurt and yet he and his dog had escaped injury. It turned out that a stray 20mm shell had hit the LST, one very likely fired by a neighbouring ship as it tried to blast one of the low-flying kamikazes out of the sky. The shell had torn across the deck and landed in the interior of the armour-plated ventilator that Wynne was in the habit of making his pillow for the night.

It had blasted a jagged, star-shaped dent in the ventilator's side, with shrapnel from the impact ripping out the top of the ventilator and scything across the deck. Anything in its path had been hit. If the shell's trajectory had been a few inches in either direction it would have missed the ventilator and torn into Wynne and Smoky's place of hiding. As it was, their taking cover where they had – guided, Wynne felt certain, by Smoky's sixth-sense – had saved them from injury or worse.

In reflecting upon all of this, Wynne felt convinced that he'd been saved from the bullet with his name on it – the one that the tail-gunner from the Jolly Rogers had warned him about back in Sydney. He also felt certain that it was Smoky's doing. She had directed him to take cover in a place that had put them both out of the line of fire.

Dusk settled over the convoy. Somehow, everyone knew the attackers weren't done yet. Their destroyer escort dropped back until she was riding directly astern of LST-706. Wynne decided to wander aft to see what the warship was up to. He put Smoky on her lead and gave her a walk along the full length of the ship. There was now an odd, unearthly stillness about everything.

For some reason Wynne was struck by Smoky's appearance: her hair, gummed up with rust and salt, stuck out in all directions. It was peculiarly fitting – like a cartoon of a dog that had been electrocuted or suffered a severe fright. And for sure, there were few scares to compare with being targeted by kamikazes.

As the light faded, extra guns were set up toward the rear of the LST. Wynne noticed that on the destroyer riding in their wake, every man had remained at action stations.

Then, from out of nowhere a lone warplane appeared. It made for a bizarre, ghostly apparition in the half-light. It was almost dark by now and the pilot had switched on his landing lights and lowered his undercarriage – though where on earth he intended to land in the middle of the ocean was anyone's guess.

The warplane seemed to glide soundlessly across the sea, lights flashing, as it drew ever closer to the rear-end of the destroyer.

The crew of the destroyer appeared mesmerized by the bizarre apparition. The scene was so curiously reminiscent of a friendly aircraft coming in to land that no one seemed able to bring themselves to open fire. And then suddenly, it was as if the spell had been broken. Beside Wynne and Smoky, one of the guns that had just been erected on the rear of LST-706 roared into action. As the whole ship woke up to the threat, every gun zeroed in on that lone kamikaze.

The warplane was almost at the rear of the destroyer, with the ship's crew staring up at it in astonished horror, when it juddered in the sky, taking multiple hits. Moments later it keeled over, fell hard and smashed into the sea. The plume of water it sent up rained down onto the aft section of the warship that it had so very nearly managed to strike. A cheer went up from those manning the vessels.

As darkness cloaked the convoy it was time to take stock. The captain of LST-706 announced that the vessel and her crew were credited with shooting down two, and possibly three kamikazes. Another massive cheer swept the ship's deck. Maybe the dreaded Japanese suicide pilots could be beaten after all.

Tellingly, the squadron war diary recorded of the kamikaze attacks: 'We had all experienced bombing at bases. An attack at sea was another story. Our squadron insignia seemed all too appropriate: we were indeed sitting ducks. We had worried about this eventuality. Now it was here . . .'

The 'sitting duck' reference was to the 26th's badge – a camera-wielding Donald Duck riding on a cloud.

CHAPTER 18

White Beach was the codename for the convoy's intended landing point at Lingayen Gulf. The town of Lingayen itself, the provincial capital, lay just beyond the beach. A fierce naval barrage had preceded the assault, lasting from 6-9 January 1945. Studying the town via binoculars from seaward, it was possible to make out a shell-shattered church spire, and the cratered ruins of the scores of civic buildings that lined the town's main square.

'Our enemy had been completely surprised,' recorded the 26th's war diary of their arrival at Lingayen Gulf, 'as he had thought it completely impossible to land ships at that place. We were inclined to agree with him, when we saw the difficulty encountered in beaching the LSTs during the high and rough tide.' Fortunately, the rugged and utilitarian flat-bottomed vessels proved able to brave the fiercest of seas.

But even here in Lingayen Gulf, the dangers of suicide attack remained acute, and not just from the skies. After the LSTs carrying the 26th had dropped anchor, awaiting orders for the troops to go ashore, the men aboard were warned to mount watch over the waters to either side. Thick, billowing smoke screens were being deployed to shield the convoy from an assault from the air, but there were few such defences at the waterline.

The Japanese were known to be sending *fukuryu* – suicide divers – to hit the convoy at anchor. The kamikaze swimmers concealed themselves beneath unremarkable-seeming flotsam, such as old wooden packing cases and crates. Once they'd paddled out to reach the hull of a warship, they'd detonate their explosive charges. Wynne and his fellows had to stand sentry at the ship's rail, carbines at the ready. All that night there were sharp cracks of rifle fire, as the watchers opened up on threats real or imagined on the bay's dark waters.

All through the following day the tension among those awaiting the call to go ashore kept rising. It was the middle of the night when the order finally came. Having won the battle for Biak Island, General Krueger had been placed in charge of the Lingayen Gulf landings. As soon as he learned that the 26th had yet to land, the frustrated general ordered the men of the photo recce squadron – his eyes in the sky – to get moving, and pronto.

The Japanese had put up only sporadic resistance along this stretch of coastline. General Yamashita had positioned the core of his forces along the spine of ridges and remote mountainous terrain lying inland, ready to fight a long war of attrition, as they had on Biak Island. General Krueger wanted the P-38s of the 26th up and running over those enemy positions, bringing back the vital images that he needed to plan the coming campaign. It was crucial that the Lightnings got airborne as soon as possible.

As the squadron's war diary makes clear, the word of General Krueger, Commanding General of the US 6th Army, the forces spearheading the landings here and the coming advance on Manila, was not to be gainsaid. 'General Krueger himself had ordered that we debark immediately, as his scheduled operations were dependent upon our aid ... We did suddenly pull for shore, bumping a neighbouring LST in our haste.'

The order was passed around the men of the 26th in more forceful terms: 'Hit the beach!'

LST-706 had slipped her anchor shortly after midnight; it was still hours before daybreak by the time her blunt prow ploughed into White Beach – a stretch of steep sand pounded by rough seas. The bow doors swung open, the ramp dropped, and before the ship lay a roaring tumble of white water, breakers surging back and forth. To Wynne it was obvious what would happen if he lost his grip on Smoky among the dark and chaotic melee of the landing. Heroic and spirited though she might be, his little dog would be swept under in seconds and dragged out to sea.

He slung his kitbag over one shoulder, gripped his rifle in his left hand, his cot in the other, and tucked his dog firmly under one arm, where he knew she would be most protected. He headed down the ramp, squeezing her warm body closer to his chest. He could get another rifle, kit bag or cot. He could never find another Smoky. Steeling himself, he dropped off the ramp into the seething swell, trying to nudge Smoky higher and keep her out of the reach of the hungry waves.

Struggling to keep his footing, he turned for the shore, which was some forty feet away. A pair of lights mounted on poles had been planted on the sand as a rough guide. He fixed his gaze on those, getting buffeted first this way and that by the powerful breakers, and knowing that Smoky was getting torn at by the wave tops. Finally, his feet found firmer ground, and he was able to drag both himself and his dog onto dry land.

A pile of rations was heaped on the beach. Not knowing when they might be resupplied with food, he grabbed as many cans as he could carry – sustenance for him and his dog. He sat on the damp sand and levered open a can with his bowie knife, as figures milled about, awaiting orders. It was a first rule of such missions to eat whenever you got the opportunity, for you never knew when the next chance might come.

Suddenly, an alert was hissed from soldier to soldier. Enemy movement had been detected further up the beach. Wynne took cover on a darkened stretch of sand, with Smoky held close and low beside him. Man and dog waited, tense in the silence, the roar of the surf behind them, a dark wall of vegetation to their front.

Suddenly, a massive explosion erupted from further along the shore, fiery detonations tearing apart the night skies. An ammunition dump had been hit, sending plumes of flame and smoke rippling across the heavens, and lighting up the bay a ghostly orange.

Wynne, Smoky and the rest of the 26th dashed for cover among the palm trees that fringed the sands. But they could afford little delay. Tempting as it was to remain in the small patch of safety they had found, they had their orders, direct from General Krueger. As soon as the tide receded and the water level began to drop a little, they got busy unloading the trucks and jeeps from the guts of the LST. They had hit this beach around 3.00 a.m. By first light the first of the trucks had been loaded with gear and was on its way, heading inland for an airbase freshly seized from the enemy.

With dawn breaking, Wynne and his dog caught a ride atop a ten-wheeler Army truck that was loaded high with kit and supplies. It churned its way up the beach before reaching the hard-surfaced road that ran to its rear. The first sign of human habitation was the barrio, or slum, on the outskirts of Dagupan, a town lying inland of White Beach. As the truck turned right swinging west towards Lingayen town, more and more battle damage became visible.

The three-day naval bombardment that had preceded the landings had been fearsome. Church steeples and high buildings had taken the brunt of the shelling. In Lingayen itself, townspeople had raised the American and Filipino flags and paraded through the square to show their support for the liberation forces anchored offshore. As a result the Navy's shells had been directed away from that part of the coast.

Facing such a fearsome onslaught the Japanese defenders had put up little resistance on land, but at sea the Lingayen landings had cost the Allies dear. A total of twenty-four warships had been sunk and another sixty-seven damaged, all due to kamikaze strikes. Those vessels hit included the battleships the USS *Mississippi*, *New Mexico* and *Colorado*, the heavy cruiser HMAS *Australia*, plus numerous light cruisers, destroyers and cargo vessels.

Further south, in Leyte Gulf, the Japanese had launched a series of surprise counter-attacks. Paratroopers and amphibious forces had landed from the air and sea in an effort to retake the US-held airfield. The enemy had planned to use it as a base from which to mount a wave of further attacks. Savage hand-to-hand fighting had ensued, as US rear echelon units were hastily deployed. Though the counter-attack had finally been repulsed, it reflected how resilient the Japanese forces in the Philippines remained. Their spirits were far from broken.

The drive to Lingayen town was no more than ten miles, the road running through verdant rice paddies. Several times the truck had to pull over to allow the bulky forms of Sherman tanks to thunder by. At one point the truck rumbled past a prisoner of war compound – a makeshift wire enclosure with dejected-looking Japanese POWs kicking about inside.

They reached the shattered streets of Lingayen town, where here and there the odd fire still smouldered among ruined buildings. The truck carrying Wynne and Smoky nosed through streets strewn with rubble and busy with Filipinos clearing up the debris of recent fighting. As the vehicle eased past, locals stopped to stare, some waving and smiling a welcome. Pushing ahead, they made for the far side of town where the airstrip was located.

After almost three years of Japanese occupation the people here looked to be in a sorry state. Stick-thin figures thronged the streets. Japanese troops had carried out periodic raids, seizing the local staples of rice, chicken and pigs from wherever they could find them. The villagers had been driven to the brink of starvation, and to Wynne their plight appeared utterly desperate. Men, women and children looked as if they had been ravaged by malnutrition.

The truck reached the airbase, which was already a hive of activity. Bulldozers shunted back and forth, as combat engineers worked feverishly to get the airstrip serviceable again. For the moment their activity centred on laying down steel matting, which represented the quickest way to repair bombed-out stretches of runway. Known as Marston Mat, it consisted of interlocking lengths of perforated steel, which were used for the rapid repair of landing strips. Each steel sheet was pegged down with iron stakes to give it added stability. Aircraft taking off made a noise not unlike tyres on a motorway's rumble strips, but it was perfectly serviceable.

The number one priority for Bill Wynne and the rest of his team was to get the photo lab up and running, so they could start to process images just as soon as the P-38s took to the skies. They set up billets in a cluster of palm-thatched buildings adjacent to the runway. The local Filipinos had been asked to temporarily vacate those huts, in return for rent paid by the US Army. Time was so tight that if the laborious effort involved in pitching camp could be avoided, so much the better.

The huts weren't exactly a home from home. Traditionally, the long, feathery leaves of the nipa palm were used to roof over the wooden-framed stilted buildings common to coastal settlements. With roof and sides made of overlapping strips of palm leaves, the huts provided basic shelter from the elements. Movable palm panels could be slid aside, to offer ventilation during drier spells. The floor was of split bamboo, which was flattened out to form rudimentary boards.

Wynne climbed the bamboo ladder to enter the hut that he'd been assigned. He surveyed his and Smoky's new home. The bamboo platform shook and creaked when anyone moved. The bamboo 'floorboards' had half-inch gaps between them. Beneath them, chickens and pigs foraged for discarded food. The smell left something to be desired, and no one was about to venture below in a hurry for anything they might have dropped, but Wynne's chief concern right now was for the well-being of his dog.

His biggest worry was the hut's floor. Smoky's paws – delicate, and small enough to caress between thumb and forefinger – could easily slip through the cracks and get trapped. Despite its size and strength, bamboo is a grass with a hollow stem. When cut, the sides can be left sharp as a razor's edge, and minutely serrated to form a saw-like blade. Wynne couldn't bear to think how much Smoky might suffer if she got a paw jammed between those bamboo floorboards.

Retrieving a wooden plank from one of the trucks, Wynne slid that beneath his cot, forming a solid base for Smoky in the space that she always claimed as her own. Her sanctuary. As long as she stuck to that while in the hut she should be reasonably safe from injury.

The plight of the locals was so desperate that a decision was taken to employ those who were capable of doing any work. One party was detailed to dig a trash-pit and latrines. Another was put on pot-washing duty, and another was made responsible for hauling in the squadron's supplies. They stopped short of allowing the Filipinos to cook, because the squadron medic, having run checks, discovered that the locals were riddled with gut parasites.

Once that first garbage pit had been dug and the first waste thrown into it, Wynne was shocked to see locals scavenging for anything that might be vaguely edible. His heart went out to them. It was a powerful reminder of how much they had suffered under the Japanese. Wynne was struck by the Filipino women in particular: they had retained an extraordinary dignity and poise, in spite of the privations they had suffered. They had been brutalized, and the chance to earn a little money, or a little food in lieu of cash, was a real godsend.

The airstrip lay to the rear of White Beach, running just behind the sand dunes, with wild breakers rolling in from beyond. It was flat, open, windswept terrain, with little cover anywhere apart from a scattering of palm trees. Both the airbase itself and the makeshift hut accommodation were wide open to enemy air attacks. That first night the men of the 26th were serenaded by the familiar, hollow thud of explosions and the roar of gunfire, as Japanese warplanes screamed out of the night in a frenzied counter-attack.

The trauma of running kamikaze alley had stayed with Smoky, and she was no longer able to hide her nerves. At the first sound of distant explosions she started spinning in circles, like a tiny whirling dervish. The violence of the blasts was getting to her, fear starting to take an iron hold. In an effort to block out the worst of the noise Wynne took to cupping the little dog's ears with his hands whenever there was an air-attack. There was one comforting thought: at least here on land they were immune to the terrible kamikaze strikes.

Dogs can suffer from a canine equivalent of post-traumatic stress disorder. Most commonly, animals exposed repeatedly to combat become over-active and hyper-sensitive, losing their ability to focus or to stay on task. They might shy away from places in which they were once comfortable, but where they have experienced repeated trauma. Some become overly clingy or aggressive. Smoky wasn't at that level yet. She still sought out sanctuary beneath Wynne's cot. But she seemed increasingly nervous and anxious, and Wynne worried that if he let her go during one of the raids she might bolt in fear.

There was to be little peace at Lingayen. That first morning Wynne and Smoky were woken by the thunderous clatter of a column of heavy tanks moving along the road that lay adjacent to their hut. Dust billowed thickly from the tracks and exhaust fumes clouded the air. The column's commander was jammed in the turret of his tank, a thick cigar gripped between his teeth, his head bare to the wind. He yelled out triumphantly to the men of the 26th that they sure were winning this war.

The town of Lingayen lay around eighty miles away from Manila, across fertile rice-growing plains. With US armour and troops advancing on the capital city, the focus of the ground battle had already begun to shift in that direction. General Yamashita had ordered that Manila should be evacuated and yielded to the Allies, judging his forces too weak to make a stand there. He'd ordered all available men to take up defensive positions in the high ground that ringed the city.

But some 10,000 elite Japanese marines, under Rear Admiral Sanji Iwabuchi, had refused to obey Yamashita's orders. They remained in Manila, determined to hold it or die in the process. As the Allies closed in on the city, the besieged forces gave their most bestial instincts free rein – carrying out mass rapes, horrific torture and massacres. They targeted schools, hospitals, convents and churches for the worst of their war crimes. In one instance, Rear Admiral Iwabuchi's marines rounded up 3,000 men and killed them all.

Surrounded, trapped and facing annihilation, Iwabuchi's

forces retreated to the historic, centuries-old Intramuros area of Manila, a quarter-square-mile district made up of twisting alleyways, grand buildings and thick stone-built walls. Anxious to avoid causing civilian casualties, MacArthur had resisted using air strikes and artillery in the battle for Manila. But with die-hard Japanese marines holed up in such a concentrated area as the Intramuros, he feared a ground assault without air support or artillery would prove hugely costly.

The Japanese defenders had taken thousands of Filipinos – men, women and children alike – hostage, and were holding them as human shields. Many died in the bombardment and subsequent battles that followed, as the walled city was cleared in bitter street-to-street fighting. Over a thousand US soldiers lost their lives, with five times that number wounded. Anything up to a quarter of a million Filipinos would die during the battle for Manila, mostly due to Japanese atrocities. Facing death or capture, Rear Admiral Iwabuchi and his senior officers committed *seppuku* – ritual suicide.

The siege of Manila was the most significant and devastating episode of urban warfare in the entire southwest Pacific campaign. Few cities in Europe had witnessed the kind of brutal street-to-street fighting that took place in that city, which many likened to the horrors of Stalingrad. The bestial acts of the Japanese troops earned untold infamy, becoming known as the 'Manila Massacre'. But even when all of Manila finally lay in Allied hands, the wider battle for the city was far from won. General Yamashita had established his fortified positions in the surrounding hills, and in doing so he had seized control of Manila's water supplies.

Even as he had gone about liberating Manila, MacArthur had half his mind on the next great challenge: keeping the surviving inhabitants of this war-blasted metropolis alive. He figured there were around ten days' water supplies remaining in the city. Normally, Manila's reservoirs would be topped up from the lakes in the highlands, the flow from which was controlled by a series of dams. But now, those lakes and dams lay in Japanese hands, which meant that General Yamashita could deprive the city of vital drinking water.

Having witnessed the dark horrors that Japanese commanders and their troops had visited on the citizens of Manila, few doubted that the enemy would wage their resistance across the rest of the Philippines with any less savagery. Depriving the citizens of Manila of water was quite within their capabilities. What MacArthur needed above all else were photographs of those highland reservoirs, so he could plan how best to wrestle them from enemy hands and before Yamashita was able to dynamite the dams.

The battle for Manila had been launched in the first week of February 1945. Just days earlier, the first Lightnings of the 26th had flown into Lingayen Airbase, which had just been declared fully operational. Within twenty-four hours the squadron was busier than it had ever been, the pace of operations proving relentless and punishing. In just eight days seventy-one photo reconnaissance missions were flown – which would have accounted for a month of missions back at Nadzab. From those eight days of flights 44,174 prints were processed.

Despite the daily air raids, and the need to dig new shelters in the soft sand, the crew at the photo lab – Smoky included –

were tireless in their endeavours, churning out images day and night. In one forty-eight-hour period the lab was asked to process 19,000 prints, with 7,000 of them listed as top priority. They pulled it off, even though they ran short of the fresh water the lab needed to continue processing film.

Reconnaissance flights over mountainous terrain were plagued by navigational issues: rich deposits of iron ore in the hills caused the P-38's compasses to go haywire, 'resulting in flight lines being flown in error'. And yet still the photo recce missions continued. General Krueger demanded a record number of reconnaissance sorties be flown in support of 6th Army operations. A Piper Cub light aircraft was kept on standby at the Lingayen airstrip, ready to rush those prints to senior front-line commanders just as soon as they were dry.

As the days progressed the 26th kept up the furious pace. The men of the squadron – the photo lab teams especially – came in for fulsome praise. A pair of 6th Army captains was transferred to the 26th, as permanent liaison officers. Their role was to work with the squadron to coordinate requests for photo recce missions, to brief the pilots, and to keep aircrew informed of the rapidly changing situation on the ground, ensuring the photos got to the right commanders as quickly as possible. Under their watch, prints were rushed direct into the hands of General MacArthur, at his command post, and to Admiral Nimitz, the US Naval commander, as well as to their senior officers.

Time after time, the 26th kept delivering. When MacArthur had needed detailed images to plan his final assault on the Intramuros district of Manila, he'd turned to the pilots of the

26th. On 15 February 1945 he got the photos he'd requested, and as the result of an outstandingly brave flight mission. It was none other than Lieutenant William Bishop who had been tasked to shoot the images – the pilot who had flown Smoky to Hollandia some eight months earlier, to save her from the long sea voyage from Nadzab.

Bishop had been sent into the skies to capture the labyrinthine terrain of the Intramuros in as much detail as possible. It involved executing a high-speed dash across the city's rooftops, capturing the last redoubt of Iwabuchi's marines on film. It was a miracle that he hadn't been shot down as he skimmed through the fiercely contested airspace.

Despite the intense workload, spirits remained high. The men of the 26th felt they were at the heart of something – a campaign of major significance and maybe even a turning point in this internecine war. As their war diary recorded, 'The opportunity to work in close support of the ground troops and to observe the successful results obtained . . . served not only as an incentive for greater production but as a valuable asset in maintaining good morale.'

By the third week of February, MacArthur's overriding focus had become the battle for Manila's fresh water supply. As US troops endeavoured to drive the Japanese from the jungle-clad highlands, General Krueger threw all available forces into the savage fighting. The crucial battleground had become the valleys of the Ipo Dam, the key fresh-water reservoir serving the nation's capital.

MacArthur and Krueger hungered after the kind of highly detailed images of the Ipo Dam and surrounding terrain that would enable them to plan their final assault, mapping out the enemy's cave positions and bunkers. But in the battle for the Ipo Dam, the pilots of the photo reconnaissance squadron would be forced to make their greatest sacrifices yet.

And so too would a small dog who would prove to have the world's biggest heart.

CHAPTER 19

As the pace of operations accelerated throughout January 1945, Counselman, freshly promoted to major, was relieved of his command, and moved into a headquarters role. He too had fallen victim to the furious demands of flying duties coupled with command. Captain George B. Gathers Jr took over as the fourth commanding officer of the 26th Photo Reconnaissance Squadron in three years.

With his jet-black hair, dark eyes, strong Roman nose and classic good looks, Gathers had the typical air of a dashing and daring recce flier. Formerly the pilot of a B24 Liberator serving with a combat-mapping squadron – one tasked to draw up detailed maps of war zones based upon aerial photography – he was a hugely experienced aviator. He, like his predecessors, seemed fearless, and before long he had entered into the same punishing flight regime, which he tried to juggle with the pressures of command.

Gathers encountered his first major challenge in the skies above the Ipo Dam. The enemy were so craftily hidden among the sheer-cut ravines and caves burrowed deep into mountain passes, that General Krueger wanted images of a much higher resolution than could ever be captured from 28,000 feet, the height at which they were now generally forced to fly, to avoid ground fire.

To provide such detailed images the 26th would have to execute a series of what were known as 'low-level oblique' photo runs over the Ipo Dam area. Filmed with a K22 camera positioned to shoot out the port side of the P-38's nosecone, the pilot would have to bring his aircraft down almost to roof-top height. The engine and propellers of the aircraft would be clearly visible in the shots, framing each of the photos so captured.

A technique first perfected by British photo reconnaissance pilots, it took a rare combination of bravery, consummate flying skills and cool focus under fire. But the risks were matched by the rewards: successful 'low-level oblique' photo runs could provide unparalleled battle intelligence.

The craft of low-level recce flying had been developed during the summer of 1940, when cloud cover over the Channel had prevented the RAF from photographing the invasion fleet then being assembled by Hitler. The answer was obvious: if the recce pilots flew at a very low altitude, they would be able to sneak in below the clouds. The trouble was this put their aircraft in range of enemy flak and also made them easier targets for fight-ers. Survival depended on split-second timing, lightning-fast reactions and not a small degree of luck. Appropriately enough, the pilots had nicknamed these flights 'dicing' – as in 'dicing with death'.

Once it had been established that this type of low-level sortie was able to capture terrain in minute detail, the focus turned to another key enemy target. For many months there had been

fierce debate about whether the Germans possessed radar technology, and if they did, whether it had reached the same level
of sophistication as its British counterpart.

The majority of those involved had concluded that the Germans didn't yet have radar, but there were a handful of top
scientists who disagreed. They argued that the enemy had developed a highly accurate, short-wave system. There were references
in decoded German signals to a mysterious device known as
the 'Würzburg'. In November 1941 a mystery object had been
spotted on a reconnaissance photo filmed at high altitude over
the French coast. It showed a tiny pinprick set atop the cliffs at
Le Havre, with paths converging upon it. Positioned adjacent
to the village of Bruneval, some believed this might be the
mysterious Würzburg apparatus.

RAF Medmenham, an RAF station based at the grand country
manor of Danesfield House, in rural Buckinghamshire, had
become the centre of wartime British photo reconnaissance
analysis. It was also where increasing numbers of US photo recce
teams were being trained. The mysterious Bruneval pinprick
was scrutinized by the analysts at Medmenham. One, Claude
Wavell, suspected it was actually a paraboloid – a shape that
resembled a large dish turned on its side.

Wavell, who'd previously worked for an air survey company
in Brazil, had a reputation for brilliance. But what he needed
was a low-level oblique photograph of the mystery pinprick,
so revealing it in far greater detail. A day or so later, Tony Hill,
a flight commander and a veteran recce pilot, was sent out to
see if he could secure one. Skimming along at 300 mph and
at no more than fifty feet, he had to somehow fly at the same

level and to the right of the pinprick, firing off his photos as it passed beneath his wing.

That first mission failed. Undaunted, Hill returned the following day, taking one of the most iconic shots of the entire war. The image he captured revealed a clifftop manor house with a path leading from it to a bowl-like structure that pointed out to sea. Though the Würzburg apparatus was no more than ten feet in diameter, Hill had nevertheless found it and captured it on film.

At Medmenham a photo montage of the target was put together, along with a highly detailed scale model. On the night of 27 February 1942 Major John Frost led 150 paratroopers on a raid on the Bruneval station. Dropped just inland they took the small German garrison by surprise, and a British radar expert was able to begin dismantling the key components of the Würzburg bowl. While he was doing so German reinforcements arrived, but Frost and his men kept them at bay for long enough for the top-secret Würzburg radar circuitry to be snatched, along with a German radar technician as a bonus.

This allowed British scientists to study the Würzburg apparatus and establish just how it worked. Not only did this mean that they could decide whether they wanted to replicate the technology for use by the Allies, it also gave them a chance to develop the means to block and scramble the Würzburg signals. This would be key to winning what was known as the 'Radar War', most notably playing a vital role during the D-Day landings.

It was this kind of breakthrough that was needed now, to break the impasse over the Ipo Dam. Only here, a whole series of photographs was required. As the battle for the terrain around the dam became ever more grinding, bitter and murderous, the demands for pinpoint intelligence became ever more urgent. Yamashita had committed the 80,000 men of his Shimbu – *martial spirit* – force to defend the dam. They were well dug-in among rugged high terrain, cut through with sheer cliffs, knife-cut gorges and plunging river valleys.

Krueger faced a gargantuan task if he was to seize this terrain in the timescale demanded by MacArthur. His advance was frustrated by rough ground and poor roads, and once again the Allies had badly underestimated the numbers and strength of the enemy. The Japanese troops had fortified the ridges with mortars, machine guns, anti-aircraft defences, anti-tank guns and 105 and 155mm howitzers. They also boasted 447mm rocket batteries, the warheads of which were charged with picric acid, more commonly known as 'Explosive D' or Dunnite – a highly combustible form of the chemical.

Their ridge-top defences were honeycombed with caves. Some had dozens of well-defended entrances. The American forces had one significant advantage: a relatively new invention called napalm – gasoline thickened with soap. Low-flying aircraft attempted to lob fiery napalm bombs directly into cave entrances, in an effort to burn the Japanese soldiers out. But it still took boots on the ground to clear and to seal off the caves. Flamethrowers and bazookas were employed to blast and scour the entrances, after which they were dynamited shut.

Such horrific close-quarter action was a painstaking process, and MacArthur warned General Krueger that time was running out. The water shortage in Manila was acute. 'Cutting daily consumption in Manila,' he informed Krueger, urging him to greater efforts. 'Outbreak of disease of real magnitude might well prove great military disaster . . . Capture of Ipo Dam would provide definitive solution.'

A total of 250,000 gallons of napalm had been dropped on Japanese positions around the Ipo Dam, the largest amount used anywhere in the southwest Pacific up to this point. And yet still the enemy held out. After months of sustained combat, Krueger's forces were overstretched, demoralized and exhausted. Early rains turned the few existing roads into quagmires. Daily advances were less than a thousand yards, and it took twenty hours to carry wounded from the front line to the nearest medical stations.

Canine warriors were also seeing action in the battle for the dams – with war dogs being sent forward to scout enemy positions and help clear the caves. And in Lingayen, the 26th's own diminutive K9 was about to prove how she, too, could make a major contribution to ensure victory.

Several attempts had already been made by the fliers of the 26th to capture those elusive low-level oblique shots of the terrain around the Ipo Dam – ones which would enable Allied air-power to identify and blast apart the enemy's hidden defences. But those heroic efforts had ended in tragic failure.

On the morning of 19 February 1945, Lieutenant Karl M. Booth had set out to capture the Ipo Dam on film. A veteran flier, Booth had been with the 26th almost since the day of its foundation. But on this day his Lightning had failed to return to the squadron's Lingayen airbase. Typically, the new CO, Captain Gathers, took to the skies to search for him, but he had no luck. Booth joined the unit's ever growing list of MIAs.

'Two days later,' the squadron recorded, 'Lieutenant Madison E. Gillespey was reported missing in action while attempting the same minimum altitude mission in the same area.' The balding Gillespey, who always seemed a little more mature than his comrades, was another major loss for the 26th. But despite two deaths in as many days, further volunteers stepped forward to attempt the Ipo Dam reconnaissance mission, one that truly was dicing with death. It was at this vital juncture that Smoky was called upon to save the squadron's air operations from serious disruption, or worse.

If for any reason the Lingayen airbase were to be deprived of the ability to send and receive messages, it would be rendered next to useless. The squadron relied upon its ability to communicate with headquarters units almost-instantly, something usually achieved by teleprinter, a very early form of typed communication similar to texting.

The teleprinter was an electromechanical typewriter that enabled short messages, pages of text or even basic black-and-white images to be transmitted via phone lines or radio signal. Teleprinters represented the squadron's quickest means of disseminating the intelligence they had gleaned from flights. A light aircraft could then follow this up, shuttling the photographs themselves into the hands of the key commanders. The nerve centre of operations at Lingayen was the communications suite, which consisted of a radio station, switchboard and a room packed with ranks of teleprinters.

Because they were invariably handling sensitive information, nearly all of the squadron's messages were sent in code. Cryptographers worked side by side with teleprinter mechanics/ typists, radio technicians and switchboard operators. Messages coming in from pilots had to be decoded, and assessed for their significance, before a newly encoded message was sent on to headquarters. The communications centre also raised the alarm if an air raid was expected. It was a highly complex and fraught operation, and keeping it running smoothly was no mean feat.

Sergeant Bob Gapp was one of the main people in charge. He worked at the switchboard, but also had responsibility for stringing the teleprinter wires from the communications centre to all relevant departments. Gapp, thickset and athletic, was accustomed to shinning up telegraph poles and palm trunks to make sure that the messages kept flowing. The signals sergeant had joined the 26th on 14 July 1943, and he'd faced all kinds of challenges since then, but the problem he'd just discovered had foxed even him. That was why he had come looking for Smoky.

By now the men of the 26th had moved into their tented accommodation. Some had even started to build their own native-style nipa palm huts-on-stilts, so taken were they with the breezy local style of living. Gapp sought out Bill Wynne and Smoky, and Wynne could tell straight away that the signals sergeant was worried. A real man's man, Gapp shifted about uneasily and hemmed and hawed a little, before giving voice to what was on his mind.

'Say, Bill, we have a problem down at the airstrip,' he began. The enemy onslaught had taken a heavy toll on the airbase's communications systems, Gapp explained. He needed to run a telephone line through a culvert – an underground drainage channel – to enable him to establish direct communications with three separate squadrons, something that was vital to the continuance of rapid and effective air operations. The problem was that the culvert lay directly under one of the airstrip's main taxiways. He couldn't string the wires across on poles for obvious reasons – aircraft zipping about would very likely blunder into them.

The only way to lay the cable manually was to dig up the culvert, which meant removing the steel matting that had been laid to form the taxiway, excavating a channel beneath, inserting the wire, then reversing the entire process. That would involve several days, during all of which time the dozens of men and the machines involved would be working in the open and at the mercy of enemy air attacks. It would also seriously hamper air operations, putting part of the airbase out of action for days at a crucial period.

The culvert ran for seventy feet below the taxiway, Gapp explained. Now he reached the delicate part. He'd once seen a news report about a similar challenge they'd faced in Alaska. Those involved had tied a length of string to a cat's collar, placed him in the pipe and then proceeded to frighten him through with bursts of compressed air from behind. The string could then be used to drag the line through. Not exactly the kindest way of doing things, but it had proved mightily effective.

The taxiway enabled the squadron's own P-38s, plus P-51 Mustangs and P-61 Black Widow night-fighters to get airborne, all of which were in very high demand at this time. It would take at least three days and cause untold disruption if a body of men were to lay the cable by digging up the culvert; Smoky might be able to perform the task in a matter of minutes.

Gapp glanced from Smoky to Wynne, his embarrassment plain to see. 'Seems to me Smoky is a very smart dog and, you know, maybe we could coax her through,' he ventured.

'Can you see daylight through the pipe?' Wynne asked.

'Yeah, but only in the upper part.' The rest was clogged with silt, sand and other debris.

Wynne explained that he was willing to consider it on one condition. If Smoky got stuck halfway, Gapp's men would dig down from directly above her, excavating a hole through which the little dog could be plucked to safety. Gapp readily agreed. Right now, he had few other options.

They hopped into Gapp's weapons carrier – a three-and-a-half tonne Dodge light truck – and raced for the airstrip. En route, Gapp suggested they might try a similar technique to one the guys had employed with the moggie in Alaska. He'd clearly thought about this long and hard. They'd tie an extremely lightweight string to Smoky's collar. Should it snag on anything inside the culvert it would sever itself, allowing her to break free and escape.

Wynne figured he needed to see the culvert for himself, before he could green light any such a plan. They reached the location at the same time as a number of P-38s were getting their engines revved up and tested by the squadron's mechanics. As with just about everything they did at the 26th, aircraft maintenance was a round-the-clock business. Wynne winced at the thunderous roar of the Allison V12 engines. They'd need to choose a quiet moment if they were to coax Smoky through the culvert, that was for sure.

Wynne crouched down at the entrance to the passageway. There were three drainage pipes, set side by side, each about eight inches across and boxed in with wooden shuttering. Each consisted of a length of galvanized steel tubing about five feet long, the individual sections of which were pushed into the next to form a series of rough overlapping joints. At those junctures sand and debris had worked their way into the pipes, forming a series of ridges that stretched for the entire length of the culvert.

Shining his flashlight along the central of the three pipes, Wynne decided it was the least obstructed. As best he could tell, the regular sandy ridges left some three to four inches of free space, providing just enough room for Smoky to squeeze through. With his flashlight extinguished, he could actually see a dim glow of light filtering in from the far side. By contrast, the two flanking culverts showed little if any illumination bleeding through from the distant end of the tunnel.

Just then a P-51 Mustang – a fighter aircraft that was fresh into theatre – taxied over the steel matting that ran above the culvert. The noise was deafening. It sounded as if a thousand dragon's teeth were being scraped over a tank's armoured hull, the noise reverberating horribly down the galvanized steel channels.

One thing was for certain: all traffic would have to cease while Smoky ran the gauntlet of the tunnel. The little dog was still shaking from the effects of her close encounter with a P-51, and if an aircraft passed right overhead while she was in the depths of the pipe, the sound would be magnified many times over.

'We'll wait until it quietens down,' Gapp suggested, stating the obvious.

'For sure,' Wynne replied. He eyed the signals sergeant for a long second, searchingly. 'You promise you'll dig her out, if we need to.'

'Absolutely.'

'Okay, here's what we'll do. Bob, you'll have Smoky here, at this central opening. I'll be over on the far side. When we're ready, I'll call her through the pipe.'

Wynne reckoned it was the sound of her master's voice that was most likely to get Smoky through the task that lay ahead of her – just in the same way that messenger dogs would carry a signal across a thousand yards of the battlefield, so as to reach their handler waiting on the far side.

Sergeant Gapp's right-hand-man, Sergeant Casalino, another expert cable-layer, was also on hand. He began to pay out the lightweight string across the taxiway, making sure it was long enough to see Smoky the entire way across. That done, the cord was wound back onto its spool and one end was tied securely to Smoky's leather-belt collar.

Wynne settled his dog as best he could by the open end of the culvert. The entrance to the central pipe loomed before her, an empty circle of black shadow as high as her head. Smoky crouched in the bright sunlight, gazing up at Wynne, questioningly. Nobody had the faintest idea what might actually be lurking inside the dark recesses of that pipe. It was daunting.

But finally Wynne could delay no longer. Gapp had got the revving of the P-38s, engines under control and the taxiway was cleared of all traffic. It was time for Wynne to dash across to the far side; time to see how strong the bond between man and dog really was. Over the last few months Smoky had met every challenge that he'd thrown in front of her, proving that inside her tiny frame beat a heart bigger than anyone could ever have imagined – but now she was going to be put to the test as never before.

'All set?' Wynne cried, once he'd reached the far side.

'Yeah! She's ready!' Gapp yelled back. 'Good to go!'

Wynne got his face down as close to the exit of the pipe as possible, worming onto his belly as if he was about to try to squeeze through himself. 'Come, Smoky, come!' he cried.

Peering inside he could just make out a tiny little head silhouetted against the distant light. 'Come, Smoky, come!' he yelled again.

He saw her hesitate for a few seconds at the tunnel entrance, as Gapp tried to coax her inside. Wynne repeated his exhortations, and finally the tiny little dog began to inch her way into the dark pool of shadow. The pipes acted as a drainage system for a small creek, which ran alongside the airstrip. The men just had to hope that no giant centipedes, no scorpions or venomous snakes had chosen to make it their home.

'Is she coming?' Wynne yelled into the enclosed space.

'Yeah!' Gapp's voice drifted back to him, sounding strangely muted and muffled. 'I'm feeding the line!'

The seconds ticked by. Was there the sound of a distant scrabbling, as a tiny dog fought her way across, scrambling over sandbanks and wriggling through the gaps? Everyone thought so. But all of a sudden the spool of string stopped unwinding. Gapp tried feeding Smoky some more line, but she wasn't dragging it forward any more.

He gazed into the pipe. He could see a tiny little face turned back towards him, the expression on Smoky's features seeming to say: *what's holding us up here?*

'*She's caught!* She's snagged on something!'

'Smoky! Stand, stay!' Wynne yelled in response.

If the line truly was trapped somewhere, the last thing he wanted was Smoky to keep struggling forward, straining at her bonds. He peered into the depths of the shadows, desperate for a sign of his dog, but the entire expanse of air inside the pipe seemed clogged with a shifting miasma of fine, drifting dirt. Struggling to free herself, Smoky's tiny, scrabbling paws had kicked up a dust storm.

She was nowhere to be seen.

CHAPTER 20

Again and again Wynne called to Smoky. He cried out words of reassurance. He hoped that his voice would carry across to her even though he couldn't see her any more. He just had to trust that his little dog, ensnared by the cord in the depths of the tunnel and blinded by thick dust, would trust him enough to stay calm and focused and to find a way through.

At the far end of the culvert Sergeant Gapp wiggled and jiggled the line, trying desperately to loosen it.

Finally, Wynne heard the burly sergeant's voice drifting through to him. 'Okay! Okay! She's free!'

His heart leapt. 'Come, Smoky, come!' he urged her. 'Come on, baby, you can do this!'

His eyes strained to cut through the gloom, yet he still couldn't make out a damn thing. He had no idea if she was heading his way, or if she had turned back to Gapp and his companion.

'Is she still moving?' Wynne yelled. 'My way?'

'Yeah!' Gapp's voice echoed back. 'I'm still feeding out the line . . .'

'Come on, baby, you can do it!' Wynne repeated, breathlessly. With all the tension the sweat was dripping down his neck and shoulders. 'Come on! Come on!'

He gazed into the murky depths of the pipe. He figured he caught a blur of movement. Sure enough, a pair of shining amber eyes seemed to dance among the gloom, piercing the haze. Smoky was about fifteen feet away from him, her forepaws scrabbling at the floor of the pipe as she struggled to drag her dust-enshrouded form through, tugging the line after.

'Atta girl! Atta girl!' Wynne yelled in relief. 'She's coming! She's almost here!'

Spurred on by the sound of his voice and the sight of his features, Smoky broke into a run. She bounded down the final sections of the pipe, her hair sticking out in dusty tufts in all directions as she vaulted over the last of the sandy barriers. Moments later, she'd leapt into Bill Wynne's outstretched arms in a puff of sand.

Wynne stood up so that Gapp could see that the little hero of a dog had made it through. The signals sergeant broke into a wild laugh. Cheers rang out across the taxiway. Gapp dashed across to join them. He reached down, grabbed the line and dragged several more feet through, before cutting Smoky, the valiant cord-puller, free.

'Boy-oh-boy,' he declared, breathlessly, his voice thick with relief. He gestured at the thin line gripped in his hand, then at the dog cradled in Wynne's arms. 'She deserves a great big steak! I'll get the mess hall to sort it!'

Somehow, Smoky knew she had accomplished something truly special. She responded to all the smiles and the praise in typical fashion. With her entire back end waggling back and forth excitedly, she kept boxing Wynne's ankles with her forepaws, her eyes shining up at him as if to say: 'Look what I've done! Look what I've done!'

Under the War Dog Programme, big, powerful hounds had been trained as line-laying dogs. They were taught to follow a strict route while a reel attached to their hindquarters played out the cable behind them. Of course, Smoky had had no such specialist instruction. All she'd benefited from was the training that she and Wynne had managed to squeeze in between the relentless photo-lab shifts, air-sea rescue sorties, enemy bombing raids and kamikaze attacks.

She had executed the cable-laying mission almost without a hitch – testament to the extraordinary bonds forged between man and dog. While sergeants Gapp and Casalino worked at the culvert – attaching a thicker cord to the line before pulling that through, and eventually getting three thick communication cables run through the pipe – word of Smoky's heroic endeavours spread throughout the camp.

A big steak for a seven-inch-tall dog was about the size of a small burger. In short order it was served up for the 26th's heroic little mascot. In fact, Smoky was no longer just the squadron's mascot any more. After the cable-laying mission – which had saved as many as two hundred and fifty servicemen and forty aircraft from being targeted by enemy warplanes – in the minds of the men she had graduated to the role of Squadron War Dog.

With Smoky's coming of age, the 26th could forge ahead with the task at hand – capturing the Ipo Dam on film. It was late February by the time the recce mission fliers were finally able to bring back the first precious rolls of film shot at low level over the target area. As soon as the planes touched down the photo lab team rushed the negatives through the development process. Now was the moment of truth: had those daring 'dicing' sorties captured what MacArthur and Krueger so hungered to see?

The images had been filmed at such low altitude that entire frames were filled with precipitous mountainsides, thick jungle and clearly defined ridgelines. So detailed were those images that individual footpaths could be traced through the trees, like white scars twisting this way and that and cutting through the thick shadows. Individual soldiers could be seen moving on those tracks; even small animals. The images were perfect for identifying the enemy's hidden defences, so they could be hit by airstrikes and ground assaults.

'A number of requests for low obliques were completed,' the squadron's war diary recorded, stressing 'the dangerously low altitude and difficult terrain over which these missions were flown'. This was something of an understatement. In fact, from 14-21 February the squadron completed a staggering 246 photo recce sorties. Not only that, but as much as seventy-five per cent of the photos secured were judged as being of 'excellent' quality.

Some 4,800 negatives were developed, from which 44,000 prints were made. Not all were low-level obliques, of course, but so overworked were the laboratory staff that power plants and driers suffered repeated breakdowns. The squadron's technicians and mechanics were forced to work miracles in order to get the machinery up and running again. That February the 26th received a special Letter of Commendation, praising the squadron for its incredible achievements.

The photo lab came in for special mention. 'I wish to commend the officers and enlisted men responsible for the operation of the photographic laboratory,' the Letter announced. 'The commendable performance of all who made this outstanding accomplishment possible has contributed much to the success of the Philippines Campaign and reflects great credit on your organization as a whole.' Among all those who had made this possible there was, of course, one small but very heroic dog of war.

It wasn't simply those operating on the front lines of war who were dicing with death. The sheer, simple mortality of all – from the lowliest trooper to the senior commanders – was about to be brought home most powerfully to all in Lingayen. At the end of the second week of April 1945 a notice was posted on the squadron's bulletin board, one that was as unexpected as it was shocking. The President of the United States, Franklin D. Roosevelt, had passed away.

Months previously, most of the GIs – Bill Wynne included – had sent in absentee ballots, to re-elect Roosevelt for an unprecedented fourth term, which had begun that March 1945. But Roosevelt had long suffered from a paralytic illness, and his health had been declining throughout the war: upon reflection, his death from a massive haemorrhage struck many as being tragic but inevitable. March was also the month of Wynne's twenty-first birthday. His girlfriend, Margie – since July 1943 also his fiancée – had written to him from the States, stressing how ill Roosevelt had seemed. He had steered the nation through the long years of war and brought it so close to the end. But here in the Philippines the fighting would have to go on without their revered Commander-in-Chief at the helm.

On the ground around the Ipo Dam troops were sent in for

the final push. Krueger and MacArthur's chief fear was that the Japanese would blow the dam to pieces before it could be captured, and every effort had to be made to prevent that from happening. On 13 May 1945, a small patrol of Filipino guerrillas reached the dam itself, under the cover of darkness. Unable to seize it, they were still able to report back vital news: the dam wall remained intact. It had been rigged with explosive charges, but General Yamashita was clearly holding on until the last moment before ordering its detonation.

P-38s and P-47 Thunderclaps – a fighter-bomber and ground attack aircraft – flew repeated sorties to hit the patch of terrain surrounding the dam that was still held by the enemy. They saturated a five-square-mile box with napalm, dropping down to one hundred feet and skipping the bombs onto their targets, leaving trails of fiery devastation in their wakes. Over 100,000 tonnes of napalm was unleashed in forty-eight hours, P-51 Mustangs following up to strafe those enemy troops trying to escape the carnage.

On 16 May ground troops moved in, using bamboo scaling-ladders to climb the fortified cliffs around the dam and root out the last of the Japanese defenders. The saturation bombing with napalm seemed to have done its task, burning most of the enemy out. The dam was taken, just as a party of Japanese soldiers prepared to detonate hundreds of pounds of TNT. They were shot dead even as they twisted the wires and raised the levers to trigger the explosives.

The remaining defenders launched a series of banzai suicide charges in a desperate attempt to re-take the dam and destroy it, but each was repulsed. By 21 May all organized Japanese resistance was over. The failure to destroy the dam was put down to a communication problem. General Yamashita had almost certainly issued the order, but the message had failed to make it through quickly enough for the men on the ground to act.

By the time the battle of the dams was won, Yamashita had lost almost half of his entire force in the area. The survivors were scattered and exhausted, plagued by disease and hunger. They were reported to be resorting to cannibalism in an effort to stay alive. Yet still there were few who chose to surrender. Japanese soldiers believed the longer they held out, the longer the military would have to ready their homeland to repulse the coming American invasion, which in turn would safeguard their families. In that belief they held on tenaciously, fought with suicidal ferocity, and died.

But American losses had also been severe. Few other campaigns had suffered such high casualty rates, which were exacerbated by the diseases and the hellish conditions in which the troops were forced to operate. Many of these units had been operating for three years of unbroken service. While MacArthur's return to the Philippines was a significant victory, it had been won at tremendous cost.

As with most units in theatre, the fliers of the 26th had lost comrades: five had been killed flying missions over the Philippines, but the squadron's work continued. By now, a US Army major had been assigned as permanent liaison to the 26th Photo Reconnaissance Squadron. He flew a light aircraft that shuttled fresh images directly to MacArthur's headquarters as soon as those photos were dry. He was immediately taken with Smoky, charmed by her role in the lab, and also by the tugs-of-war she had with the lab workers during their rare moments of downtime, in which a sock was still her favourite 'tug toy'.

The major fell into conversation with Bill Wynne. Naturally, the chat turned to dogs. Before the war he had loved to hunt waterfowl on Chesapeake Bay, a vast estuary lying on the east coast of the US. He'd been accompanied on those trips by his beloved Chesapeake Bay Retriever – a breed that looks similar to a Labrador, and which originated around the choppy waters of the estuary.

One day man and dog had sallied forth when the wind was high and the bay unusually rough. The dog had put to flight a flock of ducks and the major had brought one down with his shotgun. As the downed bird was carried away from shore on the waves, his dog went after it. He'd battled wind and surf, heading further and further away from shore. The major was forced to watch, horrified, as his powerful retriever slipped from view.

He'd waited for over an hour, but still there was no sign of the missing animal. Eventually, he'd had to turn for home, believing that he'd lost his dog to the chilly, storm-lashed waters. He lived several miles away, and he was saddened beyond words on the journey home. Several hours after his return he'd heard an odd noise outside his door. He'd opened it, only to find his Chesapeake Bay Retriever standing there wagging his tail, the duck held softly in his jaws.

The major's retriever had executed his courageous acts at sea and at a time of peace; Smoky's recent heroics had taken place underground and at a time of war. But both demonstrated a similar kind of canine dedication and endurance, not to mention the extraordinary bonds these dogs had formed with their masters. Plus for the major and Bill Wynne their love of dogs was the bridge: the passion they shared in common had enabled them to open up to each other.

By late May, there were only isolated pockets of enemy resistance remaining, and the pace of operations for the 26th began to abate somewhat. After supper each night, Wynne took to having a stroll with his dog, enjoying the balmy air of the evening. In the peace and quiet on the palm-fringed streets and on the pristine beaches, he found the time and space to reflect on all that had come to pass in this war.

With the Japanese having been driven out, local life was reverting to something like normal. Evening was such a peaceful, scenic time of day here. In the fields behind the beach, locals tended to their livestock, small boys riding atop hulking great water buffalo as they ploughed and tilled the ground. In the rice paddies, farmers knee-deep in water waved, acknowledging the presence of one of their liberators. In truth, of course, there were two: Smoky, too, had played her part.

As they strolled along the beautiful stretches of sand, with the tropical sun going down over the sea, Wynne took the opportunity to refresh some of Smoky's obedience training. There had been little chance to do so in recent months. Wherever she might have hailed from originally, Smoky seemed to be maturing. She'd stopped chasing after most fowl, as she'd liked to do in the jungle of New Guinea. A while back she'd dashed after a mother hen with chicks, but the bird had turned on her in a rage, stomping all over the little dog. She now gave all such flocks of feathered avengers a wide berth.

On another occasion Smoky had made a heedless dash across

a dirt road. She must have felt she had good excuse: she'd spotted a dog on the far side. What she hadn't seen was the GMC two-and-a-half tonne Army truck bowling along right in front of her. Fortunately, Wynne was alert to the danger. As Smoky had darted forward he'd yelled out: 'Stand! Stay!' The tiny dog froze in her tracks just as the GMC truck had thundered past, the massive wheels a bare six inches from the tip of her tiny nose.

That was just one of many times when the training had saved Smoky's life. As they strolled along the Lingayen Gulf sands, Wynne wondered whether there were other lives they might save via Smoky's training, right here and now. Many of the GIs serving on the front line had been fighting for years. Some had seen thirty-six months of brutal back-to-back combat, with precious little leave. The trauma levels were reaching gargantuan proportions, not to mention the numbers of sick and physically injured.

The needs for the kind of therapy that Smoky could deliver had to be acute, and he wondered how they might up the entertainment factor by expanding their repertoire of tricks. Costume had to be one way. The local women were skilled in needlework, and Wynne was impressed with their beauty and their dignified poise. He contacted one and asked her to embellish Smoky's coat of many colours, so as to make it fit for what he had in mind.

She embroidered onto it by hand: 'SMOKY – Champion Yank Mascot SWPA 1944.' SWPA stood for the southwest Pacific area of operations. The seamstress was inventive and she was able to add more to Smoky's 'circus' wardrobe. She fashioned a pair of clown suits, one in bright yellow and one in verdant green, using salvaged pieces of parachute silk. The zips, designed as they were for fully-grown males, were enormous in comparison to Smoky's size, but they were all that came to hand. As a final flourish the seamstress embroidered a bar of music and assorted notes onto the suits, lending them a suitably theatrical air.

Next Wynne sought out a local man who could build Smoky a slide. He found a Filipino carpenter who spoke good English, which meant he could explain exactly what he wanted. The slide should be six inches wide, to accommodate his diminutive dog, and be a good eight feet long, with a graceful arch in the middle, so she'd accelerate quickly but slow at the end as the slide levelled off. It also needed a ladder for her to climb, plus a platform for her to sit on before launching herself into motion.

He asked how much it would cost. The carpenter grinned, a little self-consciously. He didn't want money, he explained. Instead, he wanted a camera. In the war-torn Philippines cameras were like gold dust. Luckily, Wynne happened to possess a simple box camera which came with a primitive, plug in flash unit. He showed it to the carpenter, who seemed more than happy with the trade.

Three days later he presented Wynne with the slide. It was an astonishing piece of work, expertly crafted from glistening Filipino mahogany, a rich tropical hardwood. Kitting Smoky out in such a way and with such equipment served another purpose, too. It helped inject some liquidity into the economy, which had imploded under the long years of Japanese occupation.

Indeed, the local Filipinos were working everywhere that the US troops could find them gainful employment. Large workgroups had been organized to load and unload cases of food and other supplies, to sweep the bases clean and to launder uniforms. The local men, often skilled craftsmen, were employed wherever possible as carpenters and painters. The villagers traded chickens, fruit and other fresh food with the GIs.

War had thrown together these two very different populations – Filipino villagers and US troops. In Lingayen, as in much of the Philippines, they had become close neighbours and sometime work colleagues. The relationship seemed to work well on both side. Friendships had been forged, and after the dark predations of the years of Japanese occupation, it felt good.

After their evening stroll on the beaches man and dog would make their way back to their accommodation tent. They had new room-mates here in Lingayen. Alan Kuzmicki was a camera repair technician and a former lecturer in art at the University of Georgia (in the southeastern USA). John Barnard was a fellow photo-lab technician and a former art student from sunny California. Of course, Barnard was also an old Smoky hand: he'd held one side of the landing-blanket, during Smoky's parachute training back at Nadzab. Jack Tankersley, a native of Oklahoma, was another lab technician, and the seasoned sailor who'd helped steer their drop-tank catamaran on its near-fateful voyage. Last was John Graham, a Michigan native and the squadron's mail clerk.

One of their first tasks had been to dig a bomb shelter in the soft sand adjacent to their tent. It had to be large enough to accommodate five men and one dog, and sturdy enough to survive a near-hit from a Japanese 551-pound bomb. It was roofed over with thick coconut palm trunks and covered by a layer of nipa palm leaves, which supported the twelve inches of sand they piled on top. When finished, it was solid and substantial, and it had become a decidedly popular hangout during the air raids.

One evening Wynne and his buddies had been busy writing letters home, when the comparative peace was torn apart by the wail of the air-raid siren. Grabbing Smoky, Wynne and the others had dashed for the shelter. It was pitch dark beneath the coconut-log roof, and the five were all but bowled over when a sixth companion dived in to join them.

Once they'd lit some candles, the newcomer was instantly recognizable. It was Norman Smith, the man who'd been wounded aboard LST-706 during the kamikaze strikes as they steamed north to Lingayen Gulf. Smith had long poo-pooed taking cover during air raids. He'd argued that if a bullet had your number on it, then there was little you could do about it. But it seemed he'd changed his mind. As the enemy warplanes rained down bombs on the Lingayen airstrip, Smith had become a foremost believer in the virtues of such sturdily-built shelters.

When not under attack, one of the alternatives to an evening's letter-writing was a quick burst of Radio Tokyo. The various Tokyo Roses were still cranking out their propaganda, but in light of recent Allied victories it was sounding increasingly desperate. The men tuned in more to see how the enemy was trying to spin things, as the fortunes of the war turned against the Japanese.

The squadron's monthly Intelligence Summary (No. 12) reflected this. 'Entertainment emanating from Radio Tokyo has a new significance. Curious individuals tune in on the enemy version of current requests for amusement ... They are curious to hear what pretext ... the Japanese Government has to offer for its latest defeats.' Despite Radio Tokyo's best attempts to paint losses somehow as victories, their efforts proved hollow. 'The morale has been very good during the period covered by this report.'

The Lingayen movie theatre was making a great contribution to squadron morale. Built by the GIs working in tandem with locals, and made mostly from bamboo, it was managing a thrice-weekly showing, something that had been impossible back on war-torn New Guinea, due to the challenges of getting movies flown in. Not only that, but it was able to screen newsreel reports showcasing the progress the Allies were making in all theatres of the war.

As a bonus for Smoky, movie nights were when the squadron's war dog was on ultimate downtime. Wynne allowed anyone who wanted to pet and to play with his dog. She was excellent company and she loved the attention. But he wouldn't allow anyone to try out any of her tricks. As far as he was concerned the trainer–trainee relationship they had formed was sacrosanct. Wynne and Smoky were a close-knit, unbeatable team, and he couldn't allow any confusion or uncertainty to get in the way of that.

At around this time – May 1945 – a large rat began interrupting the movie nights. It took to scaling a coconut tree and climbing out along a phone wire that ran above the outdoor screen. It was bizarre – almost as if the rat sought a ringside seat. The wire lay between projector and movie screen, and once the rat was halfway across he would be silhouetted by the flickering light. Generally, he'd stop there, his tail flicking back and forth as he eyed the scenes, before trotting across to the far side, and then coming back a little later for a repeat performance.

One of the squadron's more talented artists sketched an evocative black-and-white cartoon of Ratty on the move. 'Each show night the rat would walk the wire ... about fifteen minutes after the show started,' the squadron captioned the sketch, in a moment of rare levity. 'Then, just before the show ended he would travel back. No one knows whether he was going to see his girlfriend or to get a better view of the show.'

One night a GI scaled the rat's coconut tree and got a hand on the wire. When Ratty was in position he pulled the wire down like a bowstring and let rip. Ratty flew into the air, his shadow shooting across the movie screen, before disappearing from view with a thud. Needless to say, the audience were in hysterics. Ratty clearly didn't appreciate the joke. He never put in an appearance after that.

Spirits were high in the squadron, but in a sense this was the calm before the coming storm. The Philippines had been taken, and MacArthur was turning his attention to the next steps in the march towards Japan. The 26th was about to be called upon to reach further than it had ever done before, flying reconnaissance missions over distant China, where the Japanese military had some of their last major foreign bases. If those could be captured, or at least rendered unusable, the passage to the Japanese homeland lay open to the Allies.

Yet as all were painfully aware, the entire Japanese nation had vowed to fight to the last in the defence of their emperor. Preparations were underway for a devastating final stand. Alongside the thousands of Nakajima *Tsurungi* – sabre – kamikaze aircraft and pilots that had been readied, the Japanese military had developed the *Kaiten* – 'return to heaven' – a fast kamikaze submarine-torpedo fitted with a 1,550-kg warhead. But perhaps most worrying was the development of the Yokosuka MXY-7 *Ohka* – 'cherry blossom' – a kamikaze rocket-bomb.

The *Ohka* was similar in appearance to a V1 doodlebug, but with a pilot's cockpit set amidships. Designed to be carried slung beneath a bomber, the *Ohka* was released when still miles distant from its target. From there it would glide until close enough for the pilot to trigger its solid propellant rocket motors, by which time it would be all but unstoppable. Under full thrust the *Ohka* was capable of speeds in excess of 650 mph, which meant that no aircraft the Allies possessed could come close to catching it, and it packed a devastating 1,200-kg warhead.

Between the Philippines and Japan lay the coastal islands and landmass of China. Japanese bases there would have to be identified and photographed by the high-level recce fliers, before they could be mapped and finally neutralized. Once that was accomplished, an invasion fleet could sail for Japan. The massed warships and landing craft would hit the western fringes of the Japanese homeland first, including the islands of Iwo Jima and Okinawa, with the 26th doubtless riding in the vanguard.

The Japanese had vowed to rain down kamikazes upon the Allied invasion forces, from land, sea and air. It was a daunting proposition, and the fear of what was coming loomed large. To die in what had to be the last months of the war would be the ultimate, and some might argue a senseless, sacrifice.

No one was immune to death, and as all knew, the kamikazes – thousands of them – lay in wait.

CHAPTER 21

In the first weeks of May rumour and counter-rumour swirled around the Lingayen base concerning the squadron's forthcoming move and the grim prospect of the action to come. Victory in Europe was already secured. VE Day – 8 May 1945 – had marked the moment Nazi Germany formally surrendered to the Allies. But it had proved a bittersweet experience for those serving at Lingayen, who knew plenty more fighting must lie ahead.

On 17 May an Army propaganda film was shown in the Lingayen movie theatre, entitled 'Two Down and One To Go'. It talked about how Hitler's Nazi Germany and Mussolini's Fascist Italy had been defeated, which left Japan the only remaining Axis power. Yet if the battle for the Philippines had been defined by savagery, this would surely pale into insignificance when compared with the bloody struggle that taking the Japanese homeland would involve.

At one point there was talk of how a thousand die-hard and suicidal Japanese soldiers had infiltrated the Lingayen area, filtering down from the mountains disguised as Filipino civilians. The rumour had reached the squadron by means of the 'grapevine method', according to the monthly Intelligence Summaries, which suggested that the idea was both 'absurd and impracticable'. There were precious few Japanese troops remaining in the Philippines, let alone many with the ammunition, weaponry, energy or the will to fight.

Indeed, the Japanese military had drawn back its claws, rallying all who were able to the defence of the Empire of the Rising Sun. In response, MacArthur would need to further extend his grasp, and at the vanguard of that effort would be the pilots of the 26th.

From the Lingayen airstrip a pair of P-38s took to the skies. At the controls of one sat Lieutenant Oliver, and in the cockpit of the other was Captain Gathers, the squadron's commanding officer. Their target lay over 800 miles away, on Hainan Island, which was situated on the southern coast of China. Practically the entire flight would be executed over the open expanse of the South China Sea.

Taking off at 0840 Philippines time, the 1,600-mile round trip would last seven hours in total. Their destination was the port of Sanya, on the southern tip of Hainan. In 1941 the Japanese military had seized the area and changed its name to Samah. The port had become the base of the Second Fleet of the Imperial Japanese Navy, and it was from there that they had orchestrated the invasion of Malaya (present-day Malaysia), Thailand, and subsequently Burma (Myanmar) and Singapore.

Between 1140 and 1225 the two pilots fired off 165 photos, tearing through the skies above Sanya harbour at 26,000 feet. This was one of the first ever recce flights executed over China, and Gathers summed it up with typical taut understatement in his Final Mission Report: 'SUCCESSFUL'. The squadron would go on to complete dozens more missions over China, capturing on film those enemy bases that might menace MacArthur's coming thrust towards Japan. Indeed, as much as eighty per cent of all wartime intelligence regarding China was secured from such flights.

These daring sorties were executed at enormous risk to those flying them. The Japanese nation was like a cornered rat, and those probing recce flights met with ferocious resistance. The Final Mission Report of Lieutenants Cahall and Brown, who flew over Chinese territory just days after Oliver and Gathers, was somewhat more forthcoming. It recorded how they had experienced 'Intense, heavy, accurate to inaccurate ack-ack . . . at 25,000 feet.'

That anti-aircraft fire was now reaching as high as 25,000 feet provided a stark warning that even sticking to altitude was no longer any guarantee of safety. The China sorties spurred a new rumour – that the 26th was poised to deploy to China, which at least should save them from the hell of the coming invasion of Japan. But the loss of another of the 26th's pilots – Lieutenant Clarence E. Cook – reminded all of the ever-present dangers of the war, no matter where it might be fought.

The loss of that young but talented flier – Cook had only just won his commission – drove home the sense of impending danger. The savagery involved in the battle for the remote island of Iwo Jima reinforced this impression. Iwo Jima is positioned between the Philippines and the main Japanese landmass. Lying some 750 miles south of Tokyo, it is part of Japan itself. The island was an obvious stepping stone for MacArthur, and it was heavily garrisoned by Japanese troops.

The taking of Iwo Jima had come at great cost. Despite enjoying complete air superiority, the total American casualties had exceeded those of the enemy. The island's defenders had fought as the Japanese Emperor had pledged they would – with suicidal ferocity and very nearly until the last man. Of the 21,000 enemy troops garrisoning the island, only 216 were taken prisoner, and many of those only because they had been knocked unconscious by explosions, or otherwise incapacitated.

Injured GIs had been brought back to hospitals in the Philippines in their thousands. Manila was overflowing with wounded, and where there were traumatized and injured soldiers, Bill Wynne felt certain that he and Smoky might well be called to serve. Despite the febrile atmosphere at their Lingayen base, or perhaps even because of it, this was something that he was determined to prepare for.

The Lingayen movie house doubled as a theatre – it came complete with conical-shaped stage lights crafted out of old tin, plus a bamboo stage. But Wynne craved a better, more controlled and private environment in which he and Smoky could rehearse and train. There was another incentive, as well, to do so: by intensifying the obedience training, Wynne hoped to hone Smoky's discipline so as to better the chances of keeping her safe for the remaining months of the war.

The answer was to find a bespoke training house, and Wynne set about doing so. He asked First Sergeant Joyce Howell, the hard-charging Texan cowhand who was prone to wearing cowboy boots around camp, if he could requisition a nipa palm hut solely for the purposes of training. Howell was one of Smoky's many devoted fans in the unit, so was delighted to help.

He selected a hut, clambered up the ladder, took a perfunctory look inside and told Wynne to go right ahead.

'It's all yours,' he enthused. The squadron's supplies were at Wynne and Smoky's disposal, Howell added. 'And if you need anything else, y'all just give a holler.'

Next, Wynne solicited the help of the photo lab chief, Irv Green, to convert the stilted hut into a bespoke training facility. Green secured a load of plywood lumber with which to plank-over the rickety bamboo floor. When bent into shape, discarded cardboard boxes that had once held photo paper made for excellent hurdles. Henry Wickham, the squadron's painter, decorated them with the 26th's iconic insignia – Donald Duck riding on his cloud, camera at the ready.

The plywood flooring was sturdy and smooth, and it made a great surface upon which to mount Smoky's show kit – her mahogany slide, her tightrope walk, her rolling drum, as well as a tiny little scooter that Wynne had had made for her. In their designer training house, Wynne and Smoky began to polish their skills. He even taught Smoky to leap through a bamboo hoop that he'd scavenged from an old fishing net.

Smoky was such a fast learner that Wynne figured maybe they could develop an act where the little dog actually spelled out her name. He'd never seen it done before, but he reckoned she was smart enough to grasp what he intended. He grabbed some old photo-paper boxes and cut five letters, each fourteen inches high, which together spelled 'S-M-O-K-Y'. Braced with strips of cardboard set at right angles to the backs, the letters were self-standing.

With the letters lined up on the floor, Wynne carried Smoky

over to the start, tracing the 'S' with her head repeatedly and each time pronouncing a firm and clear 'S' out loud. The following day he repeated the process with the 'M', then together they revised the first two letters. Over the next few days they completed the final three. With the 'O' he even put Smoky's little head inside the circle of the letter each time, to better impress it upon her memory.

Finally, he figured they were ready to give it a whirl. He started with the letters in their proper order, and with Smoky sitting in front of them. 'Smoky, spell your name,' he announced. She didn't so much as budge. He tried calling out the letters in order – 'S-M-O-K-Y'. Still she seemed none the wiser. He tried mixing the letters up, to see if that would trigger her interest. Still, she barely moved a muscle when he told her to spell her name.

He tried standing behind the letters, so he was facing her, to coax her into action. No joy. He tried starting early in the morning, before the heat began to build. It made no noticeable difference. He tried rainy days, which made for ideal training days – for the air was cool and most often the recce flights were grounded. Still she didn't get it. After two months of trying to master the 'spell your name' trick, Wynne gave up. For some reason it just hadn't clicked with Smoky at all.

On one level Wynne was surprised. She was normally so clever and quick, not to mention eager to learn and to please. But this time it was as if she just hadn't engaged. Almost as if she just didn't care whether she got it or not, or won any praise as a result. Almost as if she was jaded from all the training that had gone before and didn't very much give a damn. Smoky seemed to know something about the spelling trick that Wynne didn't, but as matters transpired there was no time to winkle that out right now.

A new and frightening disease swept through Lingayen. It was to be the animals who were the foremost victims of the deadly but mysterious plague. Chickens were the first to be hit. From out of the blue they began to keel over in their droves. One moment they were fine, the next they dropped dead. And just as the troops were trying to work out what the killer illness might be, it began to assail the canine population too.

As soon as Wynne got word about the mystery plague he put Smoky into isolation. Within days at least thirty dogs in the area had been wiped out. The squadron's fortunate survivors – Smoky, Topper, Duke, plus an Irish Setter freshly arrived with the men, and a little, sickly puppy adopted by a soldier called Zeitlin – were some of the few left alive. Still the mystery illness lurked and festered.

One night Wynne spotted some highly unusual goings-on. He was working the graveyard shift at the photo lab when he noticed a group of shadowy figures about fifty feet away, gathered beneath some palm trees. They appeared to be digging a hole. It was 0300 hours, a very odd time to be excavating anything. He went to investigate. To his dismay he found that his buddy, Frank Petrilak, and some others had formed a burial party for a fresh canine victim, and this time it was to be one of the squadron's own.

On the sand lay the body of Smoky's six-month-old puppy, Topper. Topper had inherited his mother's spirit, with bright eyes and perky, pricked-up ears. He'd already grown as big as her, and he'd been blessed with a beautiful black-and-tan coat of shortish, rufty-tufty hair. He'd braved six months of war. Losing him to the killer plague was heartbreaking. It was clear that no dog was safe from the scourge.

Wynne became even more protective over Smoky. Heaven forbid that he lost her now, in the final act of the war. Amid the mounting tension of the coming invasion of Japan, and with sickness ravaging the camp's animal inhabitants, there were to be other challenges, too. Chief among them was the fate of Colonel Turbo, the notorious macaque. Maybe it was due to all the cumulative stress and strain, or perhaps Turbo himself was growing shell-shocked after the years at war – but either way he truly overstepped the mark, when he turned on and badly mauled his keeper.

There were various species of macaque native to the Philippines, but Turbo possessed few survival skills and he had no experience of living in the wild; he could not simply be set free. And yet at the same time he'd become a real liability around camp. So it was that a firing squad was formed, and Colonel Turbo was read his service record, his final orders and his last rites. With that he was dispatched with a volley of rifle fire.

Eventually, the mystery disease that had ravaged the animal population of Lingayen faded away. In its aftermath a variety show featuring a mostly Filipino cast was planned, in an effort to lift the spirits of those serving at the base. The line-up of singing, dancing Filipino girls was to be one of the undoubted highlights, but so too was the moment that Bill Wynne and Smoky would step into the limelight.

At first Wynne had hesitated when asked if they would

perform. He was used to hospital audiences of a few dozen war-wounded – not the hundreds of boisterous GIs that were bound to attend a show such as this. He was no professional performer and he'd never had to face a mass audience before. But at the same time this was a perfect opportunity for him and Smoky to shine and to serve, and he didn't feel that he could say no.

He figured they needed to deliver an absolute showstopper, and for that he would need support. Henry Shacklette, one of the squadron's electricians, possessed a working Solovox – then a state-of-the-art electronic organ, incorporating a key-board, amplifier and speaker – and he was a talented musician. Together, they worked on a repertoire of tunes to which Wynne and Smoky might take to the stage. Come show night, having musical accompaniment should help settle their nerves.

They intended to walk onto the stage performing the 'through the legs' routine, to the tune of 'Pretty Baby', singer and pianist Tony Jackson's lively music hall classic. They'd switch to the dead dog act, with Shacklette playing Chopin's haunting Funeral March. Smoky would miraculously come alive and switch to hurdle-jumping next, accompanied by 'Oh Where Oh Where Has My Little Dog Gone', the popular nursery rhyme.

'Beer Barrel Polka', one of the war's biggest pop hits, would usher in Smoky's barrel roll, while Shacklette would belt out 'The Daring Young Man on the Flying Trapeze' – the timeless circus classic – for Smoky's grand finale, as she walked the tightrope wires, after which, with blindfold removed, she would ride down the slide to finish with a flourish. It was a fine act. A dead cert of a winner. But sadly it was not to be, at least not this time.

A few days before show night, Wynne sought out the show's director, Sergeant Krog, and told him they were pulling out. Wynne's excuse was Smoky. He claimed the diminutive canine performer just wasn't ready. But the truth was quite different. It was him: he wasn't ready. The thought of facing an audience of hundreds of fellow GIs had thrown Wynne completely. In his head he knew the truth: at the eleventh hour he'd chickened out.

The director was apoplectic. He told Wynne to go to hell. Wynne was truly shaken. He went and found the guy the next day and tried to argue that he'd changed his mind. But the director was having none of it. He couldn't risk building a show around the two of them, only to have them succumb to stage fright at the last minute. And that was final.

The show went ahead to a packed audience. The fresh-faced Filipino dancehall girls – resplendent in their grass skirts and with bright flowers in their hair – took to the stage to a suitably raucous reception, serenaded by male singers in smart suits. But the night was sadly bereft of the squadron's own – Bill Wynne and their famed mascot-cum-war dog, Smoky.

Shortly after this bruising failure to perform, Wynne received a letter from Barbara Wood Smith, the Red Cross nurse who had persuaded him to do the rounds with Smoky on the Brisbane hospital wards. Wood Smith asked if he might bring their act to the Santo Tomas University in Manila. During the Japanese occupation, the university had been transformed into a prison camp, with some 3,500 prisoners, mostly Americans, being held there. On 5 February 1945 a 1st Cavalry Division tank had rolled up to the main gates and blasted them off their hinges, liberating the POWs.

Shortly thereafter, Santo Tomas University had undergone another makeover, being transformed into a vast General Army Hospital. It was June 1945 by the time Wynne had received his invitation to perform there, and the hospital was packed with casualties from across the Philippines, and from Iwo Jima and further afield.

In response to Wood Smith's request Wynne boarded a truck bound for Manila, with Smoky at his side. Apart from the small bamboo hoop, they took little of their show kit with them. Instead, they would revert to the simpler, less fraught acts that had been so popular in Brisbane.

Or so Wynne hoped – that was if he found the courage to perform at all.

CHAPTER 22

As it turned out, Bill Wynne and Smoky's tour of the Manila wards proved as much of a hit as they had in Australia. As an addition to their regular act, Wynne had decided they'd perform their own version of the Jitterbug. He and Smoky began by facing each other, each lifting an opposing foot/paw several times, before spinning around in unison in opposite directions and coming face-to-face again. That seemed to bring the house down.

Wynne and Smoky performed in fifteen wards, without a single misstep or mishap, or even the slightest hint of stage fright. The other major hit in Manila was Smoky's crooning. One injured GI asked if he might take the little dog to serenade the patients in another ward, and a Red Cross photographer fired off some snaps of them in action.

Once they were done, Wynne carried Smoky to the lawn outside, where he popped her into a GI helmet, to recreate the winning *Yank Magazine* image for the Red Cross photographer. But Smoky's tongue was hanging out exhaustedly, and it struck Wynne that she looked more like a dog-tired, war-bitten soldier, than what she had been back then – namely, the gift that never stopped giving.

Here on the Manila hospital wards man and dog had brought the house down. In light of their unreserved success, Wynne felt even more regretful about the stage fright he had succumbed to in Lingayen. That bout of nerves continued to trouble him. When Barbara Wood Smith asked if they'd like to feature on the weekly Red Cross radio show, which broadcast right across the US, he jumped at the chance. Anything to help bury the memory of that vexing failure of his to perform; to measure up to his dog; to serve.

In a downtown Manila recording studio he was interviewed about Smoky winning the *Yank Mag* contest, plus her legendary exploits running the wire beneath the Lingayen airstrip, and her subsequent performances for the injured servicemen in Santo Tomas hospital. Wynne was able to alert both his mother, and his fiancée Margie, to the forthcoming broadcast, which would go out on Cleveland's Mutual Network radio, together with dozens more such stations across the US.

At the same time ACME Newspictures, then one of the world's leading press agencies, syndicated the story of the tiny dog with the big heart who acted as a miraculous entertainer for wounded GIs. It was illustrated with the picture taken on the Santo Tomas lawn, with Smoky sprawled in the helmet. It was an instant hit. Once they were back at their Lingayen base, Wynne came across scores of fellow soldiers who'd received letters and news clippings from home, showcasing the squadron's 'wonder dog' that had made thousands happy, if only for a moment, so they could forget.

Those were the highs of their return to Lingayen. The low was the news that two more of the squadron's fliers had lost their lives. Lieutenants Henry R. Willis and James L. Wilson had been through flight training together and they'd come to the 26th as young officers. Inseparable ever since, they'd been tasked to fly a low-level recce mission over Kiangan, a mountainous wilderness in the Philippines where General Yamashita himself was believed to have made his final redoubt.

Willis and Wilson never returned from that mission. Both aircraft were shot down, crashing in a remote mountain valley practically side by side. Just days after Willis and Wilson's fateful sortie, the Japanese general would walk out of the battle-scarred hills with a small retinue of staff, and surrender to the US 32nd Infantry Division.

By June 1945 the squadron's rumour mill was practically in meltdown. All talk was of Okinawa, Okinawa. The island of Okinawa lies roughly 400 miles south of the rest of Japan, and at the time it was populated by approximately 300,000 civilians. After Iwo Jima, it was the next obvious stepping-stone for MacArthur. Once conquered, the plan was to use Okinawa as a launchpad for bombing raids over Japan's major cities, and for the final invasion of the Japanese mainland.

In the largest amphibious assault of the entire Pacific campaign, US Marines and infantry units had fought their way onto the first of the Okinawa beachheads. But the fighting would rage for almost three, terrible months. Christened *tetsu no bofu* – the violent wind of steel – by the Japanese, the name embodied the sheer ferocity of their defence, which was being spearheaded by the legions of the kamikazes.

Repeated waves of suicide attackers had swept in on the US invasion fleet. Among the vessels attacked was USS *Louisville*, the cruiser that had been struck three times by kamikazes during the Leyte Gulf landings. Hit by anti-aircraft fire and in flames, the kamikaze pilot targeting the cruiser still managed to strike home, the impact ripping the ship's seaplane off her deck, crushing a smoke stack, and killing eight sailors and injuring forty-five.

Ohka rocket-planes were also in the vanguard of the attack. Mounted aboard flights of Mitsubishi G4M twin-engine bombers, they were launched in waves. On 12 April 1945, nine G4M bombers had unleashed their rocket-borne kamikazes against the US fleet steaming off Okinawa. One had hit the destroyer USS *Mannert L. Abele*, closely followed by a second. Suffering catastrophic damage, the vessel broke in two, with her midships obliterated and her bow and stern sections sinking quickly.

This was the first US warship to be sunk by one of the rocket-powered kamikazes. Throughout May and June, more rocket-planes broke through the fleet's defences, damaging and sinking a number of other warships. In one attack, an Ohka passed clean through the hull of the destroyer USS *Stanly*, exploding beside her in the sea. It was a narrow escape, but another destroyer wasn't so fortunate. USS *Hugh W. Hadley* was hit by a speeding Ohka, causing massive damage that left her beyond hope of repair.

Yet, Okinawa was as nothing, compared to the coming defence of mainland Japan – and into this violent wind of steel would sail the 26th.

Towards the end of July Captain Gathers called the men of the squadron together. The Philippines party was over, he told them. The move to Okinawa was now. And beyond that, they were destined to join the battle for Japan.

'We must strip ourselves of personal property,' Gathers informed the assembled men, his voice sombre. Anything remotely big or bulky would need to be left behind. That meant that all of Wynne and Smoky's lovingly crafted performing kit – mahogany slide, painted drum, tightrope walk and more – would have to be abandoned. While man and dog hadn't got to use the equipment much, still they lived in hope. But there was worse.

'No animals will be permitted to go,' Gathers added, ominously. Wynne felt his heart skip a beat: leaving Smoky behind was simply unthinkable. As if reading his mind, Gathers' eyes seemed to seek him out among the crowd of anxious faces. 'All except for Smoky,' he added. 'Smoky – she's been with us forever, she's the squadron mascot and she doesn't take up any space.'

Gather's surprise announcement raised a ragged cheer from his audience.

The men began to dispose of their possessions among the locals, though those who owned dogs vowed defiantly that they would take them with them, whatever Gathers might have ordered. Of course Topper, Smoky's only offspring, would sadly remain in his Lingayen grave. Filipino friends watched morosely as tents were taken down and requisitioned huts returned as much as possible to how they had been, before the 26th had moved in. Despite the air raids and the losses of their brothers in arms, the men had been happy here.

As trucks were loaded with gear a dark and funereal atmosphere descended upon the men. Finally, the long column of vehicles rolled slowly out of a place that had been home for approaching six months. Figures perched atop the heavily laden trucks waved goodbye and forced a smile. Most knew they were never going to return; that friendships made here would never be rekindled.

'When our trucks pulled out, the roads were lined with "the neighbours" and their expressions of sorrow at our departure indicated that we had helped implement the American "good neighbour" policy in a small way,' the squadron's war diary recorded, trying to sound an upbeat note. It was not one shared by the rest of the men.

At the docks they were greeted with a wearingly familiar sight: heavily laden figures shuffled aboard an old and rusting LST, in preparation for a crowded and uncomfortable passage into the unknown. The dark and potent form of a US attack submarine lay alongside. She would be sailing with them on the coming voyage. The convoy formed up. All knew their final destination lay beyond Okinawa. The massive seaborne force was heading far beyond the battle-blasted island, for the landings on mainland Japan.

The convoy set sail. As they ploughed across the South China Sea, there was more disturbing news. The famed war reporter Ernie Pyle had been killed at the height of the battle for Okinawa. Along with President Roosevelt, Pyle had been a towering figure to the GIs, earning widespread renown for his eyewitness accounts of the rank and file of US soldiers at war.

Pyle had been killed on Ie Shima – present-day Iejima – a small island lying just to the northwest of Okinawa itself. Embedded with the US Army's 305th Infantry Regiment, Pyle had been pinned down by an enemy machine-gunner, taking cover in a ditch with other troops. When he'd risked a swift glance to check out the lie of the land, he had been shot in the head and killed instantly.

The new US President, Harry S. Truman, would praise Pyle, declaring that: 'No man in this war has so well told the story of the American fighting man as the American fighting man wanted it told.' Bill Wynne was shaken by the news. Pyle had shared the soldiers' front-line privations and their darkest fears. He had understood them. Now he, too, was gone. If a man of Pyle's stature could perish among this stretch of war-blasted sea and islands, so could anyone.

So too could any dog.

By the time the convoy had steamed into the seas around Okinawa it was the first days of August 1945. The LST ran ashore, its bow-doors opened and the men of the squadron began a repeat performance of their arrival, months earlier, at Lingayen Gulf. Inland they could see a camp surrounded by mines and barbed wire, which had been constructed by some of the first troops to land here. The fence was lined with tin cans half-filled with gravel, which would rattle if anyone so much as touched the wire, giving advance warning if any enemy tried to sneak up under cover of darkness. Hand-grenades were rigged to the wire, with the intention of blowing any would-be attackers to pieces – testament to the ferocity of recent fighting and the fear that it had left in its wake.

When that first day's unloading was complete, Bill Wynne and his fellows joined the exhausted chow line. This would be their last meal aboard the hulking great LST, and few were lamenting the fact. The voyage had been irksome, the 'hardships of crowding, lack of showers, and the rest following the old pattern', the squadron's diary noted. And the food had been little better.

Men were lining up with their mess-tins when a long piece of yellow teleprinter paper was unceremoniously tacked to the ship's bulletin board. Most thought little of it, until the murmur of the few who'd gathered to read it bled into a stunned silence. It was the quiet that only ever descends on a crowd when gripped by utter shock and disbelief.

Wynne joined those gathered at the board. The teleprinter message announced the use of the world's first-ever atomic bomb. It was 6 August and the 'Enola Gay', a US B-29 Super-fortress, had dropped the Little Boy uranium bomb on the Japanese city of Hiroshima. The initial explosion, and the resulting cataclysmic firestorm that had engulfed the city, had killed in excess of 100,000 people. Many more would die from radiation poisoning.

Wynne and his fellows read the news in a state of dazed disbelief. That one aircraft dropping one bomb could unleash the power to level a city seemed impossible, but surely the teletype didn't lie. Their reactions ranged from a great regret at the massive loss of civilian life, to a quiet elation that here surely was promise the war might be over soon. President Truman called for Japan to surrender, or it should expect a 'rain of ruin from the air, the like of which has never been seen on this earth. Behind this air attack will follow sea and land forces in such numbers and power as they have not yet seen . . .' Yet still Japan gave little hint that it was even considering capitulation.

With every hour further teletyped reports were pinned to that bulletin board. Hiroshima was a legitimate target, they declared:

it had been garrisoned by some 40,000 Japanese troops, and it had provided the headquarters to many of the regiments tasked with the defence of the Japanese mainland. A port city, it had also served as a key trans-shipment point for military supplies and personnel.

In the run-up to the bombing, the 300,000 citizens of Hiroshima had been warned to evacuate their homes, in leaflets dropped by overflying US aircraft. Those warnings had been largely ignored. A day after the blast, Japanese experts inspected the ruins of Hiroshima and confirmed that an atom bomb had caused its destruction. But the Japanese war cabinet argued that the Allies could possess only 'one or two' more such nuclear devices, and so their resistance should continue.

Two days later there would be further shocking news, which would result in the work on constructing the squadron's new photo lab being put permanently on hold. A second atom bomb had been unleashed. This one, codenamed "Fat Man", was a plutonium-based implosion-type device, and it had been dropped over the port city of Nagasaki, causing even greater devastation.

Realizing that the US possessed further such devices, Japanese Emperor Hirohito finally mooted surrender, but upon one condition: on no account was his sovereign rule to be threatened. With this agreed, on 12 August 1945 Hirohito announced to the disbelieving Japanese people that the nation was to lay down its arms. In his speech he stressed how 'the enemy now possesses a new and terrible weapon with the power to destroy many innocent lives . . . Should we continue to fight . . . it would result in the ultimate collapse and obliteration of the Japanese nation.'

A Japanese delegation was to fly into Ie Shima – the island

lying adjacent to Okinawa on which Ernie Pyle had lost his life – en route to the battleship USS *Missouri*, anchored off Manila, where the peace accords would be signed. The Ie Shima landing strip was in full view of the squadron's new camp. On the morning of the delegation's scheduled arrival, Bill Wynne found himself standing with several of his expectant fellows on the bonnet of a jeep, with a ringside view, and with Smoky at his side.

They'd tuned their radio into the air-to-ground traffic, to monitor the progress of the Japanese aircraft carrying the peace party – a pair of Mitsubishi G4M bombers. At the orders of the US military they had been stripped of their weapons and painted white, and both displayed large green crosses. A phalanx of six P-38s escorted the Japanese peace party and Wynne could hear the countdown as the flight of aircraft neared the island.

The air traffic controller on Ie Shima came on the air, requesting the two Japanese aircraft identify themselves with their agreed call-signs – Bataan I and Bataan II, a clear reference to the reviled 'Bataan death march' on which so many Allied and Filipino troops had lost their lives. The American radio operator sounded tense as he demanded they come up on air.

'Bataan I and Bataan II, come in. Repeat, Bataan I and Bataan II, come in.'

After a short delay there was a halting and heavily accented response. 'Sorry, cannot hear you. Cannot hear you.'

'Come on, you son of a bitch, or we'll knock you out of the skies!' a second voice butted in over the radio.

'I hear you!' the Japanese pilot answered, nervously. 'I hear you.' Then, with clear reluctance: 'Bataan I and Bataan II, in-bound.'

Moments later, the two Japanese warplanes hove into view, flying over the northeastern shoreline of the bay.

'It's over!' someone yelled.

'DAMN! It's OVER!' another voice echoed.

'That it is,' Wynne confirmed, laughing with relief and joy that he and his death-defying war dog had made it through alive. Finally, impossibly, the war was over.

But on Okinawa, the trials and tribulations of one man and his dog were only just beginning.

CHAPTER 23

News of the surrender was greeted by those assembled on Okinawa with unreserved jubilation. At the 26th squadron's camp they unhooked the grenades and the tin-can rattles from the wire. With the war finally over, news spread that the famed war dog Smoky had arrived on the island. Wynne was approached to perform his and Smoky's act, at a servicemen's hall run by the Red Cross.

This time there were to be no stage nerves. As matters transpired, Wynne had managed to smuggle most of Smoky's performing paraphernalia onto the LST, so they could attempt something close to their full act. Shacklette still had his Solovox with him, so there could be musical accompaniment too. A big ten-wheeler truck loaded up all of their kit, plus those members of the squadron who wanted to go see the show.

Staff Sergeant Howard Kalt – Smoky's official photographer during the Nadzab parachuting stunt – was something of an amateur magician, and he came along to help compère the evening's entertainment. When Bill and Smoky's turn came, they hustled onto stage together with Shacklette, dragging all of their kit into position. As he eyed the audience, Wynne couldn't deny that he was nervous.

'And now . . .' Kalt announced, with suitable theatricality, 'Corporal Bill Wynne and Corporal Smoky!'

The show opened exactly as they had rehearsed it so exhaustively back at their Lingayen base. The music was superbly timed, switching tunes to provide the perfect soundtrack to each of their subsequent acts. Once Smoky had completed the tightrope walk, Wynne removed the blindfold and she slid down the mahogany slide with a flourish. That done, Wynne gave a quick bow and scurried off stage. Shacklette gave a final fanfare on the Solovox, but it was drowned out by the cheering and applause.

Here on Okinawa their show had proved to be the hit that Wynne had always believed it would. Here on Okinawa – on Japanese soil – man and dog had slain the ghost of their stage fright, which had haunted them in the Philippines. They had done so on the land of the former enemy, but in a time of peace. Maybe that was what had made the crucial difference: the lack of wartime tension and nerves had freed them up to perform and to shine.

Altogether, the squadron's casualties were the heaviest of any recce squadron serving with the 5th Air Force Group. The 26th had suffered thirteen dead and ten wounded. But their losses were thankfully light compared to some of the front-line infantry and marine units. Had the invasion of Japan gone ahead – had the atomic bombs not precluded that necessary evil – millions more would have died. The men of the 26th were fortunate, and they were slated to be returning home any day now.

Via a stopover in Korea, the squadron was to sail back to the USA, the country whose shores they had left almost three long years ago. A handful of men volunteered to remain on Okinawa, so as to avoid the sea voyage to Korea, and to wind down the squadron's affairs on the island. Bill Wynne was one of them. He didn't feel he should subject Smoky to long days at sea. Instead, they'd catch a flight, just as soon as a transport became available. In the interim, their duties would be to dispose of what remained of the paraphernalia of a photo reconnaissance squadron at war.

They bulldozed the photo supplies, and whatever else they could dispose of. But in the process of demolishing the camp Smoky fell ill. She developed a sinus infection, her nasal passages becoming blocked. She was constantly coughing and sneezing. Within days it had worsened so that her nose was permanently clogged with thick mucus. Though she wagged her tail and seemed energetic and in good spirits, Wynne grew increasingly worried. What a bitter irony it would be to lose her now.

The 4th Marine Regiment's War Dog Platoon was camped not so far away. These were the famed 'Devil Dogs' – patrol, message and tracker K9s that had served on the front lines and beyond, operating side by side with their handlers. Wynne walked to their camp, hoping to find a veterinarian. He was directed to the tent of a medic whose role it was to care for the dogs. To every side German Shepherds and Dobermans were barking wildly and straining at their leashes.

Wynne found the medic in his tent seated at a desk. He explained what was wrong with Smoky. The medic said that he had nothing with which to treat the dog's sinus infection, but suggested that if Wynne fed her a mixture of raw eggs and fresh milk it should clear up. He escorted Wynne off the War

Dog Platoon's camp, giving him a quick tour of some of the more famous inhabitants.

He pointed to one, a grizzled German Shepherd. 'That one saved his patrol twice,' he announced, simply.

Another dog was barking wildly. 'He's a one-man dog,' the medic explained. His handler had been killed in a foxhole and the traumatized dog wouldn't let anyone near the body. Eventually, another handler had wooed the dog in his own, inimitable way. That handler was the only guy the dog would let near him now. Fiercely loyal and protective beyond reckoning, the dog had had an uncanny ability to alert patrols to danger long before any of the other canine warriors seemed able to sense it.

There were other dogs who'd been cited for their brave actions, and still more who were recovering from the wounds they'd suffered in combat. For Wynne, it was a humbling and sobering experience. These dogs – they were yet more canine heroes of this war.

Back at camp all he could find in the mess hall were some dried milk and powdered egg. He whisked them together with water, and set the bowl for Smoky. She wolfed down the thick, gloopy liquid. The next morning she seemed a little better. He began to feed her the mixture morning, noon and night. Within three days the sinus infection seemed to have gone.

But Zeitlin's sickly puppy had caught the bug real bad. No matter what anyone might try, he just went from bad to worse. Eventually, it was clear that they would need to put the sad little fellow out of his misery. He was constantly wracked by fits and shakes and he was suffering horribly. No one had any experience of how to do this, so they formed a support party to help Zeitlin through what was coming.

They decided to dig a shallow hole and place the sickly puppy in the bottom of it. Zeitlin insisted on carrying out the mercy-killing himself. He took his carbine and ended his beloved dog's life with one bullet. He was utterly devastated, and everyone around him felt terrible as they threw soil into the tiny animal's makeshift grave.

There wasn't long to dwell on the loss. A warning came in that a typhoon was on its way. Okinawa, like most of Japan, is subject to a typhoon season from May to November. Powerful tropical cyclones blow northwards from the Philippines, gathering power and force over the South China Sea and sucking up water in their wake. On average, a dozen such storms hit Japan and its surrounding seas in a year. August just happened to be the peak of the season.

Tellingly, the local Okinawans had laughed when they'd seen the men of the 26th erecting a tented camp, and nailing corrugated iron to the roofs of the mess hall. They'd explained about the 'big winds' that regularly hit the island. The locals lived in tiny houses with massive walls. There was no glass in the windows and thick red tiles lay heavy on the roofs. Taking heed, Wynne and his fellows had weighed down the corner of tents with sand bags, but other than that there hadn't been a great deal more they could do.

Now, with the majority of the squadron already departed for Korea a typhoon was poised to hit. US military forecasters warned that Okinawa was slap-bang in its path. Wynne and his few fellows prepared as best they could. Using leftovers scavenged from the remains of the photo lab, they build plywood walls to shield their twenty-by-twenty-foot tent. Lashing the plywood to the uprights, they hoped they were ready for the storm.

At 2300 hours that August night it struck. The first blasts of almost horizontal rain slammed into the plywood 'walls' and . . . they held. Wynne and the others who shared the tent felt reassured. They drifted off to sleep, relieved that their defences seemed up to the task. Four hours later they awoke to utter silence and stillness. Had the storm passed? They sat on their cots chatting about what this unnerving calm might signify, but eventually they dozed off again.

At 0500 hours Wynne was jolted violently from his sleep. There was an almighty crash, and a stupendous gust of wind simply tore their tent out of the ground and whisked it away into the dark and howling heavens, like a giant kite. The calm had been the eye of the storm and the typhoon was back with a real vengeance.

Soaked to the skin, Wynne grabbed his blanket, slung Smoky on his cot, and with that gripped firmly in his grasp he dashed for the nearby mess hall, which was still standing. All of a sudden a massive gust caught the cot, ripped it from his hands and spun it into the air. Gripped by fear, he watched as it rose higher, turning two cartwheels in mid-air, Smoky somehow managing to hold on resolutely to the material.

All around torn sheets of corrugated iron were hurtling through the air, like giant, jagged-edged arrows. If one of those struck Smoky, she was a goner. Wynne sprinted after the cot, eyes skywards, as it continued to perform its aerial acrobatics and Smoky clung on. Maybe it was due to all her circus training – the drum-roll, the slide, the scooter, the high wire – but for whatever reason, Smoky seemed able to ride that demented rollercoaster of a flying carpet with miraculous ease.

For fifty feet or more she held on, before the cot dropped low enough for Wynne to lunge and catch hold. He dragged cot and dog to earth. With the little dog jammed tightly under one arm and the cot pointed dead ahead like a spear, he sprinted the last few remaining yards to the mess hall. The building was ruined. The roof had been ripped clean off and it was open to the howling sky. Even the heavy sandbags had been taken by the storm. But the rain wasn't coming in that way. Driven by winds of nearly 150 mph, it was hammering in horizontally, blasting through what remained of the plywood walls.

Wynne placed his cot against what appeared to be the least damaged section of wall and set Smoky on top of it. For two days and two nights they huddled in utter misery, eating whatever cold canned food came to hand, as the wind howled and the rain lashed relentlessly. Finally, the wind settled to something like half of its peak. Battling seventy mph gusts the small, bedraggled band of survivors struggled across to an adjacent building: the mess hall of the Army Air Force's 6th Group headquarters, it was a somewhat more substantial, sturdy building.

There they were served their first decent hot meal in three, storm-lashed days. But the news was far from encouraging. A second typhoon, believed to be just as powerful as the first, was headed in their direction. It hit that night, and once again the rain and wind found its way through every defence, soaking man – and dog – to the skin.

Wynne decided enough was enough. Extreme measures were called for. He'd heard that there were caves burrowed into the nearby hillsides, which the locals used as tombs. Deciding to brave the spirits of the dead, he grabbed Smoky and dashed for the nearest dark opening. He crawled inside, only to discover a line of ornate ceramic pots secreted deep in the shadows, no doubt packed full of the bones of deceased Okinawans.

In the local Buddhist tradition, the locals would lay the body of a dead family member in such a cave, waiting for the natural process of decomposition to take its course. Some years later they would return to it, gather up the bones and clean them in a ceremony called *senkotsu lit* – washing bones. After that they'd put them in one of the clay or stone pots arranged next to their deceased relations: their final resting place. The tombs – known as *hafu baka*, or roofed graves – doubled as the family shrine.

The *hafu baka* in which Bill Wynne and Smoky had taken refuge was only about four feet high, but it was deep. Wynne set the pots outside to make room for himself and his dog. It was a decidedly eerie place of refuge, but at least it was dry and they were safe from the storm, which thundered and raged outside. Trying his best to rest, an exhausted Wynne woke several times in the night to find Smoky growling, her gaze fixed accusingly on the darkest recesses of the cave.

It was unnerving. Wynne had brought a candle with him. He struck a match and lit it, peering about anxiously. Deep in the guts of the cave a row of eyes gleamed in the light like ghostly coals. Thankfully, it turned out that this was not the enraged spirits of deceased Okinawans, fearing they had been summarily ejected from their place of eternal rest. It was instead a flock of goats, who, like man and dog, had found the only safe refuge from the storm in the house of the dead.

One night of this was about all that Wynne could stomach. With the storm abating, the following morning he returned to what remained of the mess hall. There, he found Duke's owner, John Hembury, together with his plucky little terrier. Together, the two men gathered up what remained of their sodden belongings and hitch-hiked a ride to the airport. Five GIs had been killed in the storms; they didn't want to risk joining their number.

At the airbase the moorings of the Curtis C46 Commando cargo-planes had been torn loose. Wingtips were battered and broken, and any number of rudders had been ripped clean off. Not an airframe among them was still serviceable. As the winds died down, replacement aircraft were flown in. Wynne and Hembury persuaded one of those pilots to fly two men and two little dogs away from the path of the typhoons.

They wanted out of Okinawa, and they weren't too picky about how they managed it.

CHAPTER 24

After a largely uneventful flight, they landed at Kimpo Airport – known today as Gimpo Airport – to the far west of Seoul, the South Korean capital, from where they caught a ride to the squadron's new base, situated in a farming area on the outskirts of Inchon Harbour – now known as Incheon – Seoul's main port. Quartered in an abandoned Japanese military barracks, after the hell of Okinawa at the height of the typhoon season this seemed to them like sheer luxury.

There were four men to each room, each of which boasted a pair of pot-bellied kerosene stoves set dead centre, to keep it toasty. At night those sleeping closest to the burners roasted. Periodically, the stoves' pot bellies would issue deep booms, belching forth clouds of black soot-balls, which would cover everything, sleeping man and dog included. Neither Wynne nor Smoky minded particularly. The rooms were warm and free of wind, and they were dry.

Their existence in Korea became a waiting game. Every day, the men of the squadron expected to receive orders to board a waiting transport at Inchon docks. Every day, no such order came. It was frustrating. Some of the squadron's fliers began taking to the skies again, this time executing air recce missions over Korea.

'In September we moved to Korea,' the squadron's war diary recorded, 'and during a period of uncertainty and waiting, mapped US occupied Korea, and pinpointed airfields, ports and major cities.'

With the end of the war the world was changing. New alliances were forming, new enmities raising their ugly heads. It was good to be ready, especially as Korea would become such a flashpoint for American-Soviet rivalry. In the coming Cold War, Korea would be divided in two nations (present day North and South Korea).

Understandably, those Korean recce flights were a low-key and secretive affair that involved only a handful of men. Most were stuck in their quarters with precious little to do. A highlight was the moment when trucks pulled up at the barracks, distributing Japanese military paraphernalia. Wynne grabbed a rifle and a bayonet from the heap, which included several officer's swords. They would serve as souvenirs of all that had gone before, and all that might have been, had the battle for Japan not been halted by the dropping of the atom bombs.

Wynne kept packing and repacking his kit, restlessly, in preparation for the journey home. One day he emptied out his barracks bag, a kit sack that had gone on ahead of him by sea. Near the bottom he discovered the cardboard letters that he'd cut out at their Lingayen base, when he'd tried – unsuccessfully – to teach Smoky to spell her own name. What had he kept those for, he wondered?

There was little else to do, so he figured he'd try them on Smoky one last time. Intrigued, bored, kicking their heels, a crowd of fellow soldiers gathered. They watched curiously as

Wynne set the letters up near the entrance to their dorm. He decided to start with a real mix-it-up. He arranged the letters so they spelled 'M-K-O-S-Y'.

Gazing at them, he told his little dog: 'Smoky, go spell your name.'

With barely a moment's hesitation Smoky trotted over to the fourth letter in line, which stood twice as tall as her, and plonked herself down, facing it. It had to be a coincidence, Wynne told himself. It simply had to be.

'Next,' he ordered.

Smoky got up, stepped across three letters and sat down opposite the 'M'.

'Good lord,' Wynne muttered. Surely, there couldn't be two such coincidences in a row.

'Next,' he commanded.

Smoky shuffled right two letters, coming to a halt facing the 'O'. Incredible.

'Next.'

Without hesitation she moved left one, to the 'K'. Wynne didn't doubt it any more. Smoky knew this. She'd known it all along. For some reason she just hadn't wanted to show him she did, when they'd trained for it so relentlessly back at their Lingayen base. Here, in the relaxed and relatively peaceful atmosphere of the abandoned Japanese barracks, she'd decided to let him know.

'Next,' he commanded.

Sure enough, Smoky moved sharply right three, and came to a halt facing the last letter of her name: 'Y'.

'Well, I'll be . . .' Wynne exclaimed, under his breath.

The room exploded into applause. Wynne grabbed his dog

and gave her an almighty great hug, praising her for being so clever. Then he got her to do it all over again, just to be absolutely certain. It was quite simply amazing. Their greatest show yet.

He turned to his audience and explained how he'd tried to get her to learn to do this trick back in the Philippines, but no matter what he'd tried his dog had refused to play ball. As he spoke, it dawned upon him what he had been doing wrong. He'd been force-training her. He'd been forcing it and she'd hated it. Smoky had wanted to show him a better way – that she would learn when she was good and ready.

Wynne knew well how at times even top athletes needed a break from the relentless pace of training, to re-ignite their enthusiasm for and dedication to their craft. Smoky was no different. In addition to which, he had been trying to force the trick upon her in the midst of the trials and tribulations of war. Smoky had known all along what he was trying to achieve. Refusing to be taught and to perform had been Smoky's rebellion.

One of the guys seemed to take umbrage at the story Wynne had just related. 'That poor dog can't defecate unless you say so!' he objected. 'What the hell d'you think you're training her *for*?'

Wynne felt chastened. After all, Smoky was the mascot of the squadron. Every man in the 26th felt as if he owned a tiny little part of her. In a way, her well-being was the responsibility of every single one of them.

He shrugged. 'I don't know. I'm not sure. Maybe we can do some shows when we get home.'

The guy glared. 'You know something? You get a wife, she's gonna hate that dog!'

Wynne didn't reply. Clearly, at one time or another he had

pushed Smoky too hard. He'd not been aware of it back then. He'd felt as if he was doing the right thing for all the right reasons, first and foremost of which was to protect her. But here in Korea, Smoky had found a way to let him know that he'd gone too far. At times.

Yet even so, he *had* got her through this war unscathed. At least, so far.

One last hurdle – and it was a major one – lay before them: the homecoming. Orders had already been posted, making it clear that 'No dog or mascot will go back to the US on a War Department ship.' Wynne had feared that such orders were in the offing. He'd heard horror stories of dogs being removed from such vessels, or worse still, thrown overboard. In truth, he was scared, but he was equally determined that Smoky was going home with him, come what may.

He got hold of an oxygen mask case, of the kind that pilots use to carry this vital piece of kit to their aircraft. It was made of a soft green canvas and was fitted with lots of zippered pockets and buttoned flaps. He cut a hole in the bottom of it, just the right size for a Yorkie to sneak inside, and attached a flap to seal it closed.

Just as they had with the haversack that he'd used to smuggle Smoky into Australia, they practised repeatedly with the gas-mask bag. Wynne had Smoky crawl in through the bespoke opening, and spend long periods lying absolutely quiet and still. It was pliable and adjusted well to her movements. If she stood, the bag stood with her. If she chose to lie down, it crumpled and creased to suit. Once she was settled, she tended to stay settled in there for long periods of time.

Wynne decided to put the gas-mask hideout to the test. He got Smoky to crawl inside, placing some personal items, including toiletries and a few pairs of socks, on top. Thus armed, he strolled across to the mess hall, setting the bag on one of the tables. Cooks bustled about and the odd soldier paused to chat as Wynne proceeded to unload the bag's contents, as if searching for something deep inside.

Then, on the command of 'Okay!', Smoky wriggled out of her secret door, and as if by magic she appeared.

They'd drawn a small crowd. People laughed and applauded. All understood exactly what Wynne was preparing for, and one or two remarked on what an ingenious set-up it was.

'No one will ever know she's there!'

Wynne figured they were right. If his buddies in the squadron hadn't even realized what was in the bag until Smoky had emerged, surely those policing the ships against canine stowaways wouldn't stand a chance. He taught Smoky to sleep in the bag. She grew fond of her place of hiding. Upon reflection, the delay in their setting sail for home had been a good thing. They'd needed time in which to train and to prepare for perhaps the greatest threat yet, which sadly emanated from their own side.

On 1 November 1945, a notice was posted declaring that everyone from the squadron would be departing the Inchon base the following morning. Embarkation time was 0700 hours, on the USS *General W H Gordon*, a grey-hulled troop transport sporting two enormous, black-rimmed funnels.

That night, as Wynne cuddled up to Smoky for their final night in the barracks dorm, he let his mind drift to thoughts of home: of his mother, and of his fiancée, Margie. After years away, he wanted to surprise her, stepping off a bus or a tram and walking in through her front door to give her a massive hug.

Following a pre-dawn breakfast of pancakes, bacon and coffee, the men boarded a convoy of waiting trucks. Wynne had Smoky safely cocooned in her gas-mask sanctuary. His buddy, Hembury, had had to give Duke to a fellow GI, for he didn't have a place to keep the terrier at home in the US. Needless to say, he was devastated at having to do so. Another soldier carried a pet monkey with him, secreted in an ammo box. Sod the rules.

Despite her cunning place of concealment, Wynne was worried sick about Smoky. He had the letter that Barbara Wood Smith had written him, commending Smoky on her performance with the wounded. He had photos of the little dog at work on those hospital wards. But would that mean anything to those who had been ordered to police the military's draconian rules? Smoky meant so much to those who knew her. But to those who did not? It didn't bear thinking about.

Upon arrival at Inchon Harbour they caught a barge to the waiting ship. Wynne saw figures mount the gangplank. One was Shorty Randall, the guy to whom Hembury had chosen to give Duke. The terrier was too big and boisterous to be carried concealed. Randall had him gripped in his arms. At the top of the gangplank a ship's officer started shouting and gesticulating at the dog. Randall barged past, waving a sheet of paper in the face of the officer.

Wynne stepped up to the gangplank. It was narrow and steep. At the last moment he'd exchanged the gas-mask bag for a heavy kit bag owned by a buddy of his. Ed Piwarski had hurt his back and was in need of the help. Wynne kept his eyes glued to Piwarski, as he stomped up the gangway ahead of him, the still form of Smoky slung in the gas-mask sack over his shoulder.

Ten yards short of the inspecting officer, Wynne felt one of the heavy bags he was carrying slip. It jammed at his feet. Angry voices yelled from below: 'Hurry up! Hurry it up!' The inspecting officer fought his way down to Wynne. He grabbed one of the heavy bags, wrestling it out of Wynne's struggling grasp.

'My buddy's injured!' Wynne exclaimed, by way of explanation, nodding towards the figure of Piwarski, nearing the top of the gangplank. 'I gotta carry his bag too!'

The officer didn't seem to give a damn. He just wanted everyone to hurry up and board. Moments later Piwarski had made the top of the gangway. So, too, had Smoky.

Wynne hurried after them, being reunited with his dog when safely below decks. He chose a top bunk set far into one corner, away from prying eyes. He placed Smoky on the mattress, still in her pack, and settled back to wait. The ship could carry 5,000 troops and it would take all night before she was fully boarded. But just prior to setting sail, the loudspeaker crackled and there was an announcement as unexpected as it was unwelcome.

'Will the man who brought the dog aboard report to the troop office. Will the man who brought the dog aboard report to the troop office.'

Wynne's heart nearly stopped. Surely, the message couldn't refer to Smoky? No one had even seen her come aboard. The guys all around glanced at him, anxiously, but he raised a pair of crossed fingers. He told himself that he was going nowhere. A worried-looking Randall headed top-deck. Shortly, he was back. He'd been called before the ship's Transport Commander and ordered to take his dog Duke ashore.

As he'd exited the guy's office, one of the ship's crew had dragged him to one side. He could hide Duke, the sailor had told him, but only deep in the bowels of the ship. He had two other dogs down there already. So it was that Duke was sent to the depths of the *General W H Gordon*'s hold. He would have to ride out the coming voyage secreted there.

The ship weighed anchor and set sail. As soon as they were out of the harbour the sea became rough and Wynne fell victim to seasickness. He felt so bad he couldn't even leave his bunk for meals. A group of fellow soldiers from the 26th, seeing that her master was out of action, volunteered to serve as Smoky's protectors. They took her top-deck for fresh air and walks, screening her with the mass of their bodies.

Despite their best efforts, come day four of their voyage the Tannoy barked again: 'All men who have brought aboard either dogs or monkeys, report to the ship's office, immediately!'

A sickly Wynne was gripped by horror. He had visions of Smoky's tiny form being hurled over the ship's rail. Surely, no one could know that she was aboard. Though he was barely able to walk, he made his way to the ship's office, staggering and reeling drunkenly as he went. He might as well see what all the fuss was about.

Five men were there ahead of him. The Troop Commander was yelling at them, his face puce with anger. 'No dogs and especially no monkeys travel back on this ship!'

'But sir,' one of the soldiers pleaded, 'these are war dogs. I have a letter from the Colonel—'

'I don't care if you've got a letter from MacArthur himself!' the Troop Commander roared. 'No dogs go back on my ship!'

Wynne felt too sick to even try to join in the heated debate.

'Do you have any idea what it will cost to bring a dog into the States?' the Troop Commander demanded. 'A thousand dollars – that's what customs will charge you!'

The soldier drew himself to his full height. 'But sir, I have a thousand dollars and I'm quite happy . . .'

Wynne wasn't listening any more. He felt so sick he had to return to his bunk. To hell with it. He decided to keep absolutely schtum about Smoky. If the Troop Commander didn't get to hear of her presence or see her, he could hardly object or do anything about it, could he? The men of the squadron offered to lend Wynne whatever cash they had to cover the $1,000 quarantine fees that the Troop Commander was banging on about.

On day seven of the journey a group of ship's officers began to search the decks for stowaways. A pair of GIs had been scheduled to leave the vessel in Inchon, but they had reportedly hidden themselves aboard so as to secure an early ride back to the US. The search party didn't find the two fugitives. But one of them, a Navy lieutenant, did spot Smoky.

'Whose dog is that?' he demanded, accusingly. All eyes turned on a sickly Bill Wynne. 'Is the dog registered on the ship?' the lieutenant challenged.

Wynne shook his head. 'No, sir.'

'Didn't you hear it piped on the PA system?'

'Yes, sir. But I've been too sick to move. I haven't even made it to chow but two times since we set sail.'

Wynne was telling the truth about his failure to make any

meals and he must have looked sick as a dog, for the lieutenant believed him. Nevertheless, he was told to report to the ship's office in quick order.

An hour later Wynne found himself standing unsteadily before the ship's captain. He was warned that he might have to pay a bond if he was determined not to give up his dog. Wynne said that he would gladly do so. He was made to swear an oath, raising his right hand and averring that he was telling the 'whole truth, so help me God'. That done, he signed a paper that exonerated the captain and crew of USS *General W H Gordon* from any responsibility for 'One dog'.

With that paper grasped in hand, Wynne made his unsteady way back below decks. He showed the paper around Smoky's support crew, triumphantly. It seemed that for now at least their worries were over.

The USS *General W H Gordon* had been sent to Korea to join the invasion of Japan, carrying troops for the landings. The captain was determined to break his own record for the journey home. Steaming at thirty knots he had fast rounded Japan, headed past the Aleutian Islands, before proceeding south along the western Canadian seaboard.

On day ten out of Inchon seagulls swarmed around the ship's deck. Wynne was feeling a little recovered and he'd taken Smoky for a stroll in the fresh air. The little dog barked furiously each time a gull swooped in close and low. Smoky and Wynne proceeded to perform one or two of their tricks, as sailors and soldiers laughed and cheered. He noticed the ship's captain watching from the bridge and smiling, indulgently.

At dawn on day twelve, the ship steamed past the islands

of Puget Sound, an estuary on the northwestern coast of the USA, in Washington State. A little harbour boat headed out to intercept the troopship. It was packed full of young women in gaily coloured clothes. A band began to play, as the girls danced and sang a well-rehearsed homecoming routine. They waved placards reading: 'WELL DONE' and 'WELCOME HOME'. The guys lining the deck of the *General W H Gordon* went wild.

The troopship steamed into Washington Harbour, in the city of Tacoma, lying within the heart of Puget Sound. Wynne put Smoky into her gas-mask hideaway and stowed his Japanese rifle and bayonet in his barracks bag. The vessel dropped anchor and the gangplank was lowered. As he stepped off the gangway onto American soil, he spied a customs inspector lined up with the other top brass to form the reception party.

For a moment he stiffened, drawing Smoky tighter, but all those figures did was smile and salute at the homecoming troops marching past. As the crowds cheered and waved, there wasn't the barest hint of any searches or inspections. A convoy of trucks was waiting to whisk the men of the 26th Photo Reconnaissance squadron away to a smart army barracks, in the nearby base of Fort Lewis.

There, an absolute treat was laid out: fresh milk, fresh salad, huge T-bone steaks, and real ice-cream. It was the kind of food that for approaching three years the men had only tasted in their dreams. Smoky enjoyed some milk and a slice of steak, before curling up on Bill Wynne's cot. She was safely home – or at least, she had arrived in what was to be her new home: America.

Of course, no one was any the wiser as to where the small dog with the world's biggest heart had originated from. Regardless, after the long years at war Smoky had made it through safe and sound. If Smoky's past was filled with mystery, then her future, with her companion Bill Wynne at her side, was one full of promise.

And that, really, should be the end of the story.

'That should end the story,' concluded the History & Legend of the 26th Photo Reconnaissance Squadron. 'Only it doesn't. Just as the old saying tells us that "old soldiers never die", so it is true that old squadrons never die. Those of our buddies who are numbered amongst the fallen, for us will never die. They will achieve immortality in our memories and will be alive as long as any of us are alive to remember them and cherish their memories.

'The Australians, on the anniversary of the deaths of sons or brothers or comrades, insert "In Memoriam" notices in their newspapers, usually starting with the phrase "In proud and loving memory." It was a phrase that many of us admired. It would be a phrase that would be appropriate to borrow now. In thinking of the friends we have lost by death or separation, in thinking of the days of our brotherhood and camaraderie, of the hardships, grief, work and fun we shared, we shall always be one in holding them "In proud and loving memory".

In proud and loving memory.

EPILOGUE

At the end of the Second World War, General Hatazo Adachi, who had spearheaded the Japanese resistance in New Guinea, surrendered to Australian troops. By then, only 13,000 of his original army were left alive. He was subsequently tried as a war criminal by the Allies and sentenced to life imprisonment. He testified in defence of every officer under his command who was likewise tried as a war criminal.

On the morning of 10 September 1947 Adachi used a knife to commit suicide in his cell. He had written a letter to those men and officers of his command who had survived. It read:

Notwithstanding the fact that my officers and men did their best in exceptional circumstances, surmounting all difficulties . . . the hoped-for end was not attained, because of my inability. Thus I paved the way for my country to be driven into the present predicament. The crime deserves death.

During the past three years of operations more than 100,000 youthful and promising officers and men were lost and most of them died of malnutrition. When I think of this, I know not what apologies to make to His Majesty the Emperor and I feel that I myself am overwhelmed with shame ... I have demanded perseverance far exceeding the limits of man's endurance of my officers and men, who were exhausted and emaciated as a result of successive campaigns and for want of supplies.

At war's end General Tomoyuki Yamashita, who masterminded Japanese resistance in the Philippines, was also tried for war crimes. Yamashita was found guilty and sentenced to death, even though his defence argued that in many cases he was not aware of the atrocities committed by troops and had not approved them. In some cases the soldiers in question had not even been under his command. The ruling established the legal precedent known as the 'Yamashita standard', by which a commanding officer can be held legally accountable for atrocities committed by those under his command, even if he was not aware of them and did not support such actions. On 23 February 1946 Yamashita was hanged in a Manila prison camp.

In early 1946 the 26th Photo Reconnaissance Squadron was disbanded, although it would be reformed as a reserve unit from 1947–9. It was reformed once more, in 1955, as a unit operating Boeing B-47 Stratojets, a long-range high-altitude jet-powered aircraft then known as the 'fastest bomber in the world'. The reconnaissance version flew top-secret and dangerous missions over the Soviet Union, carrying state-of-the-art radar and camera equipment. The unit was renamed the 681st Bombardment Squadron in late 1961 and converted to bombing duties only, before being permanently disbanded in 1962 (although see note on its successor, below).

At the end of the war, RAF Medmenham's work as the centre of photo reconnaissance skill and excellence – for both the British and their American allies – was kept a strict secret, as the Cold War loomed large. The skills developed for spying on Nazi-occupied Europe – or the jungles of Japanese-occupied New Guinea – were far too of-the-moment and sensitive to be made public. It was not until Constance Babington Smith published a book about Medmenham's work, entitled *Evidence In Camera*, in 1957, that the secrets started to come out.

By then, of course, high-altitude US spy planes were flying missions over the Soviet Union, their fuselages packed with sensitive electronic eavesdropping equipment and state-of-the-art camera systems. The U2 flights in particular were so sensitive that each required Presidential approval and all were under the overall command of the CIA, not the Air Force. The then Soviet leader, Nikita Khrushchev, said of those flights that they 'spat in the face of the Soviet people'.

But as with the sorties flown by the pilots of the 26th over the southwest Pacific during the Second World War, even those U2 flights weren't immune to danger. In May 1960 a new long-range Soviet missile succeeded in shooting down a U2 piloted by Francis Gary Powers, who bailed out and survived. He was captured and the Soviets retrieved cameras and other sensitive equipment from the wreckage. The Americans tried to claim the U2 aircraft had got lost on a high-altitude weather-testing mission. The story did not wash, and the temperature of the Cold War lurched another few degrees lower.

*

After their triumphant November 1945 homecoming, Bill Wynne and Smoky's story was covered widely in the US media. They became a sensation. Wynne had been unable to get most of their performing kit out of storm-swept Okinawa, so he had to re-create much of the same equipment in Cleveland, to meet the demand for him and his dog to appear on radio and news shows, and for photo calls in the printed media. They were also in high demand to perform before live audiences, all of whom were fascinated to see this famous war dog in action.

Wynne quickly saw that Smoky loved to play up to the crowd. Clever and smart, she knew she could get away with things when performing that he would never allow during practice. They had an act where she would jump through three hoops in a row. But when live on stage, she'd often dodge the second hoop, skirting around it, which invariably drew a chorus of wild cheers and laughter from the audience. Realizing how much they seemed to appreciate the famous war dog's cheeky wilfulness, Wynne worked such 'disobedience' into their regular acts.

As they had done when in the field, they began to act as a therapy man-and-dog team in the local hospital, which was full of those injured and traumatized in the war. On one occasion they performed before a group of wheelchair-bound soldiers. One began gurgling excitedly and holding out his arms to Smoky. One of the nurses asked if he might get to hold the dog. He took her in his arms, and smiling widely began to swing her back and forth, gently. The nurses were in tears. It turned out the soldier had been catatonic for two years, barely moving or displaying any emotions. Smoky had broken through all of that.

Wynne was contacted by a travelling circus. They asked if

they might book him and Smoky for eight live shows, for which they'd pay him a fee of $200. Wynne agreed. He contacted good friends, needing a carpenter to help him re-create Smoky's high-wire apparatus. They managed it in time, but on the night of the first performance the clown took to the stage, to the thundering of some circus cannons. At the sound of the blasts Smoky started to spin on the spot nervously, just like she had done during the air raids on Biak Island.

Wynne had no option but to take Smoky outside, to shield her from the blasts. It was February in Cleveland and bitterly cold, but there they were forced to stay until the firing was finished. They were to be the final act, the grand finale to round off the show. Previously, the circus owner had booked a rodeo act and it had been a disaster. The stakes were high. But by the time Smoky and Wynne took to the stage, the audience had mostly left. Just a few dozen remained. The previous acts had gone on too long and drained the audience away.

Those who remained loved the show, but it wasn't enough. After their fourth night, the circus owners called Wynne into their office. They were cancelling his act, and they offered him a compromise fee of $100. Wynne objected that he'd signed a contract for $200. The owners pointed out that he might have signed the contract, but they never had. It was a take-it-or-leave-it offer. Wynne was disgusted, and he vowed never to agree to such a performance again.

In any case, other requests were flooding in. There was a call from a local Kennel Club. Would Wynne and Smoky do their act immediately prior to the Best in Show competition? Wynne had never been to a dog show before, but the act went down a storm. Wynne was contacted by several Yorkie owners. One, Goldie Stone, was a Yorkie breeder from Columbus, Ohio. She praised Smoky for her fine lines and asked Wynne if he and his dog might be willing to visit.

They travelled to Ohio by train, together with Margie. Goldie Stone was hugely impressed with Smoky. She told Wynne that Smoky was a fantastic specimen of such a dog and that she could have sold her for $250 as a puppy. She wondered what her ancestry was, and the subject of how on earth Smoky had got to New Guinea came up. Wynne had to confess that he had absolutely no idea.

In the spring of 1946 Wynne began work on a book telling his and Smoky's story. He wrote in long hand, and found it a blessing to unburden himself of his wartime memories. Together, his mother and Margie typed and edited the manuscript. In between the writing, man and dog toured a number of hospitals. In Chicago, they were met by the Red Cross, accompanied by a phalanx of press reporters. Chicago's *Daily News*, *Sun* and *Herald* all covered their story. One reporter wrote: 'Smoky looks like the business end of your wife's favorite mop dyed in tobacco juice.' But it was all good publicity.

Wynne and Smoky did their act for GIs dying with cancer and for others who'd lost their minds during the war. They helped raise the profile of animal shelters, shooting promotional films with them. Wynne used some of his contacts to reach out to *Life Magazine*, to see if the publishers might also be interested in his and Smoky's book. The word came back that they had covered the story of several Second World War mascots, and felt that another might well be overkill.

Wynne reckoned people were tiring of the war. They'd lived its horrors and privations and losses: they wanted to get on with living the future. He shelved the idea of publishing the book that he had written. He carried on doing live shows, even returning to the Parmadale orphanage where he'd spent two years as a young child.

Wynne married Margie, his Cleveland fiancée, in September 1946. She had a good job with a veteran's association, but then Wynne spotted an advert for a trainer, to prepare dogs to act in motion pictures. The job seemed tailor-made for him. He applied and was asked to go to California, to try it out. He and Margie decided to move to California and give Hollywood a whirl. They arrived with Smoky, and Wynne signed up as a trainer on a trial basis. He was soon schooling dogs through film, and meeting some of the most famous master trainers, who worked on big budget movies.

He joined the Hollywood Animal Handlers and Trainers Association. He and Smoky performed at the Hollywood Canteen, a hangout for war veterans. The night of their first show Smoky went crazy. Instead of responding to the first acts as normal, she started racing in between the stage curtains and ignoring Wynne's every command. Every time he found her, she darted off in another direction and the audience was starting to howl with laughter.

When he dashed behind the curtain to grab her, she went out centre stage, playing to the audience. Wynne eventually managed to get her under control again and they were able to finish the act as he'd intended. The odd thing was, the entire performance – Smoky's craziness included – seemed to have gone down a storm. They were invited to do a private show for a big Hollywood producer. Other big shots began to show real interest in him plus his diminutive, but hugely spirited little dog.

The trouble was Margie. From her well-paid job in Cleveland she'd been reduced to sitting at home all day long while Wynne and Smoky were out at work, and the days were perilously long. Hollywood producers tended to save money by pushing shoots through to ten o'clock at night, rather than scheduling extra days. She was sick, she wasn't eating well and she certainly wasn't enjoying Hollywood.

Her job was still waiting for her back in Cleveland, so after just three months of marriage they decided to part ways temporarily. She'd head back to Cleveland, and Wynne would give it a while longer, hoping to break through. Days later Wynne received a letter from Margie telling him that she was pregnant. Now her sickness made a great deal more sense. She'd moved back in with her parents and things weren't so bad. They could brave the separation for a while longer.

Wynne was contracted to be a handler in a Warner Brothers movie starring Ronald Reagan – the future US president - entitled *Night Unto Night*. The dog he was handling was a mongrel named Butch. One evening Wynne returned to his car in the parking lot, and Smoky was standing on the back of the driver's seat, waiting for him. The wife of the movie's producer had spotted her, and she called her husband over. Together they admired Smoky, and Wynne got her to run through a few tricks as he explained her wartime career.

The producer's wife begged her husband to let Smoky appear in *Night Unto Night*. The producer objected she was too good to play a bit-part. He'd make her the star of his next movie, he proclaimed. He was dead serious, as well. Wynne sensed this might be the turning point in his and his dog's Hollywood career.

But at around that time Margie got in contact to inform him that Cleveland NACA (the forerunner to the present-day NASA) had been in contact, offering him a job as a flight photographer. They could hold the job for one week only and it paid $3-5,000 per year. Wynne would need to be in Cleveland by 28 January 1947 and ready to start work if he wanted to make the job his.

Wynne was all but broke in Hollywood. He'd survived on scraps of work, but there was never enough. His mother called, urging him to return home. His wife was pregnant, he had no firm prospects in Hollywood and the offer of a job with NACA was too good to turn down. Wynne's buddies in the film business learned that he was on the verge of leaving. Many urged him to stay. They made promises, but what he needed was a firm, bulletproof commitment to money and work.

Nothing was forthcoming, so Wynne and Smoky left Hollywood and headed home. Starting work at Cleveland NACA Flight Propulsion Center was pretty much like returning to the 26th Photo Reconnaissance Squadron. Nearly everyone was former military. They were flying former USAAF B-24 Liberators and B-25 Mitchell bombers, testing groundbreaking de-icing kit at altitude and in the often freezing conditions over Cleveland's Great Lakes region.

A device like a mini-furnace blew hot air through ducts, playing it over the leading edges of the bombers' wings. The sheer power of the heat it produced could melt off almost any ice that formed. The icing test flights weren't without danger, but at least there was no risk of being targeted by ack-ack or enemy fighters, being hit by tropical cyclones or of having to bail out over hostile jungle.

In between the flight work Wynne and Smoky continued to perform. A booking agent got them shows at ice hockey matches, boxing bouts, night clubs and theatres. They were always a smash hit and the audiences brought the roof down with their applause. But it still wasn't Hollywood. One of the main Hollywood handlers called. He offered Wynne a full-time job as a trainer in his kennels. But when Wynne demanded a legally binding contract and guaranteed wages, he went silent.

Wynne called Goldie, the Yorkie breeder, and asked if he might buy a male dog to mate with Smoky. She sent him a puppy from a prize stud male, one whose coat had the strong steel blue and brilliant gold hues that are prized by breeders. That puppy earned the name 'Mr Terrific', or Terry for short. Two weeks later Smoky came into season and she and Terry fell very much in love. Smoky became pregnant, and in the excitement of the moment Terry was put out in the yard and went missing.

No one had a clue what could have happened to him. Wynne and family and friends searched high and low. They nailed up lost-dog posters everywhere. But no matter what they tried there was no further sign of Terry. Wynne understood then what it must have been like for Smoky's original owners to lose her in the New Guinea jungles, as they had done.

On 27 June 1947 Smoky gave birth to one little puppy, her second after Topper (who'd died during the mystery Lingayen plague). The very next day Margie gave birth to a daughter,

Joanne Marie. When Smoky's pup was four months old they gave her to Margie's sister, Helen. Though family life was getting very busy, Smoky and Wynne continued to perform their shows.

By 1949 Wynne and Margie had several young children to care for (they would end up raising nine). Having never known his father, Wynne was determined that his own family would never suffer from such a similarly absent parent. He had to balance the demands of travelling on show business with spending time at home with his wife and children, and to that end he was determined to stick to local 'day-jobs' to ensure he might do so. The best were those like the NACA contract, which took the skills he had learned in the 26th and put them to civilian use.

Wynne and Smoky were booked to do a regular children's slot on a local TV station. They had to leave the NACA lab early every Friday and rush over to make their appearance on Cleveland's Channel 9. In October 1953 Wynne was approached by a local paper, the *Cleveland Plain Dealer*, to take a job as a photographer with them. The money was better than he was making at NACA and with six children by now it was tempting. He spoke to his boss at NACA and was told there was no way they could match the newspaper's offer. He took the job.

The following year the Sunday paper carried the story that Smoky the famous war dog was retiring from her show business career. Smoky, who had to be a good ten years old by now, was still in fine form, but Wynne decided it was better to quit when they were still ahead.

Not long after this he was invited to take a regular Sunday morning TV slot. As Smoky was retired, she'd only be asked to do one trick, and most of the show would involve Wynne training other dogs and interviewing guests. He reckoned that was doable, and so they began to appear on the regular slot: 'How to Train Your Dog, with Bill Wynne and Smoky.' The show ran for thirty weeks and was a big hit, but eventually Smoky really did have to retire for good.

On 21 February 1957 Wynne came home from work and found Smoky apparently sleeping soundly. In truth, she'd passed away. Not a man to cry easily, this time Wynne gave vent to his grief freely. As they were about to move house and they didn't want to lose Smoky's gravesite, they decided to bury her in the Cleveland Metroparks, known as the 'Emerald Necklace', a beautiful stretch of woodland, cliffs and rivers surrounding the city.

They found a special tree where Wynne and Margie had once carved a heart and their names, as sweethearts, and dug Smoky a grave beneath it. Smoky's body had been carried there in a shoe box. As Wynne went to lower the body into the grave, his seven-year-old daughter, Susan, asked: 'But Daddy, how is Smoky going to breathe?'

Caught unprepared, he couldn't ignore her bright blue tearful gaze. 'She doesn't need to breathe any more,' he answered. 'She's in dog heaven.' He did his best to hide from her his own tears, because fathers are supposed to be strong at such times.

Wynne's employer, the *Cleveland Plain Dealer*, printed an obituary, which told the entire story of the famous war dog and her subsequent show business career. The day it was published Margie took a phone call from Grace Guderian, who had been a lieutenant nurse assigned to a field hospital during the war. She explained how she had lost a female Yorkie in New Guinea in early 1944. Her then fiancé, also serving in the military, had bought her the dog from a Brisbane dealer as a Christmas gift. Grace Guderian had named the dog Christmas.

A while later she'd deployed to Dobodora, in New Guinea, which is where the little dog had gone missing. Bill Wynne and his wife could only conclude that Christmas and Smoky were one and the same animal. Wynne remembered the time on Biak Island when Smoky had reacted with such excitement to the word Christmas. He hadn't made much of it at the time. It made perfect sense now. The breeder who had sold Grace Guderian the puppy had made a great show of the pedigree and class of the Yorkie. There could not have been two such dogs in circulation in Nadzab at around that time.

There was one mystery. How had Smoky got from Dobodora, where she'd gone missing, to Nadzab, where they had found her, a distance of some 180 miles? It turned out that Grace Guderian had taken Smoky to a show being performed at the Dobodora base by Bob Hope, then a popular comedian, actor and singer. Christmas had disappeared during the show. Bob Hope was touring bases and very likely flew on to others, including Nadzab. Somehow, Christmas must have made that journey as part of his retinue, or on one of countless other flights shuttling between the various bases.

That was all that Wynne could imagine. At Nadzab, she'd run off again, only for a die-hard dog-hater, Ed Downey, to discover her abandoned in the foxhole. Wynne could think of no other scenario to explain how the little dog had made it into his life as she had. To make a full circle of the amazing series of coincidences in Smoky and Bill Wynne's incredible – fated? – coming together, it turned out that Grace Guderian and her husband lived not a few blocks from the Wynnes' house in Cleveland.

Smoky's first owners were able to give Wynne some photos of her as she was when they had her, in which she looked about five months old. He calculated that she had to have been born sometime around the middle of 1943.

Since her death Smoky has been formally honoured in many different ways. In 2005, on America's annual Veterans Day, 11 November, a bronze life-size sculpture of Smoky sitting in a GI helmet atop a two-tonne granite block was unveiled at the Cleveland Metroparks, sited above the very spot where Smoky is buried. It is dedicated thus: 'Smoky, the Yorkie Doodle Dandy and the Dog of All Wars'.

The American Kennel Club Museum of the Dog in St Louis, Missouri, has a permanent display dedicated to Smoky. The 26th Air Space Intelligence Squadron, the successor to the 26th Photo Reconnaissance Squadron, has a memorial dedicated to Smoky at their Hickam Air Force Base, on Hawaii. The Ohio Veterinary Medicine Association has a memorial dedicated to Smoky, the 'No. 1 Dog Hero', in its Columbus, Ohio, Animal Hall of Fame. There are other such memorials across the US.

Smoky was also awarded the People's Dispensary for Sick Animals (PDSA) Certificate for Animal Bravery or Devotion in April 2011, in Britain. In May 2014 the *Animal Planet* TV show – a Discovery Communications broadcast – concluded that when Smoky did the rounds of the wards in the Nadzab hospital, she became the world's first ever therapy dog of record;

in other words, she was the first dog ever recorded to have carried out such therapeutic duties.

There is a permanent memorial and statue of Smoky at the Royal Brisbane Women's Hospital, unveiled in December 2012, to recognize her Australian roots and the role she served as a therapy dog in Australian hospitals. In July 2013 she was also awarded the Australian Defence Force Trackers and War Dog Association's War Dog Operational Medal, and in December 2015 she was given the Australian RSPCA's Purple Cross Award. The award recognizes the deeds of animals who have demonstrated exceptional courage, risking their own safety to save a person's life.

In 1996, Bill Wynne's rendition of his and Smoky's story, entitled *Yorkie Doodle Dandy: Or, the Other Woman Was a Real Dog*, was published by Wynnesome Press. For any reader whose wider interest may have been piqued by this book, it remains in print, now published by Top Dog Enterprises.

Author Damien Lewis supports the pioneering and exceptional work of the following two canine charities. He is proud to be a patron of Bravehound and in 2018 he received a Canine Partners retiree dog named Moxie, who has become a beloved member of the Lewis household. Please do join in supporting their work in whatever way you can.

Dogs can help heal invisible wounds:
A profile of Bravehound

Veterans with Post Traumatic Stress Disorder and other mental health conditions can become isolated and find it difficult to relate to other people, and to adjust to life as a civilian. Bravehound partners veterans with dogs, giving them twenty-four hour companionship and a structure to their day.

We provide training and support – and of course the dogs themselves – for the lifetime of each Bravehound.

Do please get in touch if you would like to hear more about Bravehound and how you might support our work.

www.bravehound.co.uk
hello@bravehound.co.uk
+ 44 7980631110

BRAVEHOUND

Amazing dogs. Transforming lives:
A profile of Canine Partners

Canine Partners is a registered charity that trains assistance dogs for people with physical disabilities including civilians and members of HM Armed Forces.

Our dogs are trained to help with everyday tasks such as opening and closing doors, unloading the washing machine, picking up dropped items, pressing buttons and switches and getting help in an emergency. They also increase independence, confidence, self-esteem, a sense of security and bring companionship and increased social interaction.

Canine Partners receives no government funding and relies solely on public donations.

For further information visit caninepartners.org.uk or call 08456 580 480.

Canine Partners
Amazing dogs. Transforming lives.
caninepartners.org.uk

Registered Charity No: 803680
(England and Wales) and SC039050 (Scotland)